Experience and Memory of the First World War in Belgium:
Comparative and Interdisciplinary Insights

Waxmann Verlag GmbH
Steinfurter Straße 555, 48159 Münster
info@waxmann.com

Historische Belgienforschung

herausgegeben vom

Arbeitskreis
Historische Belgienforschung
im deutschsprachigen Raum

Band 6

Geneviève Warland (Ed.)

Experience and Memory of the First World War in Belgium

Comparative and Interdisciplinary Insights

Waxmann 2018
Münster • New York

Funded by BELSPO (Belgian Science Policy Office)

Bibliographic information published by the Deutsche Nationalbibliothek
The Deutsche Nationalbibliothek lists this publication in the
Deutsche Nationalbibliografie; detailed bibliographic data are
available in the Internet at http://dnb.dnb.de

Historische Belgienforschung, Bd. 6

ISSN 2366-6927
Print-ISBN 978-3-8309-3855-2
E-Book-ISBN 978-3-8309-8855-7

© Waxmann Verlag GmbH, 2018
Münster, Germany

www.waxmann.com
info@waxmann.com

Cover Design: Inna Ponomareva, Düsseldorf
Cover Picture: PhotoNews/Maurice-Louis Branger/Roger Viollet
Typesetting: Satzzentrale GbR, Marburg

Printed on age-resistant paper,
acid-free according to ISO 9706

Printed in Germany

All rights reserved. No part of this publication may be reproduced, stored
in a retrieval system or transmitted in any form or by any means, electronic,
electrostatic, magnetic tape, mechanical, photocopying, recording or
otherwise without permission in writing from the copyright holder.

Contents

'The Great War as Cultural Heritage' 7
Preface by Annette Becker

Experience and Memory of the First World War in Belgium:
Comparative and Interdisciplinary Insights
Preface by the editors of "Historische Belgienforschung" 9

Geneviève Warland
Introduction
Emotion, Experience, Memory 11

Part I
Belgian Soldiers and Civilians in the First World War:
Insights in the History of Emotions

Rose Spijkerman, Olivier Luminet, Antoon Vrints
Fighting and Writing.
The Psychological Functions of Diary Writing in the First World War 23

Geneviève Warland and Olivier Luminet
***Nil inultum remanebit:* Germany in the War Diaries of the Historians**
Paul Fredericq and Henri Pirenne 45

Part II
Representations of the First World War in Belgium:
Literature, Poetry, Cultural and Collective Memory

Myrthel Van Etterbeeck and Karla Vanraepenbusch
War, Narratives and Memory:
The Defence and Fall of the Belgian Fort Cities in the Cultural Memory
of the First World War 81

Elke Brems, Reine Meylaerts, Pierre Bouchat, Olivier Klein
Dulce et decorum est:
Reading First World War Poetry 115

Valérie Rosoux, Pierre Bouchat, Olivier Klein
Retelling the War to Give a Chance to Peace.
A Comparative Analysis of Great War Memories 139

Part III
The Centenary of the First World War in Belgium:
Commemorations and Memory Dynamics

Chantal Kesteloot and Laurence van Ypersele
The Commemorations of the First World War
as Seen through Postage Stamps 167

Pierre Bouchat, Olivier Klein, Valérie Rosoux
The Paradoxical Impacts of the Commemorations
of the Great War in Belgium 197

Bernard Rimé
Conclusions
Traces of Wartime Emotions in our Collective Memory 219

Authors 225

'The Great War as Cultural Heritage'
Preface

One hundred years ago, Guillaume Apollinaire, the poet and journalist who had been wounded in battle, wondered: 'What should we call the current war? They have begun to call it "the War of 1914," then, upon the arrival of 1915, they said "the European War," then, once the Americans entered, they spoke of "World War" or "Universal War"…"The Great War" also has its defenders. "The War of Nations" could gain some votes. "The War of Races" would be defensible. "The War of Alliances" or "the War of Peoples." But the "War of Fronts" would possibly best express the character of this gigantic struggle.'[1] Indeed, since 1914, the image of the military fronts that was mirrored in domestic fronts formed a kind of worldwide kaleidoscope of complex situations. These included air, sea and land fronts, fronts of invasion and of refuge, fronts of work and of overwork, fronts of military and of civilian prisoners, fronts of hospitals where one fought against wounds and illnesses, fronts of grief, of cemeteries and of remembrance. Some fronts went on to form the heart of the catastrophes of the coming century: There, civilians had been at the centre of the war, invaded, occupied, looted, bombarded; they became ordinary targets in a total war. There, the Ottoman Empire carried out a full-scale test of population transfers, repressive measures, and even policies of 'systematic extermination'[2] towards the Armenians and the Assyrians. In these territories, the Great War came to transform, whether deliberately or unknowingly, into a worldwide *laboratory*, a testing ground for violence, a place to put it into practice and to optimise its effects on people and on materiel. At the heart of this laboratory lay Belgium, invaded in the earliest days of the war, then occupied by its enemies, a small part of its territory remaining a battlefield throughout the entire world war.

In a fascinating self-reflection, the Memex team makes Belgium, a laboratory twice over, between 1914 and 1918 and then in a century-long memory, a jumping-off point for the most innovative social sciences. Historians, political scientists, psychologists and literary scholars have united their efforts, on different scales, to examine the time of war with an eye towards emotions, and the time following the war with an eye towards cultural heritage, through to the present day. We can summarise their work in a phrase: 'the war as cultural heritage'. Immaterial cultural heritage such as that of emotions: fear, hatred, the discovery of the Other, rejection, accommodation, terror, disgust, compassion, tenderness. Oh so material cultural heritage such as that

---

1 Guillaume Apollinaire. *Mercure de France,* 16 November 1917, Œuvres *complètes,* vol. 3, La Pléiade, Gallimard, p. 514.
2 Formulation of the ICRC. (Archives, Geneva).

of destructions, reconstructions, commemorations. The scales are temporal, from the 'micro' of the day-to-day and month-to-month experience of the war – what smaller than the pages of a diary? – to the 'macro'; of a memory that has been reconstructed over one hundred years. The scales are also spatial: from the local of small villages and cities, through the regional, and all the way to Europe and even the world in the World War. For a century, we have pitied 'Poor little Belgium' and also celebrated the heroism of 'Brave little Belgium': a country that is perhaps small, but whose population has experienced all forms of war and its memories. The current authors – maybe *because* the country is small – have been able to analyse these experiences with such mastery, turning the complexity of comparisons and of interdisciplinarity into strengths. The populations of Belgium become an interface between the 'micro' and 'macro' scales, between very specific war experiences, such as the gasses tested at Ypres or the forced labour deportations, and the large-scale universality of tragedy, such as the hope of peace in 'the war to end all wars' or a pacifism that was just as popular yet impotent then as it is now.

In 1943, in the middle of another war, Arthur Koestler reflected: 'Statistics don't bleed; it is the detail which counts'.[3] Yes, the authors of this book know that social sciences need to work quantitatively, to establish statistics and patterns, on scales as immense as that of the Great War, to the scale of the individual and of diverse and shifting groups understood in terms of social, economic, cultural, and generational factors, and all of this over one hundred years. But they also know that neither statistics nor geography nor concepts bleed; it is people who bleed. This is the 'detail' envisioned by Koestler, which strongly resembles the 'Space of experience' (*Erfahrungsraum*) theorised by Reinhart Koselleck. We are impressed by the way in which the authors lead us through mental and physical destructions and through the reconstructions and distortions of memory with a mastery of the most varied sources. They examine these both as creations inscribed in history and through their reception by the other social sciences – from intimate poems to expositions and monuments, from landscapes to postage stamps, etc.

For all of their work, which is simultaneously precise and wide-ranging, their intellectual attention to detail in understanding and making understood, the quality of their writing, apparent even in the choice of titles, the authors of this exemplary collective deserve the utmost gratitude.

Annette Becker   Paris-Nanterre
                          Historial de la Grande Guerre (Péronne, Somme)

---

3 Arthur Koestler, *Arrival and Departure*, 1943.

Experience and Memory of the First World War in Belgium: Comparative and Interdisciplinary Insights
Preface by the Editors of "Historische Belgienforschung"

The First World War features prominently in the German-Language historical research on Belgium – and not by chance. In 1914–1918, Europe witnessed an armed conflict that was characterised by industrialised warfare resulting in 20 million casualties. 50 % of these were civilians. However, it was not only a war of armies and industries but also a war of words, of propaganda and of remembrance which lasted a long time after the cannons finally fell silent a hundred years ago.

"In a country where war was fought, it lingers, even if that war is already a century behind us." This motto borrowed from the mission statement of the *In Flanders Fields*-Museum in Ypres epitomises the essence of the research presented here. Accordingly, the objectives set by the authors of this volume are "to reflect on the legacy and memories of WW1 that are still alive and relevant for contemporary Belgian society." The focus is multidisciplinary, combining local, national and inter- or transnational perspectives. Based on thorough theoretical and methodological considerations and a plethora of sources, the contributions of this volume meet the aspirations in such a way that we, as the Working Group *Historische Belgienforschung*, take full pride in the fact that Geneviève Warland entrusted this meticulously edited book to our publication series. This volume proves that "little Belgium" has a large history in store that should no longer remain at the periphery of public and scholarly attention.

It is our Working Group's main purpose to foster the German-Language research on Belgian history. Therefore, it may seem a little paradoxical that this volume presents only research by scholars from Belgium. However, this is a reflection of the close contacts we were able to encourage between Belgian-based scholars and those working in a German-speaking academic environment outside the country. The fact that this volume is published in English is intended to make the research results available to a wider community than a publication in any of Belgium's three official languages could hope to reach. We sincerely wish this book the attention it deserves.

Tatjana Mrowka (current editor-in-chief) /
Sebastian Bischoff / Christoph Jahr / Jens Thiel   Cologne / Berlin, January 2019

Geneviève Warland

Introduction[1]
Emotion, Experience, Memory

1 Yet another book on the First World War?

The centenary of the First World War has provoked a wave of publications geared towards different kinds of audiences: the general public, schools and academia. 2014 saw an unprecedented peak in the number of publications of any sort in Belgium (as in other countries); 2018 has seen a revival of publications, but the number does not seem to be as high as in 2014.[2] Such an outpouring of books illustrates a real interest for this tremendous event that killed more than 18 million soldiers and civilians around the world. This interest is manifested in family curiosity supported by the discovery of objects and documents, which were in some cases digitized.[3] It has been sustained by local history associations that organized conferences and exhibitions and by the media that created websites dedicated to 1914–18, documentary films and historical fiction.[4] Finally, scholarly research on WWI, its manifold experiences, its political and social impacts as well as its memories in Europe and beyond has been vigorous.

As part of the overwhelming remembrance and commemorative activities around the First World War, this book helps to reflect on the legacy and memories of WWI that are still alive and relevant for contemporary Belgian society. It looks at these aspects with a multidisciplinary focus of interest in psychology, history, literature and political science. This book not only provides a historical insight on WWI, but also pays attention to the current representations of this war and to the impact of the commemorations of the conflict during its centenary. It has a truly interdisciplinary character as most of the chapters are written by representatives of two of the disciplines mentioned above. Authors crossed their methodologies on the topic that they jointly

---

1 I would like to thank Olivier Klein, Olivier Luminet and Laurence van Ypersele for their valuable comments.
2 See Tallier 2019 (forthcoming).
3 See the initiative financed by the European Commission *Europeana 1914–1918* aiming to collect objects and documents through several campaigns and digitize them in order to share individual and collective memories of the War throughout the whole European Union: https://www.europeana.eu/portal/en/collections/world-war-I.
4 As for the Belgian case, see respectively the very informative and well-illustrated website https://www.rtbf.be/14-18, the well-conceived documentary produced by the RTBF 14-18: L'histoire belge and the well-documented and moving television series In vlaamse velden produced by the VRT.

studied. Moreover, chapter drafts benefited from cross-disciplinary comments from authors of other chapters.

The analysis concerns the national level, but also the subnational, regional and local levels. For instance, the study of WWI through stamps operates at the level of the Belgian State, whereas the analysis of war memory related to the cities of Antwerp and Liège is anchored in local experiences and memories. Moreover, some comparisons are drawn with other countries like France, Germany, Serbia and Bosnia-Herzegovina with regard to representations of WWI among young Europeans, expanding the scope of the book to the European level.

Composed of seven chapters that I outline below, this book is situated in the wave of cultural history that has dominated the field of WWI Studies since the 1990s[5] and is one of the main contributions of the *Historial de la Grande Guerre* founded in 1992.[6] Its four main topics are related to individual war experiences, individual and collective war representations, war literature, and war commemorations, which are also central in cultural historical approaches. In a nutshell, it is the various ways of experiencing and remembering the First World War that are at the center of our analysis. The analysis deals with lived, intellectual, spiritual, political and emotional relationships of individuals to the war, which are embedded in their respective contexts.

Besides its interdisciplinary character situated in the history of the memory of WWI, the originality of this book lies in three main aspects: firstly, it depicts a history of emotions imbued with concepts and methods borrowed from psychology, which are linked to social frameworks and social norms of the time of the First World War. Secondly, it ventures onto the path of a research field that is gaining interest: the history of cultural and monumental heritage. Thirdly, it attempts to gauge the effectiveness of commemorative events understood in a broad sense: official celebrations, special TV programs or broadcasts, exhibitions, concerts, plays, books and special issues of journals.

Therefore, it is not just one more book on the First World War, but a book which takes a non-conventional stance by bringing together researchers from several fields who were eager to confront their theoretical backgrounds, hypotheses and methodologies. While being often a theoretical and a methodological challenge, it has also been an exciting intellectual adventure that I will now present in more detail.

2 The Memex WWI project

This book is the result of an interdisciplinary research project *Recognition and Resentment: Experiences and Memories of the Great War in Belgium* (MEMEX WWI) that brought together fifteen academics, researchers and PhD students from five Belgian

---

5 See Prost and Winter 2004, Jones 2013. For the Belgian case, see Benvindo, Majerus, Vrints 2014 and Vrints 2016.
6 See for instance Julien 2004 and *Historial de Péronne*'s presentation at https://www.historial.fr/en/.

universities and scholarly institutions from December 2013 to December 2018. It has been financed by the Belgian Science Policy Office (BELSPO) and is part of its program *Brain-be: Belgian Research Action through Interdisciplinary Networks*.

It is worth mentioning that the *Brain-be* selection of 2012 in the Axis 3: *Cultural, historical and scientific heritage* attests a deliberate decision of the Belgian Federal State to support large research projects on the First World War during the centennial years. As a matter of fact, another project was funded as well: *The Great War from Below: Multiple Mobility and Cultural Dynamics in Belgium (1900–1930)*, which is a research project in social history on less-studied groups – collaborators, resistance fighters, veterans, forced laborers – and on the demographic impact of the war, particularly on marriage in the interwar period. Conversely, MEMEX WWI is situated in cultural history, psychology, literature and political science.

Originally, the research aimed to bridge two perspectives on the First World War – experiences and memories – in order to enhance Belgium's WWI heritage. Four main topics of research were covered in the MEMEX WWI project: war time experience, war monumental heritage, war literature, and war memory. Each topic was studied by a PhD student who was supervised by two directors from different universities and/or different research fields and involved diverse methodologies drawn from history, political science, philology and psychology. These methodologies included historical criticism and contextualization, discourse analysis and the study of political implications, literary criticism and semantic analysis, as well as quantitative and qualitative analysis of data collection.

The chapters of this book reflect both the four MEMEX WWI research axes and the multiple methodologies, and they dealt with topics which the MEMEX WWI members have worked on during the last five years.

3   An interdisciplinary project

As a pioneer in the study of emotions in a historical-societal perspective (*gesellschaftsgeschichtlich*), Ute Frevert, professor at the Free University Berlin, underlines the fact that the First World War provoked a wave of emotions that were experienced at an intensity level never reached before. This includes negative emotions such as despair, anxiety, hate, or resentment, but also positive ones like empathy and hope.[7] She invites the study of such emotions with the help of concepts and theories developed in psychology, but equally insists on the necessity to contextualize these emotions by taking into account the social norms and values of the society of that time. In particular, she highlights a tendency among psychologists studying emotional issues of applying theoretical models and conducting empirical research with individuals with-

---

7   Frevet 2009, 196. The list given by Frevert is adapted for the sake of the argument.

out paying much attention to social and cultural – that is, collective – frameworks, which are spatially and temporally particular:

> „Völlig unterbeleuchtet jedoch bleibt bei ihnen die Frage, inwieweit solche Mechanismen kulturell geformt werden, in welchen sozialen Kontexten sie entstehen und vergehen. Welche Erfahrungen und Lernprozesse sind damit verbunden? Welche sozialen Konstellationen befördern oder erschweren welche Formen emotionaler Regulierung? […]."[8]

Conversely, historians insist on the necessity of considering the feelings that people report in their cultural environment (*Gefühlskultur*) – for instance, the *bourgeoise* of the *Belle Époque* –, as well as in their social or institutional contexts – like the Belgian army during the Great War. Professor Frevert also insists on paying sufficient attention to attitudes and representations imbued with the norms of that time.

Such interactions between historians and psychologists, the former being more relativist and the latter more universalist, lie at the heart of the MEMEX WWI project. Historians always recalled the need to adjust the psychological analysis to the context of the time and its norms and values. In contrast, psychologists emphasized the need to properly define – with the help of existing theories – emotions, attitudes and representations that they primarily approached as structural matters.

That being said, in an influential paper, social psychologist Kenneth Gergen argued that so-called "universal" (social) psychological processes are heavily dependent on the sociocultural context of the times, leading him to assert that "social psychological research is the systematic study of contemporary history".[9] He therefore called for a greater articulation between the two disciplines, which he viewed as complementary. The present book offers an opportunity to do so.

Moreover, social psychologists conduct inquiries by asking people questions in order to determine collective representations through the use of data collection and quantitative analysis. Several chapters of this book are based on this methodology. Graphs mentioning scales and proportions tend to be the pivotal point on felt emotions, on WWI representations, and on attitudes. With regard to such interpretations founded in statistics, the MEMEX WWI cultural historians and literary scholars as well as the political scientist, used to practicing discourse analysis, were at first thrown off balance. Nevertheless they recognized the usefulness of the psychological tools and methods as seen in many chapters but still kept a critical stance towards the value of statistics.

---

8   "An unanswered question remains [among psychologists]: to what extent such mechanisms are culturally formed, in which contexts do they appear and disappear. Which experiences and learning processes do they imply? Which social circumstances support or complicate what kind of emotion regulation?" (Frevert 2009, 200).

9   Gergen 1973, 319.

4 Insight into the book chapters

The first part of the book addresses the issue of emotions in a context of war and also addresses attitudes towards the Germans through the diaries of Belgian soldiers and scholars, the ones experiencing the war at the front and the others at the home front in an occupied country and during their captivity in Germany. Both chapters associate a psychologist – Olivier Luminet – with historians – Rose Spijkermann and Antoon Vrints for chapter one and Geneviève Warland for chapter two and delineate the psychological strategies and the writing strategies adopted by the diarists to overcome anxiety, inhuman living conditions in the trenches, deprivation, disillusionment, sadness and loneliness. The two chapters show how they regulated their emotions in using coping mechanisms like attention orientation and cognitive change through the act of writing, religious faith, historical reasoning, humor, concentration on the activities of daily life. They also interpret the discursive level: metaphors, processes of exaggeration or minimization. In the first chapter, a comparison is drawn between four diaries written in French or Dutch by Belgian soldiers belonging to different social backgrounds. The second chapter is based on the diaries of two well-known Belgian historians, Henri Pirenne and Paul Fredericq. It mainly deals with their attitude towards the Germans, showing a specific evolution in their feelings throughout the war and during its aftermath.

In the second part of the book, social representations of the war are analyzed using two approaches: cultural memory and social psychology. The formation of First World War memories in two fort cities, Antwerp and Liège, both during the war and in the interwar period is studied in the first chapter through literary texts, monuments, commemorative plaques and street names. The role of political and civic actors that discursively produced urban space in selecting narratives is also taken into account. Using the conceptual frameworks of cultural memory and of commemorative narrative – that insists on narrativisation processes which distort past events in order to provide a message adapted to the time –, the historian Karla Vanraepenbusch and the literary scholar Myrthel Van Etterbeeck highlight the contrasts between these two cities, the first being the embodiment of the defeat of the Belgian army and therefore the victim of "German barbary", and the second the embodiment of Belgium's glorious resistance. Two literary tropes of the First World War are then contrasted: 'poor little Belgium' and 'brave little Belgium'.

The second chapter written by two literary scholars – Elke Brems and Reine Meylaerts – and two social psychologists – Pierre Bouchat and Olivier Klein – firstly examines the literary reception of Tom Lanoye's first volume of translated international war poetry, *No Man's Land*: reviews in journals, on websites, comments on blogs and websites of online bookstores etc. Secondly, it looks at the way in which Lanoye's translated war poetry is read by analyzing through empirical research the way current Flemish students in literature at the University of Leuven react to this poetry. Its results indicate a link between the emotions of respect, sympathy, and sorrow felt by the students – which testify to the capacity of Lanoye's hybrid translation to invest the poems with new meaning and make them relevant for the 21st century reader – and their pacifist attitude, which coheres with the cultural significance of these poems.

Based on a survey conducted in the frame of a European COST project,[10] the third chapter examines current representations of the First World War among young Europeans. Carried out by a political scientist – Valérie Rosoux – and the abovementioned scholars in social psychology, Pierre Bouchat and Olivier Klein, this chapter goes beyond the spatial frame of Belgium by focusing on two groups of States with clearly different profiles – France and Germany on the one hand and Serbia and Bosnia-Herzegovina on the other. Three issues of the First World War were analyzed in the collective representations of a sample of students in history and in psychology coming from these countries: the country's responsibility for the outbreak of the war, the degree of violence of their own soldiers and enemy soldiers, and finally the suffering endured and inflicted throughout the war. The interpretation of the results makes clear how far current political and ideological context impacts on past representations. A link can be established between reconciled and not reconciled visions of the past and current patriotic or pacifist attitudes towards war in general and the First World War in particular. It clearly demonstrates that the reconciled past vision leads to a pacifist attitude and to empathy for soldiers and civilians as victims. Such a past vision is the result of the 'memory work' – that means the modification of the official narrative of the past – and of temporal dimension.

The third part of the book is devoted to the cultural memory of the Great War during its Centenary. It particularly focuses on the impact of commemorative activities. The first chapter written by two historians – Chantal Kesteloot and Laurence van Ypersele – examines the iconography of the First World War through postage stamps, and investigates the decision-making processes concerning stamp issues beginning in the war until the present in Belgium. The analysis of these everyday objects over one hundred years allows us to understand the policies of memory undertaken by the Belgian public authorities. Besides the dominant representation of the heroic figure of King Albert, the first stamps issued after the war recalled Belgian heroism – such as the defense of Liège – as well as suffering – for instance, the martyrdom of the city of Dendermonde – promoting thereby local identities within a shared national narrative. Both historians follow the evolution of stamps' illustrations, which became more diverse over time and took into account the events at the front and the war experience of civilians. They also study its various functions as in the cases of stamps carrying a surcharge for the benefit of charitable works or of current stamps issued in the context of the Centenary which are only sold to collectors.

The second chapter, which is again a collaboration between the political scientist Valérie Rosoux and the social psychologists, Pierre Bouchat and Olivier Klein, is devoted to analyzing the effects on young Belgians of exhibitions and documentaries

---

10   IS1205: *Social Psychological Dynamics of Historical Representations in the Enlarged European Union*.

produced in Belgium during the Centenary of the First World War. The main assumption is that with their scenography and their narrative these media produce an immersive experience aiming at identification and persuasion. Nonetheless, the five study cases show that contrary to the psychological rule of narrative persuasion, both of these forms of cultural mediation did not significantly contribute to reinforcing a pacifist attitude. These exhibitions and documentaries also elicited feelings of anger, opening the door to negative attitudes towards peace. The paradoxical nature of this phenomenon highlights the contrast between the objectives displayed by the designers of such cultural products and the effects observed in a psychological research based on questionnaires. It also indicates the existence of a tension between, on the one hand, the valorization of peace as an almost absolute value and, on the other hand, the accentuation of emotional devices favoring the empathy of participants called to identify with the victims of war.

The preface and the conclusion open the floor to renowned specialists in the research issues of the MEMEX WWI project discussed in this book: the historian Annette Becker (University Paris-Nanterre and Historial de la Grande Guerre Péronne, Somme) and the social psychologist Bernard Rimé (Catholic University of Louvain). The overview of these chapters leads to the observation that this book belongs to a tradition of research mainly conducted in the frame of the nation-state,[11] a frame that the historical research at an international level intended to overcome for the WWI centenary. Here are two examples: the first one is a scientific website called *1914-1918-online. International Encyclopedia of the First World War*[12], which gives a global perspective on the war through entries by areas, states and topics written by WWI researchers worldwide. The second one is a three-volume publication, *The Cambridge History of the First World War* edited by Jay Winter[13], which includes transnational chapters (as well as in the first volume dedicated to the *Global War* as in the two other volumes respectively to *The State* and to *Civil Society*). Nevertheless, the Far East (Japan and China) and Latin America remain in the background in these centenary publications. In that sense, if the centennial furthered research on the war on continents other than Europe, such as Africa[14], it did not bring a thoroughly global approach to the First World War at the political, economic, social and cultural levels. An overall synthesis still seems to be missing whereas a lot of research is still yet to be done on local, regional, national and transnational levels on less studied topics: forms of occupation during WWI and its aftermath, war economy, prisoners of war, religious faith in enduring the war, welfare and healthcare. This means that WWI research continues to have many fields to discover even after the centenary.

---

11 See for instance Boyce, Jansen, Purseigle 2014.
12 See http://www.1914-1918-online.net/
13 See Winter 2014.
14 Especially Africa. As for the Belgian case and its colony in Congo, see Ngongo, Piret, Tousignant 2018.

5 Emotion, experience, attitude, representation and memory as keywords

"The one thing a centenary history of the First World War should not be is a monument", wrote John Horne 2014 in his contribution *The Great War at its centenary* to the abovementioned *The Cambridge History of the First World War*. A retrospective glimpse of these four commemorative years indicates that the centenary history of the First World War has not been a monument. Many people participated in the various public displays (marked by some impressive artistic performances), visited exhibitions and museums, saw films, read books; along the way, they got incentives to reflect on WWI events, experiences and impacts as well as on wars in general.

This book partly documents the issue of the centenary as an important stage in the history of the memory of WWI, as in the cases of the chapters on postage stamps, on the reading of poetry, the screenings of documentaries and on visits to exhibitions. It follows the war memory in the long run through the analysis of French speaking and Flemish literature and of monuments and street names in the cities of Antwerp and Liège. Collective representations of the First World War, which form a set of knowledge and concepts shared by groups of people or a whole society are the focus here. Several past or current collective representations of WWI are disclosed and discussed: negative representations of the war time with deaths, cruelty, privation, positive representations conveyed by solidarity, hope …

The book further looks at experiences, which is the second topic of the MEMEX WWI project: experiences of the war in itself as lived by Belgian soldiers and renowned historians; experienced memory of the war leading to collective representations of soldiers and civilians as victims and to pacifist attitudes. As indicated in the overview and developed in the book, the key notions associated to the concepts of experience and representation are emotions and attitudes. The book argues that emotions are at the basis of positive or negative attitudes, which correspond in psychological terms to appraisals that individuals held towards elements in their environment: both positive and negative attitudes of soldiers who resisted in the trenches, negative attitudes of rejection by historians who condemned German barbarism, and finally positive pacifist attitudes of 21st century young Europeans, who are still moved by WWI experiences of combat and suffering, but also negative ones loaded with anger.

One hundred years after its end, in a time when the communicative memory of the First World War transmitted in families is gone with the death of the last witnesses and replaced by the cultural memory constructed with documents, images, films, objects, sites, that is the whole material heritage of WWI, it is striking to see how multifaceted and prolific the range of commemorative activities and scientific research has been. It is hoped that the MEMEX WWI project with this book as an output may have contributed to this success and also foster further multidisciplinary research on the First World War.

References

Assmann, J. (2008). Communicative and Cultural Memory. In Erll, A., Nünning, A. (Eds), *Cultural Memory Studies. An International and Interdisciplinary Handbook*, Berlin, New York: Walter de Gruyter, 109–118.

Benvindo, B., Majerus, B. & Vrints, A. (2014). La Grande Guerre des historiens belges, 1914–2014. *Journal of Belgian History*, 44(2-3), 170–196.

Boyce, R., Jansen, S., Purseigle, P. (2014). Historiographies étrangères de la Première Guerre mondiale. Introduction. *Histoire@Politique. Politique, culture, société*, 22, [www.histoire-politique.fr].

De Graaf, A., Hoeken, H., Sanders, J. & Beentjes, J. W. (2012). Identification as a Mechanism of Narrative Persuasion. *Communication Research*, 39(6), 802–823.

Frevert, U. (2009). Was haben Gefühle in der Geschichte zu suchen? *Geschichte und Gesellschaft*, 35, 183–208.

Gergen, K. J. (1973). Social psychology as history. *Journal of personality and social psychology*, 26(2), 309–320.

Gross, J. J. (Ed.) (2007). *Handbook of Emotion Regulation*. New York: Guilford Press.

Janz, O. (2014). Einführung: Der Erste Weltkrieg in globaler Perspektive. *Geschichte und Gesellschaft*, 40, 2: *Der Erste Weltkrieg in globaler Perspektive*, 147–159.

Jones, H. (2013). As the Centenary approaches: the regeneration of First World War historiography. *The Historical Journal*, 56(3), 857–878.

Julien, E. (2004). Antoine Prost, Jay Winter, *Penser la Grande Guerre. Un essai d'historiographie*, *Labyrinthe* [online], retrieved January 2 2019. http://journals.openedition.org/labyrinthe/215

Horne, J. (2014). The Great War at its centenary. In J. Winter (Dir.) *The Cambridge History of the First World War*, 3 vol. Cambridge: Cambridge University Press, 618–639.

Irwin-Zarecka, I. (2017). *Frames of Remembrance: The Dynamics of Collective Memory*. London: Routledge.

Ngongo, E., Piret, B., Tousignant, N. (Dir.) (2018). Congo at War. Journal of Belgian History, 48(1-2), 6–163.

Olick, J. K. (2003). *States of Memory: Continuities, Conflict and Transformations in National Retrospection*. Durham: Duke University Press.

Prost, A., Winter, J. (2004). *Penser la Grande Guerre. Un essai d'historiographie*, Paris: Seuil.

Sammut, G. (2015). Attitudes, Social Representations and Points of View. In Sammut, G., Andreouli, E., Gaskell, G. & Valisner, J. (Eds), *The Cambridge Handbook of Social Representations*. Cambridge, UK: Cambridge University Press, 96–112.

Tallier, P.-A. (Dir.) (2019). *Cent ans – et plus – d'ouvrages historiques sur la Première Guerre mondiale en Belgique. La Belgique et la Première Guerre mondiale. Bibliographie*. Tome 2bis (ouvrages édités de 1985 à 2018) / *Honderd jaar – en meer – geschiedschrijving over de Eerste Wereldoorlog in België. België en de Eerste Wereldoorlog. Bibliografie*. Deel 2bis (werken uitgegeven van 1985 tot 2018), Brussels: Belgian State Archive.

Vrints, A. (2016). Van niemandsland tot de "grote klaprozenexplosie": twee decennia onderzoek over België in de Eerste Wereldoorlog, 1995–2014. *BMGN-The Low Countries Historical Review,* 131(3), 54–73.

Winter, J. (Dir.) (2014). *The Cambridge History of the First World War*, 3 vol. Cambridge: Cambridge University Press.

Part I
Belgian Soldiers and Civilians in the First World War: Insights in the History of Emotions

Rose Spijkerman, Olivier Luminet, Antoon Vrints

Fighting and Writing. The Psychological Functions of Diary Writing in the First World War

1 Introduction

Diaries, letters, autobiographies and memoirs: 'The most dangerous of all sources'. At least, according to the historian Jan Romein (1946), and an opinion shared by other historians of the mid-twentieth century.[1] They were regarded as subjective, distorting and often written out of vanity, rancour or self-justification. A decade later, Jacques Presser (1958) did perceive these sources as valuable, and created the term 'egodocument' for these kinds of writings. He coined the word for all texts in which the author wrote about his or her own feelings, thoughts and actions. His use of egodocuments was quite exceptional for the time, considering that most other historians still perceived them as doubtful sources.[2] It took some more decades before egodocuments were fully accepted as an historical source. The development of social and microhistory in the 1970s considerably raised the interest in egodocuments. Nowadays many studies within social and cultural history are based on this kind of sources: it is acknowledged that the use and the study of egodocuments can contribute to a different, personal perspective, 'by endowing ordinary lives with agency, dignity, and texture'.[3] Whether a text is factually true, which used to be one of the main questions at the beginning of this kind of research, is no longer relevant. It is rather the subjectivity of an author's writings, the creation of a certain image of himself and his own version of reality that is of interest for contemporary historians.[4]

First World War research fits well in this larger trend. For a long time, personal texts of the main protagonists of this war, soldiers, were excluded from historical research. One of the first historians who considered these texts as sources for research was Jean Norton Cru in 1929. In *Témoins* he stated that the writings of soldiers had to be critically scrutinized in order to become useful as an historical source, and as a result examined 300 novels, memoirs, and letters published in French. In particular, Cru wanted to check the correctness of soldiers' statements about their whereabouts, and he detected other implausible and incorrect accounts and forms of expression. Although he was hypercritical about what he considered a credible testimony, fore-

---

1 Romein 1946, 204.
2 Baggerman 2005, 108. Presser 1958.
3 Dekker 2002, 7–12. Dekker quotes Mary Lindemann in the *Encylopaedia of European Social History*.
4 Dekker 2002, 7–12.

most a reaction to the exclusion of war experience of soldiers from the First World War historiography, he also presented many passages of men describing their war experiences.[5] Annette Becker and Stéphane Audoin-Rouzeau criticize Cru's study.[6] They rightly consider his method as a way of setting a rigid and selective standard regarding the trustworthiness of soldiers' experiences. Nevertheless, it should be stressed that Cru was one of the first historians that took egodocuments seriously as a source in the historic discipline as a whole. Within the field of First World War history, Cru remained an exception for a long time, since war historians remained focused on political and diplomatic history until the 1960s.

Thanks to the 'cultural turn' in war history, historians started to use soldiers' egodocuments on a large scale in the seventies. First, scholars used to select and analyse egodocuments with little consideration for the social background of the writers and with a strong overrepresentation of elite and intellectual voices as a result. Recently, growing attention has been paid to the question of the social representativeness of these sources, and this strong social bias has been corrected to some extent by integrating more egodocuments of popular origin.[7] Within French historical research, with Rémi Cazals as its forerunner, numerous soldiers' diaries were published and attracted a lot of attention. For instance, more than 60,000 copies of Cazals' publication of the diaries of barrel-maker Louis Barthas have been sold.[8] Studies based on diaries and letters of British, Austrian and German soldiers followed, such as the work of Eric J. Leed, in which personal experiences, representations and emotions are addressed, as well as explanations why soldiers persisted for four years.[9] In Belgium, research using egodocuments from the soldiers is more limited, especially with regard to the First World War. Benvindo (2005) and Amez (2009) are the only two historians who primarily used letters and diaries when describing the experiences of soldiers. Amez is the only one to devote an entire book to egodocuments he found in Belgium's Royal Army Museum in which he discusses, for example, the conditions at the battlefield, patriotism and leisure based on these sources.[10] National and international research on egodocuments has thus been used successfully to access the mentalities, perceptions and emotions of soldiers during the First World War. In particular war diaries became a central source for the cultural and social history of the front experience.

Strangely enough, far less attention has been paid by historians to the act of writing war diaries itself. War diaries have been elaborately explored as a source, but their genesis has not been taken seriously as a practice. This lack of attention contrasts with historians' interest for other forms of soldiers' writing. The dynamics of war corre-

---

5   Winter, Jay & Antoine Prost 2005, 14, 87. Cru 1929.
6   Audoin-Rouzeau & Becker 2000, 63.
7   Hanna 2006.
8   Barthas & Cazals 1978.
9   Winter & Prost 2005, 99–100; Leed 1979; Watson 2008.
10 Amez 2009 and 2013; Benvindo 2005.

spondence, between soldiers and their families and friends, and of course war literature, has been systematically analysed.[11] The same can be said about studies on trench journals – written and read by 'common' soldiers.[12] This relative lack of systematic attention for the practise of diary writing by soldiers is peculiar if one considers that the war generated a substantial boom of diary writing in the trenches. As these sources are more self-referential than letters, they offer a different access to war experiences.[13] Moreover, the motivations that explain why soldiers started writing diaries on a massive scale are only rarely addressed in historical research. This is quite noteworthy, since First World War diaries take up a complex place in the epistemology of testimony, states linguist Nancy Martin in her article on diaries and combatant identity. The genre of the diary does not follow the traditional structural form of narrative.[14] Since diaries focus usually on the immediate present, they are often serial, open-ended, repetitive and contradictory: 'Diaries often display a reshaping and revising of an individual's experiences and perceptions, illustrating what Martha Nussbaum describes as the constantly shifting self, or 'selves'.[15] Moreover, most soldiers did not keep a diary before the war, and thus were not used to diary writing. Apparently, they felt the need to start writing as many civilians did in order to 'make sense of the war'.[16] Reasons could be found in psychological studies in which various explanations have been provided to explain the functions of diary writing. Therefore, the explorative research presented in this chapter seeks to contribute to an active dialogue between history and psychology. This interdisciplinary dialogue can also be interesting for the ongoing controversy about the reasons of soldiers' capacity to fight on in spite of all deprivations of warfare.[17]

2   Diaries in psychology: functions and effects

Diaries are of great interest to psychologists.[18] According to Wheeler and Reis[19], they are designed to capture the "little experiences of everyday life that fill most of our working time and occupy the vast majority of our conscious attention". A first benefit

---

11   For example, Beaupré 2006; Hanna 2003; Roper 2009; Meyer 2009.
12   Audoin-Rouzeau 1986; Nelson 2011. For an overview of Belgian trench journals, see Bertrand 1971 and Bulthé 1971.
13   The 'writing boom' also results in the accessibility of diaries within archives. The British National Archive and the Imperial War Museum made nearly 4,000 First World War diaries online available.
14   For a literary perspective on war narratives, see Cobley 1993.
15   Martin 2015, 1248.
16   De Schaepdrijver 2014. See also next chapter.
17   Purseigle 2007.
18   Bolger, Davis & Rafaeli 2003.
19   Wheeler & Reis 1991, 340.

of using diaries as sources is that they permit the examination of reported events and experiences in their natural, spontaneous context, providing information complementary to those that are obtainable by more traditional methods in psychology, such as laboratory studies or questionnaires.[20] Secondly, because reconstructions in memories occur very rapidly, it is important that people recollect events soon after they occur. Diaries offer a very efficient way to reduce retrospection biases by minimizing the amount of time elapsed between an experience and the account of this experience. Various situations of psychological importance have been examined through diaries such as marital and family interactions[21], physical symptoms[22] or mental health.[23]

In addition, to obtaining reliable person-level information, Bolger *et al.* identified two other research objectives that can be achieved by studying diaries. Firstly, they offer a reliable way to obtain estimates of within-person change over time, as well as individual differences in such change. Diaries are thus excellent for studying temporal dynamics, such as weekday versus weekend effects, seasonal variation, or the long-lasting impact of an event. Secondly, diaries can help determine the antecedents and consequences of daily experiences. Daily diary writing is also particularly useful in understanding how people differ in their reactions to affective states as they go about their day-to-day lives.[24]

As previous studies highlighted, some important functions are involved when writing diaries. Recent research tests whether keeping a diary for some time can have beneficial effects for people encountering psychological difficulties. For instance, the intervention resource diary (RD) is a positive writing intervention designed to induce positive emotions and well-being by promoting reflection on personal memories and emotions and recognition of personal skills and potentials.[25] It is expected to activate an upward spiral of positive affect, which will then promote a more balanced style of emotion regulation and a greater accessibility of personal resources. Suhr *et al.*[26] showed that patients recently discharged from psychiatric inpatient treatment who completed the RD had significantly lower depression scores than controls and reported an increased use of the functional emotion regulation strategy 'reappraisal' five weeks after discharge. We will return later to the definition of emotion regulation and the positive effects of reappraisal.

This short overview shows that keeping a diary can have a beneficial effect on various aspects of psychological functioning. We will now examine how to apply this theoretical framework to the analysis of soldiers' diaries of the First World War in Belgium.

---

20 Reis 1994.
21 Almeida, Wethington & Chandler 1999.
22 Suls, Wan & Blanchard 1994.
23 Alloy, Just & Panzarella 1997.
24 Moeller, Nicpon & Robinson 2014.
25 Suhr, Risch & Wolz 2017.
26 Suhr, Risch & Wolz 2017.

3 Objectives and protagonists

Our main objective in this chapter is to examine the functions and meanings of soldiers' writings. This includes considering their writing practices as fulfilling coping and emotion regulation strategies. Did soldiers write in order to get a grip on their experiences in general and the deprivations of war in particular?

We analysed four diaries of combatants of different ranks: a sous-lieutenant, a physician, a corporal and an infantryman. Although diaries of the lowest ranks of the army are rarer, we tried to find diaries representing soldiers of different ranks. In addition, we searched for diaries that have never or rarely been used in other studies, as it is the case with some other published diaries.[27] As far as their social background is concerned, the quality of available information is not as consistent for the four diarists. All four diaries were written by Flemish combatants, but the linguistic background of the writers is irrelevant in this context.

Clément De Waele (1889–1918) was a doctor of law who joined the army as a volunteer immediately after Belgium was attacked in August 1914. He was born in Westkerke, a small village in West Flanders that was occupied by the Germans during the war, and was the youngest of a family of ten children. Within the period he wrote his diary, he was promoted to corporal. Later he became a lieutenant and thus achieved a significant elevation within the army. In 1917 and 1918, he was honoured with several decorations, such as the Order of the Crown and the Croix de Guerre. In September 1917, De Waele married Zulma Vandamme in Derby as she and her family stayed in England during the war. On 23 October 1918, during the final offensives and less than a month before the Armistice, he was fatally wounded and died at age 29. His diary is the shortest one, starting in January 1 1915 and ending in May 5 1915. Whether these are the only months he kept a diary is uncertain, since the way the text commences seems a continuation of earlier writings. It is therefore likely that only the part about this period of time has been preserved.

Joseph De Cuyper (1891–1918) was a physician who was already in military service when the war broke out. He was an assistant doctor in the First Army Division. The first months he spent at the front, after the battle of the Yser De Cuyper joined a 'colonne d'ambulance'. In 1915 he worked behind the front at a 'Section d'Hospitalisation', but in 1916 he returned to the front. He was born in the West-Flemish capital Bruges as the eldest son of a family of ten children. His father was the headmaster of a prestigious secondary school in Bruges. He served the entire duration of the war as a physician. As a result of his war experience, he became a committed partisan of the Flemish movement. During the Liberation offensive, he was killed at age 27 on September 30 1918. In six notebooks, his diary covers the period from July 29 1914 until

---

27   For example, Deckers 1999.

October 18 1917. There is, however, a gap in his writings between September 29 1914 and February 12 1915.[28]

Louis Hanegraef (1893–?) was born in a bourgeois family in the Antwerp suburb of Berchem. As a student of the Antwerp Institut Supérieur de Commerce he volunteered with his brother Felix at the moment of the German invasion. Originally a soldier, he was promoted to a sous-lieutenant in 1916. He lost his brother in the war, but survived it himself. His ten notebooks encompass almost the entire war, from August 5 1914 (the day after Germany invaded Belgium) until November 7 1918 (four days before the Armistice). However, from 1917 onwards his entries become more concise, perhaps because of his promotion to the time-consuming rank of sous-lieutenant. In some of the carnets, he combined his writings with drawings.

Raymond Van Aughem (date of birth and death unknown) came from a far more humble social background than the other three diary writers. Unfortunately, we know very little about this soldier; apparently he had a working-class background and came from the Ghent region. As an infantry soldier he survived the war. The part of his diary that is preserved covers the end of the war, from February 5 1917 until April 12 1918. However, his diary is quite extensive for the relatively short period that is described.

The social backgrounds of the three first combatants contrast sharply with that of the last one. De Waele, De Cuyper and Hanegraef are highly educated and stem from well-to-do families from Flemish cities. Van Aughem clearly had a working-class background. This social contrast is of importance, since the war experiences of different layers of the army diverge greatly. It is already clearly reflected in the style and language of the four diaries. Hanegraef and De Cuyper wrote most of their diaries in French, which was at that time the elite language in Flanders, even though both of them were sympathetic to the Flemish movement. During the war this movement mainly strived for recognition of the Dutch (then mainly called Flemish) language in the army. After the war it expanded its agenda with regard to the preservation of the Flemish culture and history, the autonomy of the Belgian region of Flanders or even the forming of an independent State.[29] De Waele wrote in standard Dutch, except on one occasion when he wrote some strongly emotional sentences in French. In contrast, Van Aughem wrote his diary in his East-Flemish dialect in an almost phonetic spelling. Taking into account the sketchy and inconstant nature of their writings, it is likely that the four men wrote their diaries just for themselves. They did not publish their testimonies, and these are only known because their families donated the manuscripts to archives. Three of them were kept in the archives of the In Flanders Fields Museum in Ypres. Only the diary of De Cuyper was published, but decades after the end of the war.

---

28 His biography can be read in De Cuyper 1968, VII–XX.
29 See, for example, Vanacker 2000 and Wils 2014.

Regardless of the content, we noticed in the selected diaries that their styles differ. Although soldiers describe the same battles and war environment, some are very precise and give detailed descriptions, while others only note the most important aspects. But even this changes from day to day. Their writings contain similar content, which also reflects different coping strategies: it seems that the soldiers' background did not play a considerable role, at least in this regard. However, it is noticeable that they – as many other Belgian soldiers – wrote lengthy texts about their experiences at the beginning of the war and during the war of movement, but from 1916/17 onwards, many soldiers stopped writing, or their entries are less extensive. One explanation can be that they became used to the experiences and conditions at the front. Their chores and exercises were a routine and every day the same, and this resulted in a certain numbness. As said, representativeness is not a central aim of this chapter, but one still has to be aware of the complexity of these texts when interpreting or using them as a source.

As this chapter is an explorative study of the functions of diary writing, we approached the diaries without a set framework in order to avoid theoretical biases in our search for possible authors' motivations for writing. This required extensive close reading, which explains the limited number of diaries included in our study. Based on this initial exploratory reading, we gathered and identified topics that we considered relevant regarding our central question. We came up with a list of functions and meanings that emerged from an inductive reading, without any a priori categories. After sharing this list, we examined existing theories or models that can account for these findings. We identified two relevant frameworks from psychological literature: coping and emotion regulation.

The first one is related to the presence of coping mechanisms that could be inferred from the writing. Coping strategies refer to the responses (cognitive, emotional, and behavioural) that an individual develops when appraising an event as threatening, a context that frequently occurred during the war. The goal is to control, tolerate, or decrease the impact of the event in order to maintain physical and psychological well-being.[30] A classical distinction among coping strategies is often made between confrontation, and avoidance or detachment. Confrontation strategies involve the focalisation of attention towards the sources of stress, together with the psychological and somatic responses towards the stressful event.[31] Avoidance or detachment strategies involve drawing the attention away from the sources of stress, together with the psychological and somatic responses towards the stressful event. How is the use of these two large categories of coping illustrated in the diaries?

---

30   Folkman & Lazarus 1988.
31   Suls & Fletcher 1985.

4 Detachment and avoidance

War implies the confrontation with a level of violence that had been unknown to soldiers in their prior civilian lives. They had to develop strategies to cope with these new horrible experiences. In the four diaries we noticed that the soldiers either avoided the subject altogether – in order to repress the experience of violence – or confronted or elaborated on the topic in order to process it psychologically. However, it is difficult to observe which option prevails. A strategy was to write down very short and apparently very factual sentences about the most gruesome experiences. Descriptive notes on the number of casualties of a German attack without or with very little emotional vocabulary can be found in the four diaries. This sentence of De Cuyper written down on 10 July 1917 offers a good example:

> "The number of casualties at 4, 24 and 3 at M.V.D. This number rises to 23 during the night and today."[32]

To write violent experiences down in such a detached way seems at first glance quite pointless. Why not completely omit them when it is apparently too painful to write about them, or the other way around, why not write everything down when these violent experiences are already mentioned? The frequency of detached descriptions of horror is so high that it must have some function for the diary writers. We hypothesize that writing about violence in a detached way enabled soldiers to get a grip on their disturbing experiences, while not being (overly) destabilized by it. Writing in a detached way could not only be achieved by a descriptive style, but also by allusion, writing about the violence of war in an indirect way. Hanegraef, for example, regularly mentions the odour of corpses without ever going further into the subject. Detachment can also be achieved by dehumanizing the experience of violence. De Waele describes a bombardment of a town wherein many inhabitants were killed or wounded. He directly expresses his revulsion by underlining several words, such as the horrible things they encountered upon seeing the victims, e. g., a man whose entire face was gone. But whilst describing the man with the disfigured face, he suddenly detaches himself, by writing 'thing' instead of 'man':

> "and that repulsive thing is still alive."[33]

De Waele not only addressed violence in a detached way by replacing emotion-charged words, he also changed his language. As mentioned, he wrote primarily in Dutch. However, in one diary entry he abruptly switches to French in order to address his greatest fear, the death of his mother who remained in the occupied land suffering from famine and violence. Perhaps because it was too painful to write about this in his own language:

---

32 De Cuyper 1968, note of 10.7.1917, 181.
33 In Flanders Fields (IFF), 3048, Diary Clément de Waele, note of 17.4.1915.

"For some time now, a frightful punishment tortures me. What if Maman died during my absence? Every day I think about it. No doubt, the good God would not allow such a thing, this catastrophe, the death of our mother! […] This thought tortures me and has become an obsession."[34]

Avoidance can also take other forms. One especially interesting strategy involves the use of (black) humour to address difficult topics. The ability to use humour in order to distance oneself from very stressful situations is described in psychological research as a functional strategy.[35] De Waele writes about a night in the trenches, illustrating how he and his friend suddenly find light in a terrible situation, as well as his humorous cynical comment about the conditions at the front:

"I have not slept at all. (…) My back, my neck, everything hurts. My feet are almost frozen. The night passes so slowly. We lose (my comrade and I) our courage, but suddenly we laugh at each other because we are so dirty. We are surrounded by, without exaggeration, more than 100 dead cows, which have already been lying there for more than three months; at least the crows enjoy a festive meal."[36]

Van Aughem also jokes about the war. First he writes that it does not stop raining, which affects the progress of the troops, and then he mentions that he and his comrades

"drink a fine glass of beer in honour of the birthday of the war."[37]

That the 'birthday of the war' is not the date of his entry, August 2, but two days later, is understandably no less reason to have a drink.

5   Confronting

A detached way of writing within the diaries alternates with moments in which the writers adopt confrontation strategies. Some of these descriptions are quite elaborate; at other times, one single sentence illustrates what is experienced and felt. As reported before, it is difficult to conclude whether a detached or a confronting style prevails, as the content of their writings is highly unstable, changing from day to day.

---

34   IFF, Dossier 3048, Diary Clément de Waele, note of 16.1.1915. 'Ik ben nog ziek, de hoofdpijn verminderd en de keelpijn gedaan. De eetlust blijft nog achter. Ik blijf nog den ganschen dag liggen. Depuis quelque temps déjà, une peine affreuse me torture. Si Maman était morte en mon absence. Chaque jour je songe à cela. Pauvre maman. Non sans doute, le bon Dieu ne permettra pas cette chose, cette catastrophe, la mort de notre mère! Maman, nous avons encore tous tant besoin de votre présence, au milieu de nous. La mort de Maman, ne serait-ce pas le raison pour laquelle je reste sans nouvelles de vous. Cette pensée me torture et devient une idée fixe.'
35   Abel 2002; Erickson & Feldstein 2007; Geisler & Weber 2010.
36   IFF, Dossier 3048, Diary Clément de Waele, 14.1.1915.
37   IFF, 7106, Diary Raymond Van Aughem, Note of 2.8.1917. Transcription by Jack de Moor.

Deprivations are sometimes described in short, confronting sentences that immediately illustrate their situation. For example, with regard to fights, De Cuyper states:

> "We live in a real hell: guns, cannons, minenweerfer [sic], all of these are present. The bombs are terrible."[38]

Feelings of loneliness and abandonment are also reported. De Waele writes:

> "I am sick. (…) Here no one takes care of you. One loses his courage in such circumstances. It is the same when one of us is left behind on the battlefield. One thinks so little about his comrades!"[39]

A specific moment that elicits confrontational responses is the return to the front, as Van Aughem writes:

> "The train leaves (…) and again the days of happiness are gone. The journey to the trenches begins."[40]

There are also events that at first sight might seem trivial but, due to the circumstances, deeply affect their mood such as the following situation described by Hanegraef:

> "I had the misfortune of losing my wallet, and we are terribly broke. Consequence: we are deeply depressed."[41]

Other descriptions are more elaborated and detailed. It seems that they felt the need to write down their experiences in order to cope with the tragedies they encountered. In these situations, the authors also often reflect on their feelings concerning, for instance, the conditions of trench life. In a long account, De Waele tells about going to the trenches:

> "We have to cross the Yser (…). We cannot reach our trench. We fall into the holes made by the shells. Our feet are wet, and we are muddy to our bottom. We find our trench. Never in my life have I seen anything so dirty. (…) Mud and water. We have to crawl on our bellies to the trenches and have to lie down in the mud. (…) We are to stay here for 24 to 30 hours. At first, I think I will go crazy."[42]

Earlier we mentioned that the authors mainly write about death and casualties in a factual manner. But when they themselves were involved in the events in question, chances are that they will include more details. Van Aughem, for example, conscientiously includes the tale of a particularly terrible episode in the trenches. On a bright and therefore dangerous night, he witnesses two men getting shot on the road to his post. One of them was severely injured and was not able to reach the trench unaided. When others tried to rescue him, unsuccessfully, they were wounded in the process.

---

38   De Cuyper 1968, note of 14.5.1915, 67.
39   IFF, 3048, Diary Clément de Waele, note of 15.1.1915.
40   IFF, 7106, Diary Raymond Van Aughem, note of 17.2.1917.
41   IFF, 1897, Diary Louis Hanegraef, note of 12.4.1915. Transcription by Jack de Moor.
42   IFF, 3048, Diary Clément de Waele, note of 7.1.1915.

Van Aughem sums up the men's injuries, and describes how one soldier, who was able to get back to the post, was treated with a rope around his leg. He remarks that others were not so lucky:

> "It is terrible to hear the boys scream. The boy who lay there for almost 4 hours, still screamed for help in a heart-breaking tone. Finally the boy and two of his rescuers died of their injuries and the cold; three others survived but were seriously wounded."[43]

Van Aughem is reflecting on his feelings and his sense of helplessness:

> "It is terrible to see your comrades die like this, and not to be able to help them."[44]

Another topic which elicits strong emotional responses from our writers is family. Friends and family living in occupied Belgium are a reoccurring subject in the diaries, one which receives particular attention during holidays which the soldiers used to celebrate alongside their loved ones. These are moments which highlight the unusual character of their present situation to the diary keepers. For instance, De Waele writes:

> "Today I start a bit downhearted. Tomorrow is Easter, and on other years we are all together with you, dear Mother; but now I am all alone. You will think about me, that is for sure, but I will think all day of you as well. There are no days in which I don't think very, very much about you. I will be glad when this day is over. On other days, we are not so sad as today."[45]

As the war continued, they also often reflected on the passing of yet another year in the trenches and beside their homesickness expressed their desire that the war would end soon.[46]

We noticed that soldiers regularly alternate confrontational descriptions, when they address the very hard conditions of life, with moments of avoidance during which they do not report any hardship or do so in a particularly distant and detached style. This corresponds with psychological literature demonstrating that in difficult situations such as grief, the most efficient way of coping is to alternate between confrontation and avoidance coping strategies. For instance, the dual-process model of coping with bereavement (or DPM) describes the regular oscillation that is associated with the most successful ways of dealing with the death of a close relative.[47]

---

43 IFF, 7106, Diary Raymond Van Aughem, note of 6.2.1917.
44 IFF, 7106, Diary Raymond Van Aughem, note of 6.2.1917.
45 IFF, 3048, Diary Clément de Waele, note of 3.4.1915.
46 IFF, 7106, Diary Raymond Van Aughem, note of 1.1.1918.
47 Stroebe & Schut 1999.

6 Emotion regulation

The soldiers' diaries also illustrate how diary writing sustains emotion regulation as defined in psychology, which could explain the functions and meanings of keeping a diary. Emotion regulation includes a set of processes by which individuals assess, control, and modify their spontaneous emotional responses to accomplish their goals or to express socially appropriate emotional behaviours. Regulation can operate both consciously and unconsciously and exerts its effects on the intensity, type, persistence, and lability of the emotions felt.[48] A distinction needs to be made between emotion regulation and coping. The main difference consists in the duration of the down-regulation, i.e., coping aims to decrease the negative affect for a longer time. Gross developed a model in which different regulation mechanisms occur through time.[49] We identified two of them that are relevant for the analysis of the diaries. The first one is attention orientation in which people can decide to distract themselves from unpleasant emotions either by thinking of pleasant past events or by engaging in activities unrelated to those negative emotions (e.g. reading a novel, doing physical exercise). The second is cognitive change, in which people mentally modify the way they perceive an event. The most common cognitive change is reappraisal during which the person reinterprets aims, causes and outcomes of the situation. It can involve the perception of positive aspects within a negative situation (e.g. learning from bad experiences), focusing on long-term benefits rather than on short-term costs, or relativizing the situation by comparing his/her own status with people in even more difficult settings.

In December 1915, Hanegraef sent a letter to a friend informing her that he and his comrades could stay in a little cabin during the winter. He writes:

> "To shout out our opulence: we have a stove and windows! Ask a soldier what that means if he has ever lived on the front, and he will explain. For us it means light and warmth on these cold winter days."

and he continued by saying that this felt a bit like home. In the last sentence of his letter, Hanegraef concludes that outsiders would probably be astonished by the adaptability of Belgian soldiers.[50] In this letter, Hanegraef addresses explicitly what we noticed in all the diaries: the writers often mention positive matters that they appreciate or that make them cheerful. To hear from family and friends – staying in occupied Belgium and a constant source of concern for soldiers – obviously brought pleasure, as well as relief. However, trivial things that seem normal at first sight, but are not that evident in the trenches, are also often described.[51]

---

48 Luminet 2013.
49 Gross & Thompson 2007.
50 IFF, 1897, Louis Hanegraef, letter to Maria, 6.12.1915.
51 Several historians address positive descriptions of banal events or experiences, which were important to maintain soldiers' morale: see Martin 2015, 1247–1248 and Prost 2014, 58.

We observed that the context can have an important impact on the type of event that the soldiers describe, as well as on their writing style. For instance, the diaries are often more elaborate when they are on leave. This is understandable, since they experienced more varied events compared to the trenches, and also more enjoyable ones. When they were at the front, their entries are often shorter, but it is still noticeable that within one entry, factual, negative and positive issues are often successively written down. This makes sense since the authors often summarise their entire day and this comes with different descriptions, feelings and experiences. However, what is interesting is that within their description, they almost always mention something positive. This can be explained either by their will to focus their attention on any positive aspect, even very briefly, during the day (attention orientation). It could also be the result of purely cognitive mechanisms. In that case, it is possible that nothing positive happened, but that they were able to reappraise the situation in order to find some positive aspects in it (cognitive change). For example, De Waele writes:

> "I wonder if I will make it through the war alive! When will this be done?"

But immediately thereafter states:

> "We have not so much to complain about. It is no longer freezing. We are warmly dressed, have good food and even if we have to cross the Yser, we receive a bottle of cognac."[52]

From a psychological point of view, the author uses descendant social comparison. This consists of comparing oneself with potentially less favoured people and is generally considered as a very efficient strategy to decrease negative emotions.

The diary of De Cuyper reflects his ability to highlight any even slightly pleasurable moment in very negative circumstances, which fits within the attention orientation category of emotion regulation described above. In one and the same entry he mentions that a friend has gone to Calais to have his eyes treated (which means that De Cuyper is alone once more), that a torrential bout of rain has flooded the place they are staying at and that two men were killed by a shell, not far from them the day before. Yet despite all these very painful and unpleasant events, he takes the times to mention that he ate excellent rice porridge during a visit of the village of Ramskapelle.[53]

As mentioned before, family and friends who remained in the occupied land caused a lot of worries. News from the home front was scarce, and the information they received was not very reassuring. Diaries report situations in which Germans were staying in their family houses, that there was a severe shortage of food and that cities were being bombed. Although news from home involved these negative and sometimes threatening issues, receiving letters improved soldiers' morale. Letters

---

52   IFF, 3048, Diary Clément de Waele, note of 30.1.1915.
53   De Cuyper 1968, note of 10.2.1915, 56.

brought relief, they confirmed that – at least at the moment of writing – the family was safe and moreover thought about and cared for them:

> "This morning I reread the letters I received at the beginning of the war. (…). This gave me joy, to see that over there lives a good mother, the best mother, who thinks about me day and night, brothers and sisters who care for me. I thank God for having given me such a family, and I ask Him to spare them so that I can see them again in full health after the war."[54]

This is an interesting example of attention orientation. As the possibilities of positive experiences at the front were extremely reduced, De Waele focuses his attention on one of the few available sources of joy.

Home was something they fantasised about. As mentioned before, during holidays, it was mainly in a gloomy way. For example, Van Aughem, who writes on 31 December 1917 that he is sad that he cannot celebrate a normally pleasant New Year's Eve with his family as they always did.[55] However, when he met friends from the same town, they could talk about home and happier times, which provided an escape from their current situation:

> "At night I visit Josef, but on the way I ran into Jeron de Clercq with whom I go out, and we speak of the past and, of course, also about Ghent."[56]

While the previous example of attention orientation illustrated the possibility of thinking of pleasant past events in an individual way by rereading letters, the present one shows an even more efficient emotion regulation behaviour: Van Aughem reactivates positive feelings related to past events, but this time in the presence of other soldiers sharing the same geographic background, which stimulates a sense of belonging to a community, which is an essential human need combined with the activation of positive memories. Together, these changes are likely to maintain a positive mood for a longer period of time. Hanegraef describes a similar evening and mentions the comforting effect of talking about the past. He is on leave in Vichy and stays with a family from his own hometown Antwerp:

> "As a result, we feel transported to home (…) we quickly pass over the miseries of war, to the memories of the happy life of yesteryear. The trenches are already far away after only one evening of intimacy."[57]

Fulfilling basic needs was very important in order to cope with the very adverse situations they had to deal with, as can be seen in many entries in which they write repeatedly about 'trivial' or simple things such as taking a bath or having a haircut. However, as Hanegraef mentioned in his letter addressed above, these apparently basic activities were not that evident in the trenches, and thus when they occurred, they

---

54 IFF, 3048, Diary Clément de Waele, note of 19.1.1915.
55 IFF, 3048, Diary Clément de Waele, note of 31.12.1917.
56 IFF, 7106, Diary Raymond Van Aughem, note of 3.5.1917.
57 IFF, 1897, Diary Louis Hanegraef, note of 21.6.1916.

were highly appreciated. The four writers regularly report how they felt better when they and their clothes were clean and dry, and when they could have a nice dinner. Whenever Van Aughem had the opportunity to take a bath or to swim in the sea he explicitly mentioned this, as did Hanegraef and De Waele. The opportunity to bathe was worth writing about, since it did not occur every day or even every week: our diarists reported that it could take 5 to 15 days before they could wash themselves.[58] Hanegraef noticed, in his own words, a 'repugnant detail'. He had the opportunity to put on new clothes, and take off his underpants for the first time since Christmas. He wrote this on 30 March.[59]

Other recurrent descriptions are related to interrelations between eating and weather. Both were often reported in a negative way, but when the soldiers had a proper meal, the weather was good and the landscape beautiful: this could really uplift their spirits. De Cuyper had a good day during Christmas 1914; it was a beautiful day, and he had a pleasant time at the home of the stretcher bearers, where he had dinner with wine and cognac.[60] Hanegraef writes very often about food; almost in every entry he notes what soldiers eat, often just simple meals like 'rice soup'. However, when they ate something special, he gives many details about the composition of the meal. Hanegraef writes about a

> "succulent lunch of sausages. Although our meals are rather frugal (…) we sometimes arrange our meals as we would not expect at the countryside. Like the dinner we had yesterday: the soup of the troop with boiled meat, pork (chop and stew) with bread, rice with raisins and finally a good coffee."[61]

However, this was not usual:

> "I should add that feasts like this are among the great exceptions, and they cost us a great deal of trouble to prepare them."[62]

An experience that exceeded the pleasures of a bath or food, and could ignite a moment of genuine happiness, was seeing or meeting King Albert I. Without exception soldiers expressed joy, were impressed and motivated after an encounter with the monarch. The decision of the King to stay with Queen Elisabeth near the front was a great support for the soldiers, and the concern Albert demonstrated for the wellbeing of his troops contributed to his nearly mythical status. Hanegraef writes that they were marching through the fields when suddenly their commandant talks with a man:

> "It is the King! We pass silently, impressed, our throats tightened with emotion."[63]

---

58 For example, IFF, 3048, Diary Clément de Waele, note of 17.1.1915 and IFF, 1897, Diary Louis Hanegraef, note of 26.11.1914.
59 IFF, 1897, Diary Louis Hanegraef, note of 30.3.1915.
60 De Cuyper 1968, note of 25.12.1914, 46.
61 IFF, 1897, Diary Louis Hanegraef, note of 27.11.1914.
62 IFF, 1897, Diary Louis Hanegraef, note of 27.11.1914.
63 IFF, 1897, Diary Louis Hanegraef, note of 21.11.1914.

He felt the same during a ceremony in which the King inspected the troops:

> "A very moving ceremony. The King looks very good. He traces the experiences of the regiment since the beginning of the war with remarkable precision in an emotional speech."[64]

De Waele equally describes that it is very emotional to see the King:

> "We feel proud, and everybody feels the love for our fatherland, and how we adore our King."[65]

7   Structuring time and place

Warfare is particularly disorientating; it disturbs existing notions of place and time. This may explain the urge that people felt to write down their war experiences, in order to get a grip on a situation that was generally perceived as involving an absence of structure or being disruptive. This might be particularly the case for trench warfare, since it generated literally a feeling of being lost in space and time. The apparently everlasting war in the trenches was a difficult time perspective to cope with. This was even more the case for the Belgian soldiers since they did not participate in major offensive operations for most of the war as a result of the strictly defensive strategy of King Albert.[66] Although soldiers were less exposed to injuries and death through violence, the static situation concerned them. Especially because of their families in the occupied land they longed for action. De Waele writes at the beginning of February 1915:

> "6 months of war. A month of the year 1915. And we are still at the same position. I am sometimes worried that we cannot defeat the Germans."[67]

In addition, this lack of action was an important source of boredom and war weariness. Days at the Belgian front were often very much the same. The sentiment of being bored can often be found in the diaries, as soldiers stressed the passing-by of the days. Moreover, Belgian soldiers had little opportunity to escape temporally from the everlasting army experience as they could in general not go home and the possibilities to go on leave were relatively limited as well. De Waele expressed the perception of the sameness of all days in his diary on 31 January 1915:

> "Sunday, today. One does not know. Sunday or Saturday, it's all the same. We play a bit of cards, in the trenches."[68]

---

64 IFF, 1897, Diary Louis Hanegraef, note of 3.4.1915.
65 IFF, 3048, Diary Clément de Waele, note of 25.2.1915.
66 van Ypersele 1995; Velaers 2009.
67 IFF, 3048, Diary Clément de Waele, note of 2.2.1915.
68 IFF, 3048, Diary Clément de Waele, note of 31.1.1915.

In order to structure their blurry experience of sameness, soldiers paid great attention to timing in their war writings. The war diary as a genre in many ways resembles an agenda in which the author makes short notes about his daily activities, even with a precise time schedule. A telling example is that of Van Aughem for 14 March 1917:

> "In the morning from 6 o'clock onwards the trench; at a quarter to 8 alignment and we kick off for the dunes. It is raining, but we nevertheless have to stay till 12 o'clock. In the evening, I go with Jul to the library and that way another evening passes by."[69]

The frequency in the diaries written by soldiers of this type of apparently factual notes about the timing of the day clearly reflects a need for structure. Otherwise, the practise of systematically writing down the timing of daily routines cannot be explained.

However, the time dimension of the writings is not solely used to structure daily life. Soldiers also write about time in order to express their unease about the seeming endlessness of the war. By their very nature, these writings about the *longue durée* of the war are far more emotionally expressive and confrontational than the apparently factual notes on daily life. Generally, meaningful dates act as a trigger for this kind of reflection. For example, New Year's Day of 1918 prompted Van Aughem to write the following:

> "Yet another year has passed by, a year which brought nothing but misery for me. But, I have been bearing all this without complaining. One hears only wishes of happiness in the camp. But it is the fourth time already that one hears that. We hope it shall be the last time."[70]

Also dates with a more personal meaning as in the case of Hanegraef, the fair in his native Berchem, his parents' wedding anniversary and his own anniversary provoke writings of this nature.

Soldiers also felt the need to situate themselves geographically. They systematically registered their movements in their diaries. As they had little control over their movements themselves, writing them down was perhaps one of the only ways to get a grip on them. An example is an entry of De Cuyper, who writes:

> "Housed at Capelle. Two 'aviatiks' arrive. One goes to Dunkirk, the other drops two bombs on Veurne and then disappears. Result? Three soldiers badly wounded. In front of Voorstad [Veurne], where the bomb fell, we see shreds of flesh and pieces of clothes."[71]

At times they mentioned their position with regard to the deprivations of war, as Van Aughem did:

> "I am so glad that once again I could return from hell. That's what they call the sector of Merkem."[72]

---

69   IFF, 7106, Diary Raymond Van Aughem, note of 14.3.1917.
70   IFF, 7106, Diary Raymond Van Aughem, note of 1.1.1918.
71   De Cuyper 1968, note of 6.1.1915, 48.
72   IFF, 7106, Diary Raymond Van Aughem, note of 1.12.1917.

As noted before, they also compared their situation to others: whenever possible, the situations in their own hometowns were closely observed. De Waele writes after hearing rumours about the possibility that the area around his own village was going to be bombed:

> "Supposedly, there is no danger for Westkerke. But these villages of Ghistel and Westkerke are likely to be destroyed completely within a month. How you must suffer with our enemies, all this time in your vicinity, and without truthful news about the war."[73]

As mentioned earlier with regard to emotion regulation, positive aspects are emphasized. For example, when the beauty of the landscape is addressed. Specifically, Hanegraef often mentions the scenery, and at the same time the focus on time and place can be seen. He writes:

> "Watch at the hamlet of Knesselaere. We walk for 20 km on waterlogged roads. Beautiful landscapes. At 1 o'clock we stand guard at Raverschoot with adjutant Morlet. From 5 to 7 I go with Edouard to the road before the bridge. Then from 11 to 1, from 5 to 7 and from 11 to 1. No incidents. The weather was very beautiful and I enjoyed this beautiful day of September spent in the countryside."[74]

8 Conclusion

It is common knowledge that the experience of the First World War prompted soldiers to write on a scale unknown before. This was particularly true for war diaries as the considerable number kept in archives testifies. Historians have been fruitfully using these diaries for a number of years now as a source of the experiences and perceptions of the soldiers. However, the crucial question of what urged so many soldiers to write a diary has not yet been systematically addressed. This exploratory chapter tackles this question by introducing psychological concepts in an historical analysis of the war diaries of four Belgian soldiers. While the scope and empirical basis of this article may be limited, it shows the potential of such an interdisciplinary approach. The collaboration between historians and psychologists makes it possible to really take diary writing seriously as a practice by analysing it as an emotional strategy. Of course, the functions of diaries are not limited to their psychological dimensions. However, if we want to understand what motivated so many soldiers to write diaries, these dimensions should be taken into account to a larger extent than is generally the case in historiography. Judging by our small sample of Belgian war diaries, two psychological concepts seem to be particularly promising for a better understanding of soldiers' writings: coping and regulation strategies.

The alternation of confrontational and avoiding styles of writing in war diaries could be seen as part of constant shifting of emotional coping strategy. By stressing

---

73 IFF, 3048, Diary Clément de Waele, note of 1.3.1915.
74 IFF, 1897, Diary Louis Hanegraef, note of 22.9.1914.

good experiences and by spacing and timing themselves, diary writers seemingly tried to regulate their emotions in the gruesome and disorienting context of industrial warfare. One could therefore argue that the analysis of the functions of diary writing adds yet another dimension to the everlasting debate on the soldiers' willingness to keep on fighting. Writing a diary was one of many more strategies of soldiers to take care of themselves under the gruesome conditions of industrial warfare. It helped them to keep themselves in balance psychologically, and therefore might have contributed to the capacity to fight on. The Belgian soldiers might have felt a particular need, since the vast majority of them were cut off from their family for four long years. Needless to say, these observations necessitate far more systematic research. Moreover, psychological insights on diary writing offer more clues for a better understanding, which have not been fully explored in this article, for example, the impact of passing of time on writing practices.

References

Alloy, L. B., Just, N. & Panzarella, C. (1997). Attributional style, daily life events, and hopelessness depression: subtype validation by prospective variability and specificity of symptoms. *Cognitive Therapy and Research,* 21, 321–44.

Almeida, D. M., Wethington, E. & Chandler, A. L. (1999). Daily transmission of tensions between marital dyads and parent-child dyads. *Journal of Marriage and Family,* 61, 49–61.

Amez, B. (2009). *Dans les tranchées. Les écrits non publiés des combattants belges de la Première Guerre mondiale. Analyse de leurs expériences de guerre et des facteurs de résistance.* Paris: Publibook.

Amez, B. (2013). *Vie et survie dans les tranchées belges: témoignages inédits.* Brussels: Éditions Jourdan.

Audoin-Rouzeau, S. (1986). *14–18. Les combattants des tranchées: à travers leurs journaux.* Paris: Armand Colin.

Audoin-Rouzeau, S. & Becker, A. (2000). *14–18, retrouver la Guerre.* Paris: Gallimard.

Baggerman, A. (2005). Inleiding: Egodocumenten. Dagboeken, Brieven en Memoires als Historische Bron. *Spiegel Historiael,* 3/4, 108–113.

Barthas, L. (1978). *Les carnets de guerre de Louis Barthas, tonnelier, 1914–1918,* preface by Cazals, R. Paris: Maspéro.

Benvindo, B. (2005). *Des hommes en guerre. Les soldats belges entre ténacité et désillusion, 1914–1918.* Brussels: Archives générales du Royaume – Algemeen Rijksarchief.

Bertrand, F. (1971) *La presse francophone de tranchée au front belge, 1914–1918.* Brussels: Musée royal de l'armée et d'histoire militaire.

Beaupré, N. (2006). *Écrire en guerre, écrire la guerre. France, Allemagne 1914–1920.* Paris: CNRS Éditions.

Bolger, N., Davis, A. & Rafaeli, E. (2003). Diary methods: Capturing life as it is lived. *Annual Review of Psychology,* 54, 579–616.

Bulthé, G. (1971). *De Vlaamse loopgravenpers tijdens de Eerste Wereldoorlog.* Brussels: Koninklijk museum van het leger en van krijgsgeschiedenis.

Cobley, E. (1993). *Representing War: Form and Ideology in First World War Narratives*. Toronto: University of Toronto Press.

Cru, J. N. (1929). *Témoins: essai d'analyse et de critique des souvenirs de combattants édités en français de 1915 à 1928*. Paris: Les Étincelles.

De Cuyper, J. & De Cuyper, E.H.A. (Ed.) (1968). *Journal de campagne 1914-1917. Oorlogsdagboek van een hulpdokter bij het Belgisch leger*. Brugge: Genootschap voor Geschiedenis.

Deckers, R. & Gysel, A., Verbeke, R.V. & Malfait, G. (Eds) (1999). *Deckers' dagboek 1914-1919, Notities van een oorlogsvrijwilliger*. Gent: Snoeck Ducaju & Zoon.

Dekker, R. (2002). Introduction. In Dekker, R. (2002). *Egodocuments and history. Autobiographical writing in its social context since the Middle Ages*. Hilversum: Verloren, 7-20.

De Schaepdrijver, S. (2014). Making Sense of the War (Belgium). In Daniel, U., Gatrell, P., Janz, O., Jones, H., Keene, J., Kramer, A., Nasson B. 1914-1918-online. International Encyclopedia of the First World War. DOI: 10.15463/ie1418.10450. Berlin: Freie Universität Berlin.

Folkman, S. & Lazarus, R. S. (1988). The relationship between coping and emotion: Implications for theory and research. *Journal of Health and Social Behavior*, 21, 219-239.

Gross, J. J. & Thompson, R. A. (2007). Emotion regulation: Conceptual foundations. In Gross, J. J. (Ed.), *Handbook of emotion regulation*. New York: Guilford Press, 3-24.

Hanna, M. (2003). A Republic of Letters: The Epistolary Tradition in World War I France. *American Historical Review*, 108(5), 1338-1361.

Hanna, M. (2006). *Your Death Would be Mine. Paul and Marie Pireaud in the Great War*. Harvard: Harvard University Press.

Leed, E. J. (1979). *No man's land. Combat & identity in World War I*. Cambridge and London: Cambridge University Press.

Luminet, O. (2013). *Psychologie des émotions. Nouvelles perspectives pour la cognition, la personnalité et la santé*. Brussels: De Boeck.

Martin, N. (2015). 'And all because it is war!': First World War Diaries, Authenticity and Combatant Identity. *Textual Practice*, 29, 1245-1263.

Meyer, J. (2009). *Men of war. Masculinity and the First World War in Britain*. Basingstoke: Palgrave Macmillan.

Moeller, S. K., Nicpon, C. G. & Robinson, M. D. (2014). Responsiveness to the negative affect system as a function of emotion perception: Relations between affect and sociability in three daily diary studies. *Personality and Social Psychology Bulletin*, 40, 1012-1023.

Nelson, R. L. (2011). *German Soldier Newspapers of the First World War*. Cambridge: Cambridge University Press.

Presser, J. (1958). Memoires als geschiedbron. *Winkler Prins Encyclopedie*, VIII, Amsterdam: Elsevier, 208-210.

Prost, A. (2014). *Les Anciens Combattants 1914-1940*. Paris: Gallimard.

Purseigle, P. (2008). A very French debate: the 1914-1918 'war culture'. *Journal of War and Culture Studies*, 1(1), 9-14.

Reis, H. T. (1994). Domains of experience: Investigating relationship processes from three perspectives. In Erber, R. & Gilmore, R. (Eds), *Theoretical frameworks in personal relationships*. Mahwah, NJ: Erlbaum, 87-110.

Romein, J. (1946). *De biografie*, Amsterdam: Ploegsma.

Roper, M. (2009). *The secret battle. Emotional survival in the Great War*. Manchester/New York: Manchester University Press.

Stroebe, M. & Schut, H. (1999). The dual process model of coping with bereavement: Rationale and description. *Death Studies*, 23(3), 197-224.

Suhr, M., Risch, A. K. & Wolz, G. (2017). Maintaining mental health through positive writing: Effects of a resource diary on depression and emotion regulation. *Journal of Clinical Psychology*, 73, 1586–1598.

Suls, J. & Fletcher, B. (1985). The relative efficacy of avoidant and nonavoidant coping strategies: A meta-analysis. *Health Psychology*, 4, 249–288.

Suls, J., Wan, C. K. & Blanchard, E. B. (1994). A multilevel data-analytic approach to evaluation of relationships between daily life stressors and symptomatology: patients with irritable bowel syndrome. *Health Psychology*, 13, 103–113.

Vanacker, D. (2000). *De Frontbeweging: de Vlaamse strijd aan de IJzer*. Koksijde: De Klaproos.

van Ypersele, L. (1995). *Le roi Albert: histoire d'un mythe*. Ottignies: Quorum.

Velaers, J. (2009). *Albert I: Koning in tijden van oorlog en crisis, 1900–1934*. Tielt: Lannoo.

Watson, A. (2008). *Enduring the Great War. Combat, morale and collapse in the German and British armies, 1914–1918*. Cambridge: Cambridge University Press.

Wheeler, L., Reis, H. T. (1991). Self-recording of everyday life events: Origins, types, and uses. *Journal of Personality*, 59, 339–54.

Wils, L. (2014). *Onverfranst, onverduitst?: flamenpolitik, activisme, frontbeweging*. Kalmthout: Pelckmans.

Winter, J. & Prost, A. (2005). *The Great War in history. Debates and controversies, 1914 to the present*. Cambridge: Cambridge University Press.

Geneviève Warland and Olivier Luminet

Nil inultum remanebit: Germany in the War Diaries of the Historians Paul Fredericq and Henri Pirenne

1 Belgian scholars' attitude in the First World War's aftermath

In the aftermath of the First World War, many Belgian and French academics were unwilling to resume relationships with their German fellows. They were still profoundly shocked by their nationalistic support of the German Empire's war aims. The *Aufruf an die Kulturwelt!*[1] [*Appeal to the cultural world*] in October 1914, initiated by representatives of the *Kultusministerium* and signed by 93 well-known German academics to provide a justification for the German invasion of Belgium and the subsequent destructions and injuries, provoked a wave of reactions of indignation among scholars and intellectuals in Belgium, France and Great Britain.[2]

> "Pirenne is een vulkan von woed tegen Duitsland en zijn militarisme, dat hij nationalisme noemt. Hij citeert met welgevalem: Der Weg der Menschheit geht von Humanität zur Nationalität, von Nationalität zur Bestialität." [Pirenne is a volcano of anger against Germany and its militarism, which he calls nationalism. He likes to quote: the way of humankind goes from humanity to nationality, from nationality to bestiality],

wrote the historian, specialized in the history of the Inquisition and Dutch literature at Ghent University, Paul Fredericq (1850–1920) on 7 October 1914[3] in his diary about his colleague Henri Pirenne (1862–1935), one of the most distinguished medievalists that Belgium ever had. Such a disappointment with Germany rapidly turned into resentment against its academics. It is not only the case of Pirenne, but of many scholars in Belgium and in other countries.[4] The involvement of German academics in their country's war effort was perceived as the fierce expression of German nationalism, which was viewed as constituting one of the main causes of the war. Many university professors and academicians of the invaded countries felt that their relations with their former German fellows had been irreparably damaged.[5]

---

1 See Jürgen von Ungern-Sternberg and Wolfgang von Ungern-Sternberg 2013, vom Brocke, 1985.
2 See Horne 2005, 392ff.
3 For information on Fredericq's diary, see note 30 and the section "unpublished sources" with all the details in the bibliography.
4 As for instance the French philosopher Émile Boutroux or the historian Ernest Lavisse. For an overview, see von Ungern-Sternberg 2015.
5 See Crawford 1992, von Ungern-Sternberg 2003.

Accordingly, the attitude of German scholars was morally condemned and the question of how to deal with them after the war was an agenda item at both Conferences of the inter-allied Academies of Sciences in London and in Paris in 1918, which led to the creation of the *Conseil International de Recherches Scientifiques* (CIRS).[6] In his report *Les relations intellectuelles internationales d'après-guerre*, which served as a discussion basis at these conferences, the Belgian astronomer Georges Lecointe (1869–1929) pointed out that given the fact that

> "les intellectuels allemands ont prostitué la science en l'asservissant à leurs intérêts, lorsqu'ils ont lancé leur menteur Appel au monde civilisé, les Alliés ont à rompre, pour un temps déterminé tout au moins, dans la plus large mesure possible, les relations intellectuelles avec les Empires du Centre et les peuples soumis à leur influence."[7] [German intellectuals have prostituted the science in submitting it to their own interests, when they launched their Appeal to the Civilized World, the Allies have to interrupt, at least for a certain period of time, as far as they can, the intellectual relations to the Central Empires and the nations who are under their influence].

The decision to interrupt scientific relationships with the Central Empires and to ban their academicians from their position as corresponding members of academies in the allied countries was not only taken by the representatives of the academies of science.[8] The establishing of the *Union Académique Internationale* (UAI) followed the same principles of recasting scientific networks and cooperation exclusively among the winners of the war and neutral countries.[9] It also resulted in the exclusion of the German language from international scientific organizations in favor of English and French.[10] Even a few years later, when the *Comité International des Sciences Historiques* (CISH) resumed, German (as well as Austrian, Bulgarian, Hungarian and Turkish[11]) historians were still not allowed to become members and they were not invited to the first congress after the war, which was held in Brussels in 1923.[12]

In 1926 the Belgian Royal Academy officially decided to break the boycott of the German *Wissenschaft*.[13] In doing so, it followed the line of the Belgian authorities,

---

6 This topic had already been discussed during the war, officially – as for the exclusion of the Germans academicians of the *Institut de France* (Dmitriev 2002, 640) – or unofficially as among the members of the Belgian Royal Academy who lived in Ghent and decided in a private meeting that the scientific relations with Germany should be interrupted after the war because of the German responsibility. See Pirenne, *Journal de guerre*, 13.3.1915 and 5.6.1915 and Paul Fredericq, *Dagboek*, 13.3.1915.
7 de Guchtenaere, Lecointe 1919, 8.
8 de la Vallée Poussin, Lecointe, Massart 1919.
9 See Pirenne 1919b.
10 See Reinbothe 2010.
11 The exclusion was also effective for the countries, which were allied to Germany during the War. See Schröder-Gudehus 1966.
12 See Erdmann 2005.
13 See van Ypersele 2004.

which adjusted to the strand of international *détente* implied by the signing of the Locarno Pact (1925). The Belgian Academy estimated that it was time for what historians later designated as cultural demobilization.[14] In 1927, the UAI opted to include members of the former Central Powers. Similarly, historians from these countries attended the second international Congress of the Historical Sciences in Oslo in 1928.[15]

In these three international organizations (CIRS, UAI, CISH), the most radical voices against any kind of contact with scholars from the Central Powers came from representatives of Belgium and France, two countries which had suffered greatly from the German invasion and occupation.[16]

Why did Belgian and French scholars so vehemently expel their former – mainly German – colleagues and friends from any participation in the reconstruction of a new international science? Why did they not take into account different degrees of implication of German scholars to the war effort and/or propaganda? Why did they not consider the neutral or even critical attitude held by some of them towards their government and army authorities[17]?

We argue that, in the First World War's aftermath, emotions of sadness, hate and anger played a key role in decisions about postwar international cooperation. As a matter of fact, the decisions collectively taken by scholars and academicians from the allied countries expressed the injuries linked to war experiences and were driven by a strong sense of moral outrage as expressed, for instance, above in Lecointe's quotation. From a psychological point of view, this case shows how choices, which resulted from negotiation and votes made in a professional and presumably rational context, were in fact imbued with feelings. What is illustrated here is that reason cannot be fully separated from emotion: cognitive psychologists name it broadly "situated cognition".[18]

2   Belgian scholars' war experience: Paul Fredericq and Henri Pirenne's war diaries

In order to better understand Belgian scholars' attitude in the First World War's aftermath, we consider their war experience as a potential explanation for their antagonistic positions towards German scientists. Addressing this topic of micro- and emotional history, we did not primarily rely on administrative and scientific papers like

---

14   Horne 2002b.
15   See Erdmann 2005.
16   For the best informed overviews, see Schröder-Gudehus 1966 and 1986, and Anne Rasmussen 2007 with a focus on France.
17   See for instance the historians Ludwig Quidde and Veit Valentin.
18   Scheer 2012, esp. 197. Cognitive theories of emotion have shown that emotional experiences are determined by preliminary cognitive appraisals of a situation.

the reports of the Belgian Royal Academy or distinctive speeches[19], but on diaries as a particularly revealing source for autobiographical information (as the previous chapter devoted to the act of writing already showed). Following the growing interest in cultural history, diaries have eventually become in the last decades a major way to study the everyday life in war times and to grasp the feelings and the morale of individuals enduring the war. This kind of egodocuments represents a genre per se: facing such a turbulent situation and such a rupture in their lives, soldiers as well as civilians felt compelled to write down what they experienced.[20] So doing, they tried to "make sense of the war".[21]

While soldiers' diaries have been studied in the first chapter, the focus here is on diaries of two very influential scholars, the above-mentioned Paul Fredericq and Henri Pirenne, which are particularly telling to understand the attitude of Belgian scholars and academicians in the immediate postwar. Even if Fredericq's and Pirenne's diaries were written far from the battlefields, they cannot be fully assimilated to the category of "home front diaries"[22], e. g. diaries written by civilians providing a glimpse of civilian life during wartime. There are two reasons for this: firstly, Belgium was an occupied country and not a free territory and this kind of writing could have represented a danger[23]; secondly, Fredericq and Pirenne spent the war partly in captivity in Germany, giving an insight into the home front war experience of Germans civilians. In a nutshell, writing a diary meant a war effort in itself: if it was a way of calming down emotions and fighting the lack of activity, boredom and despair; it was also conceived as a testimony on experienced events or more general facts. Both diaries of Fredericq and Pirenne best illustrate these aspects.

Diaries showing the life in occupied Belgium were mainly written by intellectuals. Some of them were published shortly after the war: for instance, *Journal d'un journaliste: Bruxelles sous la botte allemande* – by Charles Tytgat (1919); *Nos années terribles 1914–18* by Charles Gheude (1919 or 1920); *Cinquante Mois d'Occupation Allemande* by Louis Gille, Alphonse Ooms, Paul Delandsheere (4 vol., 1919); *Notes d'un Gantois sur la guerre de 1914–18* by Marc Baertsoen (1922). Others diaries were rediscovered as interesting testimonies and published much later, very often at the occasion of First World War's anniversaries. This is the case for instance with war diaries of bourgeois women – for instance, the novelist Virginie Loveling who lived in Ghent[24] and the wife of a wealthy industrialist with German roots, Constance Graeffe[25] –, and of the novelist Paul Max.[26]

---

19   See Warland 2018b.
20   See, for instance, Henwood and René-Bazin 2016.
21   De Schaepdrijver 2016.
22   See Krumeich 1997, 12–19.
23   See De Schaepdrijver and Proctor (Eds) 2017.
24   See Van Peterghem, Ludo Stynen (Eds) 2013.
25   See De Schaepdrijver 2008.
26   See Majerus and Soupart (Eds) 2006.

As for Belgian scholars, no publication exists apart from the partly published war diary of Henri Pirenne that we will discuss hereafter. It is also striking that it is only recently that some (home war) diaries from scholars of other countries were published. Worth mentioning here are the diaries of distinguished German historians who had scientific contacts with Fredericq and Pirenne: Karl Hampe (1869–1936) from Heidelberg[27] and Alexander Cartellieri (1867–1955) from Jena.[28]

If some diaries were published after the war or in recent years, others are still in their initial manuscript form kept in libraries or in private households. With the Centenary of the First World War, some were digitalized and are now available in libraries' online catalogues or on the portal *Europeana 1914–18*. Fredericq's and Pirenne's diaries are unpublished or only very partly published. Fredericq's unpublished diary is kept at the library of the University of Ghent and is partly available online[29] whereas the unpublished part of Pirenne's diary is still in the possession of his family.[30] The part, which mainly covers the period spent by Pirenne in prisoner of war camps in Germany from March to September 1916, was published by Pirenne's biographer in the 1970s.[31]

These two professors of history at the University of Ghent and members of the Belgian Royal Academy belonged to a generation that was too old to actively take part in the war: Fredericq was 64 years old and Pirenne was 52.[32] They were forced to stay in Ghent, their home city, which was part of the *Etappengebiet* (i.e. rear area) and ruled by the German Army authorities from October 12th 1914 when the German troops arrived in the city. While Fredericq had been used to writing a diary since he was 19 years old in which he recorded anecdotes from everyday life, impressions and feelings about his writings and his professional environment, as well as political events[33], Pirenne only began a diary with the breakout of the First World War on August 2th 1914 and ended it on November 29th 1918 when he left Germany. He named it *Journal de guerre* and renamed it *Journal de captivité* from the time when he was deported to Germany. During his captivity, Pirenne collected his reflections, book comments and reports of conversations in a separate notebook: *Réflexions d'un solitaire*.[34] After the war, he used this variety of notes to compose an autobiographical article

---

27 See Reichert and Wolgast (Eds) 2004.
28 See Steinbach and Dathe 2014.
29 See https://lib.ugent.be/en/catalog/rug01:000770150?i=0&q=paul+fredericq+dagboek&type=manuscript#reference-details.
30 The diary is in the possession of his great grand-son, Yves Pirenne, who lives in the castle of Cernex in France.
31 See Lyon 1976.
32 On Fredericq in general, see Coppens 1990 and Tollebeek 2008. On Pirenne, see Lyon 1971 and Keymeulen and Tollebeek 2011.
33 On the circumstances of the beginning of Fredericq's *dagboek* and on its form, see Van Werweke 1979, 73.
34 See Lyon and Pirenne 1994.

narrating his experience in Germany: *Souvenirs de captivité* (1920).[35] If Fredericq did not develop such a system differentiating private and family matters from professional ones, he nevertheless gave a new name to his diary (*dagboek*) when he was transferred to Germany: *Rapture diary* (*wegvoeringsdagboeken*).

This chapter analyzes Fredericq's and Pirenne's diaries in order to understand which emotions both historians developed towards the Germans. We argue that the war experience and the feelings that it had generated profoundly changed the relationships that both historians had with their German colleagues as well as their whole perception of Germany. This hypothesis is not new in the sense that several historians have already shown how far the Great War modified Pirenne's ideas and impacted his contacts with German scholars.[36] But so far, the war experience of both historians has not been thoroughly studied in itself, and certainly not from the perspective of emotional history. Van Werveke's study of Fredericq's diary took into account many topics (the struggle for the Dutch language, the relationship with other historians, the representation of King Albert …), but left out the voluminous diary written in captivity[37]. Moreover, it gives only a short insight into the impact of the war on Fredericq's mood and activities.[38] As for Pirenne, Lyon's biography narrates the main situations that he experienced by using his egodocuments (*Journal de guerre, Journal de captivité, Réflexions d'un solitaire*) and his autobiographical sketch *Souvenirs de captivité*. However, he does not take a critical stance on the differences between these two types of texts, which belong to distinct literary categories marked by a time gap.[39]

Our approach in this case study of two historians is not that much in the line of an intellectual history of the Great War showing the main ideas on specific topics expressed in texts and looking at agencies and networks.[40] We rather chose to work within the perspective of emotional history, which focuses on the emotional expression of the self in a particular society with its own moral code.[41] Accordingly, our major interpretative line does not merely consider *what* individuals experienced but *how* they experienced events, news and relationships. We mainly focused on how Fredericq and Pirenne perceived the impact of the German invasion and occupation in Belgium, how they felt about their experience of captivity in Germany from March

---

35 For a discursive analysis of this autobiographical text in comparison with Pirenne's journal, see Warland 2018.
36 De Schaepdrijver 2011; Hasquin 2004; Lyon 1997 and 1998; Schöttler 2004 and 2005; Violante 1987 and 1997; Warland 2004, 2008, and 2011.
37 Van Werveke 1979, 73.
38 Van Werveke 1979, 56–62.
39 Lyon 1971, 205–276. The introduction of the *Journal de Guerre* writes up the biography for the factual description.
40 See for instance Hanna 1996, Horne 2005, Iggers 2002, Mommsen 1996, Schwabe 1969, Warland 2011.
41 See for a review of the historical literature on emotion in the 19th century, Reddy 2009, 309.

1916 to December 1918, and how this experience changed their perception of the country that they most admired before the war.[42]

As illustrated by the diaries, we can distinguish three main attitudes of Fredericq and Pirenne towards the Germans: avoiding, accommodating, and rejecting. These attitudes follow their war experience chronologically: firstly, Belgium's invasion and occupation by the German troops; secondly, the captivity in Germany; thirdly, the postwar period. Corresponding main feelings expressed in their diaries and other egodocuments – such as Pirenne's autobiographical article – are respectively anger and disappointment towards the German invaders; empathy for the suffering of the German population; and again anger against the German elites and military and political authorities. The expression of these attitudes and feelings in the diaries are illustrative of social norms that dominated at that time. Due to the influence of self-control and self-restraint in the bourgeois society, the diary served as a release for the ban on the public expression of feelings.[43] In addition, to write down daily activities and thoughts helped one to find a balance in unusual living conditions.[44]

3 The Germans in occupied Belgium: anger, sadness and coping strategies

On August 3rd, the German Empire declared war on Belgium and the first troops entered the country the day after. In his diary, Fredericq wrote:

> "Duitsland verklaart der oorlog aan België! Ik werk aan Rooses voor Elsevier als troost."[45] [Germany declared war on Belgium. I am working on Rooses for Elsevier as a consolation].

His reaction gives the tone for his way to cope with the war situation and to make sense of it:

> "Nooit heb [sic] ik zoo uitsluitend bezig geweest met mijn wetenschappelijk werk als nu. Ik meen het vaderland niet beter te kunnen dienen dat met ernstige boeken te schrijven. Bella gerant allii."[46] [Never have I been so exclusively busy with my scientific activity as I am now. I think that there is for me no better way to serve my country as in writing serious books. Bella gerant allii].

Such diving into intellectual activity went on throughout the war. From August of 1914 until his deportation, Fredericq wrote a monograph on the life of Max Rooses and his major publication, *De Geschiedenis van de Inquisitie in de Nederlanden*. The

---

42 See Warland 2011. See also especially for Fredericq, Coppens 1993.
43 See, for instance, Reddy 2009, 309.
44 See Theofilakis 2016, 63.
45 Fredericq, *Autobiografie*, 4.8.1914.
46 Fredericq, *Dagboek*, 11.1.1916. In the following, it will occur under the abbreviation FD. See also Van Werveke 1979, 59–61.

fact that the University of Ghent did not reopen in October 1914 enabled him to devote his whole time to scientific work. During his captivity in Germany, Fredericq worked on two books: a history of Dutch literature written in French and intended for the French speaking Belgians and a general literature history named *Allgemeene Geschiedenis der wereldletterkunde sedert Adam en Eva*. In scholarly activity Fredericq found reassurance; and so did Pirenne. After the shock of the first months, he resumed his work in order to finish the publication co-authored with the French archivist and specialist of the history of the city of Douai in the Middle Ages, Georges Espinas (1869–1948), on the Flemish wool industry[47] and to continue his history of Belgium, volume 5, that he intended to dedicate to his son Pierre who died in the battle of Yper in October 1914.[48] In his assigned residence in Germany (and particularly during the nearly two years in Creuzburg an der Werra), Pirenne wrote an economic history of Europe.[49] It was a way to escape neurasthenia, as he confessed to a colleague and friend, the French medievalist at the *École des chartes*, Maurice Prou (1861–1930), on July 15th and November 17th 1917.[50]

Fredericq's and Pirenne's intense intellectual activities with both the continuation of previous work and the initiation of new projects can be seen as a coping mechanism in psychological terms. Coping strategies refer to the responses (cognitive, emotional, and behavioral) that an individual develops when appraising an event as threatening, a context that frequently occurred during the war. The goal is to control, tolerate, or decrease the impact of the event in order to maintain physical and psychological well-being. It is what happened with Fredericq and Pirenne. By being occupied intellectually, they could escape for a time from their worries. It was also a way to resist the Germans by not falling into depression and by standing tall.

Another coping mechanism that can be observed as a way of resisting and keeping confidence, was to believe in spiritual powers. An older friend of Fredericq told him the rule to be followed:

---

47 Pirenne, *Journal de guerre*, 15.10.1914: "depuis deux jours, j'ai repris la table de mon recueil de draperie. C'est un travail matériel qui tue le temps si lourd". See also 11.11.1914 and 22.03.1915. On this date, Pirenne indicates that he brought the finished manuscript to his bank safety box. In the next footnotes, Pirenne's *Journal de guerre* as well as *Journal de captivité* will be mentioned as PJG.

48 PJG 20.12.1914.

49 See Warland 2004 for a discursive analysis of this book in its context and reception. For a revised edition of Pirenne's manuscript, see Devroey and Knaepen 2014.

50 Quoted in Lyon 1971, 263. During the time spent in war prisoners camps, he tried to stay intellectually active, to prevent any brain standstill ("se défendre contre cette paralysie [des cerveaux]" (PJG 16.5.1916, in Lyon 1976, 100).

"Hij zelf gaaf mij bij't begin van de oorlog de leus van het dies irae op: *Nil inultum remanebit.*"[51] [He himself indulges me at the beginning of the war the slogan of the Dies irae: *Nil inultum remanebit*].

Nil inultum remanebit ("nothing unavenged remains") became the reassuring words of the protestant Fredericq who believed in the justice of God: this motto is recalled many times in his diary in Ghent as well as in Germany.[52] Pirenne, who was not a religious man, found reasons for confidence in analyzing historical evolutions.[53] His *Journal de guerre* includes long reflections on European wars in which he tried to find analogies with the current war.[54] A reassuring feature was, following Pirenne, that Germany never won a war waged simultaneously on two fronts:

"Je songe à la guerre et il me paraît évident que la défaite de l'Allemagne est certaine. Cette guerre est pour elle une guerre d'expansion comme au Xe et au XIIe siècle. Et comme alors aussi elle cherche à atteindre l'Orient. Elle s'oppose à la Russie comme au Moyen âge aux slaves et aux magyars, mais alors elle n'avait pas en même temps l'Occident sur les bras. C'est toujours de l'Occident que sont venues ses défaites depuis Bouvines. Elle ne peut le vaincre que si elle n'a rien à craindre à l'Est comme en 1870. Mais elle va périr. (…)."[55] [I think of the war and it seems clear to me that Germany will be defeated. This war is for it an expansion war as in the 10th and the 11th centuries. At that time it also wanted to reach the Orient. Germany is opposed to Russia as in the Middle Ages to the Slavs and Magyars, but at that time it did not have to fight against the Occident. It is always from the Occident that all her defeats have come since Bouvines. She can only win against the Occident if she has nothing to fear from the East as in 1870. But she will perish. (…)].

At times, a belief in moral forces which pointed to a superior order is expressed in Pirenne's diary as the following quotations from 1915 show:

"L'attentat contre la Belgique, le crime du Lusitania sont proches du châtiment. Y aurait-il une justice dans les choses humaines? En tous cas, les puissances de réaction sont dès maintenant virtuellement vaincues par les puissances du progrès. Mon Pierre n'aura pas vainement versé son sang pour la civilisation."[56] [The assault against Belgium, the Lusitania's crime are close to punishment. Would there be a justice in human affairs? In any case, the reactionary Powers are now virtually defeated by the progressive Powers. My Pierre will not have vainly shed his blood for civilization].

---

51 FD 14.12.1915. First mention on 12.10.1914 and later always in relation to Germans violence: 18.10.1914; 14.2.1915; 7.3.1915; 8.4.1915; 23.4.1915; 12.7.1915; 17.10.1915.
52 FD 12.10.1914; 7.5.1915; 23.3.1916.
53 PJG 7.8.1914.
54 PJG 26.11.1914; 4.1.1915; 14.1.1915.
55 PJG 26.11.1914.
56 PJG 24.5.1915.

"Cette lutte gigantesque ne peut finir dans l'impuissance. Elle doit aboutir au triomphe du droit sur la force brutale."[57] [This gigantic struggle cannot end in powerlessness. It must lead to the triumph of law over brutal force].

Pirenne was intimately convinced that the Central Powers could not win the war: he sought hints for hope not only in history and in the superiority of Law, but also in the news given by Belgian, Dutch, English and German newspapers that he read, compared and submitted to the historical critical method. He believed that peace should come at least as a result of the exhaustion of German and Austrian armies.[58]

How Fredericq reported German deeds at the beginning of the war illustrates how strong his anger was. Germans were compared to the most cruel Barbarians – "de krijgsdaden der Duitschers in België herrineren aan die der Hunnen en Willem II heet reeds Attila II"[59] [Germans' warrior acts in Belgium are reminiscent of those of the Huns and Wilhelm II is already called Attila II] – who acted as beasts: "beestachtige gruwelen der Duitschers."[60] [beastly atrocities of the Germans]. Considering the changes in Ghent during the first three months of the war – the arrival of Belgian refugees, the death of English and French soldiers of the marines, army, navy, and then the entry of the German soldiers on October 12th –, Fredericq concluded:

> "en dat alles onverdient door de schuld der Duitsche Schweinerei."[61] [and all of that undeserved because of the German brutality].

Among the adjectives that Fredericq mostly used in reference to the Germans, we find the attribute "revolting" (walgelijk) as in his judgment on the Appeal to the Civilized World in October 1914:

> "Het Manifest der 93 is dan ook walgelijk en ongehoord."[62] [The Manifesto of the 93 is revolting and unheard of].

The shelling of the Rheims Cathedral was seen by Fredericq as a deed which was so horrific that he asked himself whether the Germans had become insane:

> "'t is nog vreeselijker dan de verwoesting van Leuven. Zijn de Duitschers in massa krankzinnig geworden?"[63] [It is even more terrible than the destruction of Leuven. Have the Germans en masse become insane?]

The reference to Germans' insanity recurs in Fredericq's diary in order to qualify their most radical acts or attitudes. Nevertheless Fredericq had to admit that they behaved

---

57 PJG 22.9.1915.
58 PJG 27.5.1915.
59 FD 03.09.1914.
60 FD 02.10.1914.
61 FD 19.10.1914.
62 FD 19.3.1915.
63 FD 22.09.1914.

well in the city of Ghent.[64] Nostalgic moments of remembering the "good Germany" were recalled on several occasions, by the singing of German soldiers in the street[65] or the reading of his travel books through Germany in 1911 and 1913. But the war created a gap between his current feelings and the beloved past.[66]

Pirenne was not less moved by anger against the Germans as shown above by his reaction to the Appeal of the 93 reported in Fredericq's diary. In his Journal de guerre, he always mentions this document by referring to the 93 impostors.[67] The word expressing the common attitude of the Belgian population towards the Germans that Pirenne mostly used in the first days of the war is indignation:

> "L'indignation contre les Allemands dans le public l'emporte sur la fierté de voir Liège tenir."[68] [The outrage against the Germans in the public outweighs the pride of seeing Liège hold on to its position].

This term comes up again later to characterize the moral attitude against Germany among western European countries.[69] Another recurring effective word characterizes the Germans as barbarians[70], a term commonly used among the intellectuals[71] and in the newspapers of the Western countries. When the sinking of the Lusitania occurred in 1915, Pirenne's semantics gained in intensity within a few days as an expression of his anger: he qualified the Germans as murderers (*assassins*[72]).

The use of strong emotional expressions in Fredericq's and Pirenne's diaries can be seen as a way of subduing the emotion of anger through the act of writing. This type of response is considered in psychology as a mechanism of emotion regulation. Emotion regulation includes a set of processes by which individuals assess, control, and modify their spontaneous emotional responses to accomplish their goals or to express socially appropriate emotional behaviours. Regulation can operate both consciously and unconsciously and exerts its effects on the intensity, type, persistence, and lability of the emotions felt.[73] Further, a distinction needs to be made between emotion regulation and coping strategies that have been presented before. The main difference consists in the duration of the down-regulation, i.e., coping aims to decrease the negative affect for a longer time.

64　FD 22.10.1914.
65　FD 29.3.1915.
66　FD 10.09.1915.
67　See, for instance, PJG 26.11.1914; 14.1.1915; 21.2.1915; 2.3.1915; 23.4.1915; 11.6.1915.
68　PJG 4.8.1914. See also 3.8.1914.
69　PJG 1.1.1915.
70　PJG 19.8.1914; 1.9.1914; 15.9.1914.
71　See, for instance, the speech of the French philosopher Henri Bergson at the French Academy on 8.8.1914: "la lutte engagée contre l'Allemagne est la lutte même de la civilisation contre la barbarie" (quoted in Prochasson 2004, 674).
72　PJG 11.5.1915, 12.5.1915, 15.5.1915.
73　Luminet 2013.

4 An honor code: avoiding contact with Germans

As a result of the German invasion in Belgium, Fredericq and Pirenne adopted an honor code, which was actually representative of the behavior of Belgian patriots[74]: they avoided the contact with the occupiers. A German *Privatdozent* (i.e. private lecturer) at the University of Berlin, Dr. Wirth, requested several times to visit Fredericq. He always declined and wrote in his diary that

> "ik kan geene Duitschers meer voor mijne ogen zien."[75] [I cannot see any Germans before my eyes].

Fredericq expected the same conduct from his fellow citizens. It was not always the case. In his diary, he reported that his nephew Louis saw his grand aunt (and Fredericq's aunt), the famous Flemish writer Virginie Loveling, having tea with the employee of the Kommandantur:

> "Proficiat! Ik zal er haar niet van spreken. Zij is oud genoeg om te weten wat zij doen moet. 't is toch maar laf & gemeen, gegeven zij geene verontschuldiging daarvoor heeft. 't is wellicht de schuld van Alice De Keyser. Het schijnt dat de Van Trigt's in' t openbaar altijd Engelsch spreken met de Kommandantur juffrouw. Zij gevoelen zelve, dat het stinkt."[76] [Congrats! I will not speak to her. She is old enough to know what she has to do. It is only cowardly and mean because she has no apology for it. It is probably the fault of Alice De Keyser. It seems that the Van Trigts always speak English with the Kommandantur Miss. They themselves feel that it stinks].

In contrast to the very strict rules followed by Fredericq, Pirenne was more flexible in his behavior towards the Germans. On the one hand, his patriotic feelings commanded him to keep distance from the occupiers. He could not tolerate the expression of their collective presence such as the military songs, which resonated in the streets of Ghent,[77] and even less the attitude of some Belgian people who expressed positive opinions regarding their attitudes. The recording of a conversation with a colleague at the University of Ghent and member of the Belgian Royal Academy, the art historian Georges Hulin de Loo (1862–945), illustrates it at best:

> "Les Allemands se conduisent admirablement. Puisqu'il n'a pas à s'en plaindre, il trouve donc que tout est pour le mieux. Je lui dis qu'il devrait envoyer une correspondance à la

---

74 See De Schaepdrijver 2000.
75 FD 25.11.1914. See also 3.11.1914 and 1.12.1914.
76 FD 13.12.1915. Two days later, Fredericq wrote: "Bezoek bij tante Virginie. Geen woord over den thee in het Groen Kruis. Anders zeer vriendelijk" (14.12.1915). Worth mentioning is that, according to De Schaepdrijver, Virginie Loveling refused to subscribe to chauvinism: she made a point of talking to German occupation personnel and she never idealized the occupied citizenry (De Schaepdrijver 2014).
77 PJG 5.7.1915.

Vlaamsche Post.[78] C'est un incivique incapable de s'élever à un point de vue mâle. D'ailleurs du moment qu'il a un *von* chez lui, il se sent honoré et heureux."[79] [The Germans behave admirably. Since he does not have to complain, he finds that everything is for the best. I tell him that he should send a correspondence to the Vlaamsche Post. He is an unpatriotic person who is unable to rise to a male point of view. Moreover, as long as he has a *von* at home, he feels honored and happy].

On the other hand, Pirenne was still able to have private contact with some individual Germans. Very often, he tried to convince them that Germany had offended Belgium's neutrality and he invited them to take a critical stand towards the war reports (for instance concerning the *francs-tireurs*), as in the case of the young officer who was billeted in Pirenne's home, where he stayed two months and was delighted to dine at the family's table.[80] Pirenne refused to meet with the social and economic historian Robert Hoeniger (1855–1929) despite the fact that he had known him since his stay in Berlin in 1884–85 because he was angry with him.[81] However, he agreed to see Hans Müller, a disciple of Cartellieri, who wanted to discuss with a renowned historian the causes of the war from an historical perspective and not from a patriotic one. After having summarized the discussed issues and their respective standpoints, Pirenne summed up their talk:

"Nous avons causé objectivement et fort tranquillement. Il me dit qu'en Allemagne tous les esprits élevés ont le plus grand respect pour la conduite de la Belgique. Nous nous quittons bien. Il me dit qu'un de ses frères a déjà été tué. Je lui souhaite bonne chance et il en fait tout autant pour mes fils. C'a été un petit oasis que cette conversation où la haine nationale n'a eu aucune part."[82] [We talked objectively and quietly. He told me that in Germany all the higher spirits have the greatest respect for Belgium's conduct. We said farewell in a gentle manner. He told me that one of his brothers had already been killed. I wished him good luck and he did the same for my sons. This little conversation was like an oasis where national hate had no part].

This talk based on rational arguments is representative of other exchanges between Pirenne and well-educated Germans who showed a balanced judgement on political and military matters, a sensitivity for the Belgian case, and a distance towards 'reactionary' (e.g. conservative and nationalistic) trends in their own country, to use Pirenne's vocabulary.[83] Nonetheless, Pirenne's sensitivity for differentiation and relative flexibility was not appreciated by the uncompromising Fredericq. Reporting the

---

78 Published in Ghent between the 21.2.1915 and 5.5.1915, *De Vlaamsche Post. Algemeen dagblad voor Vlaanderen* was the newspaper of the Flemish activists.
79 PJG 5.6.1915.
80 PJG 7.11.1914; 9.11.1914.
81 PJG 8.1.1915. No reasons are mentioned, only sadness towards a colleague who was also a friend and nostalgia for the good old days (9.1.1915).
82 PJG 4.11.1914. Such talks were exclusively private. Pirenne declined Müller's request to publish it (6.11.1914).
83 PJG 12.3.1915; 30.4.1915; 3.8.1915.

visit to Pirenne of a young German professor who was interested in genealogical information on Protestant families of Tournai in the 16th century, Fredericq writes in his diary that Pirenne felt a little embarrassed in telling this episode which was followed by Fredericq's response:

> "Moi, j'ai jeté mon allemand à la porte!"[84] [I threw my German out and closed the door!]

Within Pirenne's family, his wife, Jenny, and even more his son, Robert kept their distance from the Germans. Robert did not even want to speak to them. The philosopher, who became a renowned educationalist after the war, Hermann Nohl (1879–1960), *Associate Professor* at the University of Jena, working as a soldier for the German administration in Ghent, experienced this attitude.[85] Acting as an intermediary between Pirenne (during his time in Jena and in Creuzburg) and his wife by giving news, carrying letters and caring for their well-being[86], he was never considered a guest when he visited her in Ghent. The exchanges with Pirenne's wife were polite, but she never suggested that he remove his coat and hat.[87]

On the way to his captivity in Germany, Fredericq was accompanied by the lieutenant Freiherr von Dalwig. In bidding farewell he thanked him for the pleasant [sic] journey and apologized for not shaking his hand: the lieutenant should not see Fredericq's attitude as a rudeness – *Roheit* [sic] –, but simply as the results of the circumstances of the war.[88] We will see that the circumstances of his forced stay in Germany led Fredericq to adopt a more flexible and nuanced attitude towards Germans. These changes contrast with Pirenne who since the beginning of the war had been more able to draw a line between war circumstances and a kind of respect towards well-educated and intelligent German soldiers and officers.

5 Disappointment towards German scholars

Sadness is a feeling that can follow disappointment. Both feelings concern the relationship with the three German historians that Fredericq and Pirenne knew the most and considered as their friends: the historian of Leipzig, Karl Lamprecht (1856–1915); Joseph Hansen (1862–1943), head of the Cologne archives and specialist of the Inquisition; and the German Jewish historian Martin Philippson (1846–1916).

---

84 FD 8.1.1916.
85 Nohl supported all kind of initiatives to release Pirenne and Fredericq from their German captivity. See Thys 2005, 32, 213.
86 For instance, Nohl helped Pirenne's wife to get the authorization to rejoin his husband with her son Robert to Germany in August 1918. See Thys 2005, 32, 41, 42, 176.
87 See the letter from Nohl to his wife in Jena from 01.02.1918 (Thys 2005, 242).
88 FD 19.03.1916.

5.1 Karl Lamprecht

The one who caused the highest level of disappointment was Lamprecht who was also the most active in supporting German imperialism and war justification.[89] One of his first articles, *Der Krieg und die Völker* (*Berliner Tageblatt*, 23.8.1914), interpreting the war as a conflict between Germanic and Slavic civilizations and arguing for the support of the European countries for Germany against the barbarian Russia, heavily shocked Pirenne and Fredericq. Pirenne noted:

> "Il est impossible d'écrire quelque chose de plus lamentablement bête et zoologique. Le bâton est rompu entre une mystique zoologique et moi. Gemeines Krieg ! […]. Dans l'article d'ailleurs pas un mot de noblesse morale, d'idéalisme. Non ! La plate antithèse: teutonisme et non-teutonisme. C'est à vomir!"[90] [It is impossible to write something more lamentably stupid and zoological. The stick is broken between a zoological mysticism and me. Nasty war! […].In the article, moreover, not a word of moral nobility, of idealism. No! The flat antithesis: Teutonism and not Teutonism. It makes me feeling sick].

And Fredericq who was not less upset asked himself:

> "Het is toch kolossaal! Is de arme Lamprecht krankzinnig geworden? En dat is een der lichten van het beschaafde Germanendom."[91] [It is unbelievable! Has the poor Lamprecht gone insane? And he is one of the lights of civilized Germanity].

Trying to collect information for the administrative division of Belgium in a Flemish and a Walloon part from the historian Guillaume Des Marez (1870–1931), head of the Brussels archives, Lamprecht was again a matter of concern in Fredericq's diary (*de zaak Lamprecht*):

> "Zijn poging aan Des Marez tot landverrader te maken is walgelijk. Mentalité à la boche. Wraakroepend. Hoe lag zijn de besten in Duitschland gevallen! Doch zij zullen gestraft worden. Nil inultum remanebit!"[92] [His attempt to make Des Marez a land-eater is disgusting. Boche's mentality. Revenge. How far the best ones have fallen in Germany! But they will be punished. Nil inultum remanebit!]

Accordingly, his death in May 1915 left Fredericq indifferent:

> "Ik kan hem niet bidden. Hij is te harteloos voor België geweest."[93] [I cannot pray for him. He has been too heartless for Belgium].

---

89   On Lamprecht's war investment, see Chickering 1993, 431 ff.
90   PJG 4.9.1914.
91   FD 3.9.1914. Following echoes of Lamprecht's speeches in Dresden show that he was not mere seriously to taken (see FD, 23.4.1915).
92   FD 7.5.1915.
93   FD 13.5.1915.

All Lamprecht's articles as well as his handling of Des Marez particularly dismayed Pirenne.[94] Meanwhile as he learned that Lamprecht was about to die, he wrote in his *Journal* a long introspective reflection on this old friend and their friendship:

> "Cette nouvelle m'afflige. Malgré tout, il avait été pour moi depuis 25 ans un ami fidèle. C'était un brave homme mené par une tête fumeuse, et il s'est cru du génie. […]. Il avait injurié notre pays en signant le manifeste des 93 imposteurs. Il est le premier qui s'en va et son sort annonce celui de l'Allemagne."[95] [This news afflicts me. Nevertheless, he had been for me for 25 years a faithful friend. He was a brave man led by a smoky head, and he thought himself a genius. [….].He had insulted our country by signing the manifesto of the 93 impostors. He is the first to die and his fate indicates that of Germany].

5.2 Joseph Hansen

Remembering Joseph Hansen, with whom he spent holidays in the surroundings of Weimar in the country house of the artist Max Klinger together with Lamprecht in the summer 1913[96], the nostalgic Fredericq noted in his diary:

> "Hansen, de goede Keulsche vriend, kan ik uit mijn hart niet verjagen. […]. Zal ik hem nooit meer zien? Het kanonnengegrol houdt mij en daarvan! Dat scheidt mij van Duitsland en mijn vroegere Duitse vrienden en kennissen!"[97] [Hansen, the good friend from Cologne, I cannot banish from my heart. Shall I never see him again? The cannons keep me from that. That separates me from Germany and my former German friends and acquaintances!]

Meanwhile, the reading of Hansen's review in the *Kölnische Zeitung* (16.–17. August 1915) of the propaganda book written by well-known historians, *Deutschland und der Weltkrieg*,[98] thoroughly changed Fredericq's mind:

> "Nu is het uit tusschen ons beide. Het is eene scheuring in mijn hart."[99] [Now it is over between the both of us. My heart is broken].

Associating irony and political reflection, Pirenne also reacted to this book review with disappointment towards Hansen who in his opinion was representative of the Liberals and a friend even if not as close as to Fredericq. The use of Caesar's words addressed to his adoptive son, Brutus, who participated in his murder, unveils a feeling of betrayal by Pirenne:

> "Le bon billet! Tu quoque fili mei. Cette concession d'un homme qui jadis se considérait vis-à-vis des Prussiens comme représentant d'une "ältere Kultur" dans laquelle il me classait aussi, en qualité de Belge, est significative. Elle montre combien la victoire de l'Allemagne

---

94 PJG 28.2.1915.
95 PJG 13.5.1915.
96 FD 7.10.1914.
97 FD 27.6.1915.
98 Published by Otto Hintze a. o. (Leipzig, Teubner, 1915).
99 FD 19.8.1915.

serait, si jamais elle devait arriver, la victoire de la plus complète réaction."[100] [The good article! Tu quoque fili mei. This concession of a man who once considered himself towards the Prussians as a representative of an "older culture", in which he also classified me as a Belgian, is significant. It shows how the victory of Germany would be, if it ever were to happen, the victory of the most complete reaction].

5.3 Martin Philippson

Finally, the relationship to Martin Philippson who taught several years (from 1879 to 1890) at the University of Brussels because he was a victim of the antisemitism of the German higher education system and of some renowned historians[101], suffered from the war no less. Fredericq's response to his New Year's greetings for 1915 that he transcribed in his diary contains the following words:

> "[….] des amitiés qui résistent à tout. Telle est la nôtre."[102] [friendships that resist everything. This is ours].

Later he noticed patriotic feelings in Philippson's letters and answered equally in a patriotic tone.[103] A copy of a letter of Philippson is transcribed in Fredericq's diary. It reveals his patriotic turn:

> "Et mes faiblesses ne me permettent plus, comme en 1870, de prendre le fusil!" om op mij te schijten? Subliem,[104] ["And my poor health no longer allows me, as in 1870, to take the gun!" to shit at me? Sublime]

as to the comment given by Fredericq. Humor seems to be a coping mechanism used by Fredericq to resist disappointment and anger: his diary illustrates this in several cases. The same is true for Pirenne who mocks German occupation rules by distorting expressions – *l'Allemagne fait notre éducation*[105] – or perverting the concept of *Inhaltskultur* developed by the German philosopher Rudolf Eucken (1846–1926) to characterize German cultural soundness as opposed to the *Formkultur* of other (Western) countries.[106]

Pirenne's diary first and only mentions Philippson in 1916. With resignation he sent him birthday greetings justifying his action by remembering his generosity:

---

100 PJG 20.8.1915.
101 See Warland 2016.
102 FD 17.1.1915
103 FD 24.4.1915
104 FD 14.5.1915.
105 PJG 28.6.1915.
106 PJG 4.1.1915; 14.1.1915 (a. o.). For an introduction on these concepts which belong to the German 'Ideas of 1914', see Prochasson 2004, 668ff.

À la demande de Hubert,[107] je me décide à envoyer deux mots à Philippson dont on célébrera le 70e anniversaire le 27 juin. Il paraît qu'il est très mal. Sa femme a écrit à Hubert qu'un mot de ses amis belges lui ferait grand plaisir. Je ne peux pas oublier qu'il a légué sa bibliothèque à mon séminaire.[108] [At the request of Hubert, I decide to send two words to Philippson, whose 70th birthday will be celebrated on June 27th. It seems he is in very bad condition. His wife wrote to Hubert that a word from his Belgian friends would make him very happy. I cannot forget that he bequeathed his library to my seminary.]

To sum up, the analysis of Fredericq and Pirenne's reactions towards German historians who were also close friends, show how deep their disillusion was. If they could partly recognize that their behavior was driven by their patriotism – a normal reaction in war times –, they nevertheless could not accept that they voluntarily supported Germany's war aims, a country which had violated Belgian neutrality. During the year 1915, Pirenne was informed at several occasions that the subscribers of the *Appeal* were compelled to sign without having an idea of the final text.[109] It nevertheless did not calm his anger against the scholars who were involved in disseminating the idea of a supposed German superiority or justifying a defensive war in the German case.

6 Fredericq and Pirenne's deportation to Germany: the war camps and the university city of Jena

In their willingness to convert Belgium into a vassal state and to be granted the favors of the Flemish speaking population, German authorities tried to meet its prewar claims. One of them was to be trained in Dutch at a high school level, a claim that was on the agenda of the Belgian parliament, just before the war.[110] The German general governor Moritz von Bissing tried to implement this demand in reopening the University of Ghent as a Dutch speaking university, while it had been a strictly French-speaking university before the war.[111] The professors were asked to teach in Dutch; this measure was discussed among them and they were not willing to adopt it.[112] Fredericq, whose mother tongue was Flemish and who was a supporter of the Flemish movement, categorically refused to meet this demand, which would mean to ac-

---

107 Eugène Hubert (1853–1931) was a modern historian at the University of Liège and a member of the *Académie royale de Belgique*. He was a friend of Fredericq and Pirenne.
108 PJG 16.6.1916 (Lyon 1976, 128).
109 PJG 2.3.1915; 23.4.1915; 11.6.1915. Fredericq never refers to this information.
110 See the draft bill Franck (De Schaepdrijver 1997, 31).
111 For the description of the motivational aspects from the side of the German authorities, see Amara, Roland 2004, 172–175.
112 For a detailed overview, see Vanacker 1991, 101ff. Fredericq's and Pirenne's diaries discussed several times this issue which encompass the topic of this chapter. See also Pirenne 1928, 215ff.

cept to collaborate with the enemy. The same patriotic feelings animated Pirenne, who belonged to the French speaking *bourgeoisie* of Ghent. Pirenne and Fredericq were considered as being the leaders of the opposition among the professors and they promptly were deported to Germany.[113]

Fredericq was first sent to the camp of Gütersloh (19 March 1916 to 7 September 1916), then to the city of Jena where he stayed together with Pirenne (8 September 1916 to 26 January 1917), and finally to Bürgel, a small city in Thuringia (26 January 1917 to 30 November 1918). Pirenne was transferred to a war officer's camp in Krefeld (19 March to 12 May 1916), then to the civil camp of Holzminden (12 May to 28 August 1916), before being moved to Jena (28 August to 29 January 1917), and finally to Creuzburg an der Werra near Eisenach (29 January 1917–27 November 1918).

Fredericq's and Pirenne's imprisonment in prisoner-of-war camps did not last long because of the international pressure as well as of the requests of German professors who wanted to ensure them good working conditions in Germany.[114] It is the reason why they were assigned to the university city of Jena by the German military authorities. They found in the camps a world of new experiences with people from different countries. They also benefited from a relative comfort and were very active, reading books and newspapers, learning Russian and teaching various audiences – although these last two aspects were only true for Pirenne.[115] They initially found themselves isolated in Jena among the German population, although several scholars stood at their disposal for making their stay comfortable and profitable for their work.[116]

Their diaries report that they were well treated. The *Oberbürgermeister* (Lord Mayor) of Jena was very kind and helpful.[117] However, the most delighted words were used for describing the curator of the University of Jena, Max Vollert (1851–1935), who offered Fredericq and Pirenne all the facilities they needed. Fredericq found in him the

> "allerliefste oude man van het vorig gemüthlich geslacht."[118] [the kindest old man of the previous pleasant type]

Vollert also made the best impression on Pirenne through his kindness and reflectiveness.[119] Reporting one of his pleasant (sic) walks with Vollert, Pirenne described him as

> "tout à fait simple et bienveillant. […]. Vollert a l'air de s'intéresser à mon livre et à sa continuation. Dans toute la promenade pas un mot de la guerre."[120] [really simple and caring. […].

---

113 See Lyon 1971, 225ff and 1976, 11ff. See also Nyrop 1917.
114 Lyon 1971, 238ff and 249ff.
115 See Fredericq's diary for the time in Gütersloh. See the published part of Pirenne's diary (Lyon 1976).
116 PJG 28.08.1916 and 3.09.1916 (Lyon 1976, 176 and 182).
117 PJG 5.09.1916 (Lyon 1976, 185).
118 FD 11.09.1916.
119 PJG 28.12.1916.
120 PJG 22.12.1916.

Vollert seems to be interested in my book and its continuation. During the whole walk not a word of the war.]

Preparing his return to Belgium after the armistice in November 1918, Fredericq sent to Vollert a letter of thanks where he underscored some of his qualities – *menschlich, brüderlich, väterlich (humane, brotherly, paternal)* – and expressed the wish to see him again.[121]

The old jurist Vollert was actually the only German with whom Fredericq agreed to have friendly talks with and join for walks – with or without Pirenne – in the surroundings of Jena. Otherwise, his attitude towards the Germans was characterized by rejection and a kind of provocation. In his diary, Pirenne thought of Fredericq as being an agitator (*provocateur*) for speaking French on the street or at the hotel.[122] As far as he categorically refused the invitations to the home of Professor Alexander Cartellieri, who took an active part in the settling of Fredericq and Pirenne in Jena, Pirenne had to find excuses for him. Once, Fredericq gave Pirenne an overall justification by telling him that he was too old to make new German relationships during the war.[123] In fact, his decision to avoid any contact with German professors, which was grounded in his resentment, had already been made before his arrival in Jena:

> "ik zal noch met Cartellieri noch met andere professors de minste betrekking hebben!"[124] [I will have no contacts neither with Cartellieri nor with other professors!]

Therefore the obstinate Fredericq also declined the visit of Ida Philippson, the widow of the recently deceased Philippson.[125]

In contrast, Pirenne was more inclined to observe the rules of politeness.[126] He accepted the numerous invitations of Cartellieri for dinner, drinking a beer and walking. Nevertheless, the reciprocal professional esteem[127] could not hide the fact that their relationship was impacted by the war. As summarized by Cartellieri who cared for Pirenne in Jena and contributed to reestablishing the correspondence between him and his wife in Ghent as noticed in Pirenne's diary[128]:

> "Wir sprechen nur deutsch und natürlich nie vom Kriege."[129] [We only speak German, and of course never about war.]

---

121   FD 16.11.1918.
122   PJG 11.4.1916 (Lyon 1976, 60).
123   FD 15.09.1916.
124   FD 30.08.1916.
125   FD 16.11.1916.
126   It is an attitude which was criticized by Fredericq as shown through an ironical remark to Pirenne that he transcribed in his diary: "on finira par vous présenter à tout le corps professoral d'Iéna en vous le détaillant par tranches" (FD 23.12.1916).
127   Cartellieri reviewed Pirenne's *Geschichte Belgien* for the *Historische Vierteljahrschrift*. See Warland 2011, 250.
128   6 and 7.09.1916 (Lyon 1976, 186 and 187).
129   17.09.1916 (Cartellieri 2014, 243).

Pirenne's view on their relationship follows the same patterns:

> "Cartellieri me reçoit aussi bien qu'il peut. Mais malgré tout il y a une gêne."[130] [Cartellieri receives me as well as he can. Nevertheless, there is a feeling of discomfort.]

Another cultivated German with whom Pirenne had many contacts in Jena was Bertha Nohl, the wife of Hermann Nohl who served as an officer in Ghent. As already mentioned, he functioned as an intermediary between Pirenne and his wife Jenny. He actually did it with the help of his wife who cared in Germany for Pirenne's well-being and delivered the news about his family. She invited him for dinner on December 5th and 18th 1916.[131] The same year, she offered Fredericq and Pirenne a bottle of wine for Christmas Eve.[132] To thank her, Pirenne ordered her a flower basket.[133] Several times she visited Pirenne, who apparently was delighted to see her as she wrote to her husband.[134] It is a feeling which is confirmed by Pirenne's diary:

> "Je lui suis vraiment très reconnaissant de son amabilité. C'est une femme charmante et je l'avais bien jugée à Iéna. Je vois qu'elle a vraiment de la compassion pour moi. […] bons moments de vraie sympathie et de conversation civilisée."[135] [I am very grateful to her for her kindness. She is a charming woman and I had judged her positively in Jena. I see she really cares for me. […] good moments of true sympathy and civilized conversation.]

In Jena, Fredericq and Pirenne were for the first time able to measure how the war affected the Germans and to confront the suffering of individuals and families: Many of the scholars and other people that Pirenne met told him about the injuries and the deaths in their family. It is an issue that illustrated the emotional side of Germans who suffered also from the war. Talking with the *Oberbürgermeister* (Lord Mayor) of Jena, who was in Pirenne's opinion a very correct person, he noticed that he distanced himself from the war:

> "À propos de la guerre il lui échappe un cri 'Wozu denn das?'"[136] [About the war he cried out 'Why all this?']

The absurdity of the war as expressed by the Mayor of Jena was approached by Fredericq and Pirenne in the last period of their captivity through the suffering of ordinary people who had restrictions imposed on them by the German government.

---

130 PJG 29.8.1916 (Lyon 1976, 177).
131 PJG 5.12.1916; 18.12.1916.
132 PJG 24.12.1916.
133 PJG 31.12.1916.
134 Letter from 31.10.1917 (Thys 2005, 227).
135 PJG 5.7.1917.
136 PJG 5.09.1916 (Lyon 1976, 185).

7   Pirenne and Fredericq among the Germans: the provincial cities of Bürgel and Creuzburg

In January 1917, Fredericq and Pirenne were accused of betraying the German hospitality in their correspondence.[137] The mediation of the Major of Jena did not prevent the decision of the German military authorities to separate the two Belgian historians and send them to small towns.[138] This decision was actually welcomed by Fredericq who did not feel well living together with Pirenne who was more successful as a professional historian and was anything but humble.[139]

For both the life in small cities of Thuringia, gifted with a medieval character and surrounded by a beautiful landscape with hills, forests and fields, represented a kind of rest. Pirenne, who was an enthusiast of the calm of the countryside[140], took long walks mostly alone but sometimes accompanied by the *Bürgermeister* (Lord Mayor).[141] In Bürgel which he described as "idyllic"[142], Fredericq found an inner peace.[143] Due to their daily physical activity – not only Pirenne but also Fredericq walked every day – and plain fare, their health conditions improved. Pirenne noticed in his diary and in letters to his wife that he was never troubled with gout.[144]

Besides the environment which recalled the romantic Germany that they used to love, they got to know middle-class Germans who did not belong to the elite that they had contacts with before the war.[145] As Fredericq notes in his diary,

> "de menschen zijn hier toch allemaal sympathiek in den hoogsten graad."[146] [The people are all likable to the highest degree].

They lived among kind people who were honored by the presence of eminent *Professoren* (professors) residing in their towns and willing to speak with them. A very typical German word often occurs in Fredericq's diary to describe the people and also the landscape as well as the whole atmosphere in Bürgel: *gemütlich* (pleasant). The lovely city of Bürgel, described in his diary and accompanied by pictures, incorporated the

---

137   Fredericq's disobedience towards the rules given for the correspondence were, in Pirenne's opinion, the cause of their separation and expulsion of Jena. See Lyon 1971, 253.
138   See the narration in Pirenne's diary as well as in Fredericq's one.
139   See his whole diary. On the competition between Fredericq and Pirenne, see Tollebeek 2011.
140   See his letter to Sam Muller (5.3.1917), quoted in Lyon 1971, 259.
141   PJG 28.7.1917.
142   For instance, FD 1.11.1918.
143   FD 31.5.1917; 30.4.1917.
144   See his letters from 12.10.1917 and 19.10.1917 as well as from 13.12.1916 (letters from Henri Pirenne to his wife, private collection, Cernex, France).
145   On Pirenne social and intellectual environment in Creuzburg, see Lyon 1971, 256–57.
146   FD 5.4.1917. The letter was transcribed in his diary.

Germany that Fredericq knew before the war. As he wrote to his brother in Liège at the beginning of his stay in Bürgel,

> "Je continue à être content ici. [...]. L'hôtel est bien tenu et plein de prévenances. Le milieu ambiant est gemütlich. Je me suis fait à ma nouvelle vie et je ne suis pas à plaindre."[147] [I am still happy here. The hotel is well run. The environment is gemütlich (pleasant). I have adapted myself to my new life and I am not to be pitied.]

One year later he had not changed his opinion as expressed in a letter to the Dutch archivist of Utrecht, Samuel Müller (1848–1922), who wanted that Pirenne and Fredericq could move to Holland:

> "[...] mon sort au milieu de la population très gemütlich de la Thuringe soit tout à fait supportable et presque idyllique en ces temps de boucherie internationale vous me dites."[148] [my fate in the middle of the very gemütlich (pleasant) population of Thuringia is quite bearable and almost idyllic in these times of international butchery that you tell me about.]

Fredericq and Pirenne adjusted easily to their new lives in these communities participating in local activities (concerts, theater) and being concerned about the events which affected the people they had to live with.[149] Fredericq rented a room at the Hotel *Zum Deutschen Kaiser* in Bürgel and Pirenne at the *Gasthof Zum Stern* in Creuzburg. They eventually became the closest guests of their host family. Fredericq developed an affection for the three daughters; so did Pirenne for Joachim and Wilhelm, the son of relatives of his host and the son of the *Bürgermeister* (Lord Mayor) of Creuzburg.[150]

Pirenne was very concerned about the fate of his wife and youngest son in Ghent as well as of his other two sons and their wives and his first grandchildren in Paris and in Switzerland – a concern which comes up very often in his *Journal de captivité*, especially from the time in Creuzburg when he stayed alone. On the contrary, the unmarried Fredericq had always showed himself more involved in relations with people outside the narrow family circle and free for activities. In Bürgel, he gave French lessons to several people (for instance to the three Gebauer daughters[151]), he shared food packages which were sent to him: he distributed chocolate to children and old ladies as well as cigars to men and sometimes to prisoners of war that he met during his walks.[152] Pirenne did the same for the children who were close to him.[153]

---

147 FD 26.3.1917.
148 FD 21.08.1918. See also FD, 24.11.1918.
149 For instance, he used kind words to describe the people with whom he shared the same fate of war: "de jonge fleurige sympathieke badmeister is heden nacht gestorven" (FD 3.11.1918).
150 PJG 22.06.1917.
151 FD 7.5.1918.
152 For instance FD 29.1.1917, 31.3.1917, 2.4.1917.
153 PJG 22.6.1917.

If Fredericq referred to several conversation partners, Pirenne's main partner was the *Bürgermeister* of Creuzburg with whom he had a good relationship[154]:

> "À 3h il pleut. Je vais cependant chez le bourgmestre et y reste à bavarder jusqu'à 5 h."[155] [At 3 o'clock it is raining. However, I go to the mayor and stay there until 5 am.]

The *Bürgermeister* offered Pirenne several times to join him on his trips to Eisenach.[156] Through him, Pirenne learned a lot about war developments, about political decisions, and more broadly about German mentality: he was struck by the lack of political consciousness and the narrowness of concerns among the population of Creuzburg.[157] The war was part of discussions[158], also with the internationally renowned psychiatrist Otto Binswanger (1852–1929), professor at the University of Jena, who invited Pirenne to his castle not far from Creuzburg.[159] Pirenne observed the restrictions imposed on the population by the war: food scarcity, the removing of some church bells of Creuzburg, the decrease of financial help to soldiers' families … He followed the growing frustration among the German people who were eventually tired of the war which cost so many injuries and deaths. Fredericq could observe the same trends[160], but did not write down as many comments on politics as did Pirenne in his diary and even more in his separated notebook called *Réflexions d'un solitaire*. Fredericq's diary mainly deals with daily matters describing the activities and persons in his close environment and of the transcription of letters to his family and friends.

Fredericq's and Pirenne's main activity as above mentioned consisted of writing, Fredericq in literature history and Pirenne in economic history. The calm and undemanding life without burdens and obligations and outside of the familiar context of Ghent placed them both in a privileged situation. Comparing his life to the one of a Benedictine, Fredericq felt very well in his

> "Eldorado van eene krijgsgevangene. Ik woon hierboven als een benedictijner der middeleeuwen. En toch niet als een egoïst […]."[161] [Eldorado of a prisoner. I live here as a Benedictine of the Middle Ages. And nevertheless not as an egoist.]

Using the reference to a French philosopher, Pirenne made a parallel between his enforced exile and that of Descartes in Holland:

> "N'ayant aucun devoir à accomplir, libre de toute besogne, débarrassé de toutes obligations mondaines et sociales dans mon isolement, je goûtais le charme de la méditation, l'élabora-

---

154 The same was also true for his relationship to the *Oberbürgermeister* of Jena. See Lyon 1971, 255.
155 PJG 7.8.1917.
156 PJG 28.5.1917; 2.7.1917.
157 See for instance PJG 12.7.1917.
158 See for instance PJG 30.6.1917.
159 PJG 31.5.1017 and 1.6.1917.
160 See for instance FD 5.4.1917.
161 FD 31.5.1917.

tion lente et progressive des idées que l'on porte en soi, avec lesquelles on vit et dans lesquelles on finit par s'absorber."[162] [Having no duty to perform, free of all work, free from all worldly and social obligations in my isolation, I tasted the charm of meditation, the slow and progressive elaboration of the ideas that one carries in oneself, with which we live and in which we end up absorbing ourselves].

Fredericq and Pirenne had distant echoes from the war through German newspapers and the information they received from their conversation partners. The most concrete impact of the war that they were confronted with was the presence of war prisoners who worked in farms or passed through their city. They took the opportunity to speak with them[163] and observed that the contacts with the Germans went generally well.[164] Pirenne wondered how his host, the innkeeper Panitz, was impressed by the French prisoners:

"je suis étonné de voir avec quelle sympathie il parle des prisonniers français qu'il admire pour leur intelligence et leur travail."[165] [I am surprised to see with what sympathy he speaks of French prisoners whom he admires for their intelligence and their work.]

Fredericq and Pirenne's living conditions in Germany were not harsh and almost enjoyable: they did not lack food because of the parcels which were sent to them by family and colleagues from Belgium, Holland and Switzerland[166], and they were able to borrow books from the university library of Jena. Moreover, after having waited for months to secure the authorization[167], Pirenne's wife Jenny and his son Robert were permitted to come and reside by him in Creuzburg from 8 August 1918 until war's end. It is an end that they were waiting for, looking for its signs as the copy of a letter of Fredericq to his brother Leon in Liege shows:

"[…] pourvu que nous nous retrouvions tous bientôt, sans avoir perdu personne en route. La paix approche, mais je tremble pour vous tous en Belgique, moi qui suis si tranquille ici dans l'idyllique Thuringe. J'en rougis presque et voudrais tant être à vos côtés."[168] [as long as we all get together soon, without losing anyone on the way. Peace is approaching, but I am trembling for all of you in Belgium, while I am so quiet here in idyllic Thuringia. I almost blush and wish I could be by your side.]

---

162 Pirenne 1920, 465.
163 For instance PJG 26.6.1917, FD 14.4.1917, 4.5.1917.
164 On the acceptance of the captive enemies who contributed to the German economy, see Hinz 2004, 781–82.
165 PJG 27.05.1917.
166 Lyon 1971, 245ff.
167 As attested in his letters, Nohl mediated for this concern in Ghent. See Thys 2005.
168 FD 15.11.1918.

8 The return to Belgium and the First World War's aftermath

During their stay in Germany, both Fredericq and Pirenne could experience that not all Germans were in favor of the war. In his diary and in his *Réflexions d'un solitaire*, Pirenne made a distinction through the war between the liberal Germany and the reactionary one, which was associated with Prussia.[169] During his enforced exile, he followed the inner politics and noted the progress of the democratic trends in Germany speaking out for universal suffrage.[170] He also welcomed the Wilson idea of the League of Nations which was approved by the 'Republican Germany' [sic], as the absolute opposite of nationalism, maintaining by the way its idea of a difference between two Germanys, the Liberal one and the reactionary one.[171]

Such a differentiated attitude towards the Germans vanished in the aftermath, when the representation of Germany that Pirenne disseminated through his article *Souvenirs de captivité*, published in the *Revue des Deux Mondes* in France and as a booklet in Belgium[172], was that of an authoritative and militaristic regime. The resurgence of a strong emotional attitude rejecting Germany as a whole finds some explanation in the shock felt by Belgium's devastation. On the way back to Ghent at the end of November 1918, Fredericq, Pirenne, his wife and his son were shaken by the destruction that they observed during their travel.[173]

As a consequence of his disillusionment with Germany and the intellectuals who were involved in the nationalizing of their fellow citizens and in the war propaganda, Pirenne resigned, already in 1918, his from membership in all German academic organizations.[174]

As for Fredericq, who did not survive a long time after the war (he passed away on 23 March 1920), he had to manage the consequences of the German politics[175] at the University of Ghent where he had been offered the position of rector (10 January to 18 April 1919). In favor of a partial introduction of the teaching in Dutch, Fredericq was confronted with the French speaking *bourgeoisie* who rejected this solution because of its continuity with the German occupation regime and who fought against any kind of Flemish activism. Fredericq, who was deeply depressed, decided to hand over this responsibility to Pirenne who held this office until 1921.[176]

How deep was Fredericq's and Pirenne's anger towards the Germans? If in 1915 Fredericq did not demand the exclusion of the German corresponding members

---

169 See, for instance, his reflection on bismarckism on 24.10.1918 (Lyon 1994, 226–229).
170 See PJG 12.7.1917.
171 On the evolution of these idea by Pirenne, see Warland 2014b.
172 See Warland 2018a.
173 Lyon 1971, 274.
174 Lyon 1971, 282.
175 One of the issues was the exclusion of the former students of the "université flamando-boche" (FD 19.1.1919).
176 Lyon 1971, 283.

from the *Royal Belgian Academy* because of its inappropriate character in war time and of the possible threat for the later international scientific community[177], he nevertheless called for the decision of the *Classe des Lettres* in January 1919 to ban all the corresponding members of the Central Powers and not only the German subscribers of the *Appeal* of 1914.[178] Pirenne also pushed for this decision which had been taken in a second meeting; Pirenne's first proposal concerned solely the scholars of the *Appeal*, the impostors as he named them during the war, but the decision failed and the more radical option prevailed.[179]

As explained in the introduction, Belgian and French scholars were strongly mobilized against Germany in the aftermath. In Fredericq's and Pirenne' s cases, their attitude can be interpreted as a remobilization after their stay in Germany where they were partly 'demobilized', mainly in Bürgel and Creuzburg: during this period, they shared the anxiety, the sadness, and the hope for peace with the German population. They saw them not anymore as the enemies as they did during the time in Ghent but more as human beings who had equally endured difficult times and did not at all or entirely adhere to the war aims of the German military authorities or government. Such attitude expresses the following psychological rule: when people have the possibility of understanding the point of view of others either intellectually (perspective-taking) or emotionally (empathic concerns), they feel closer to them. Clearly, this occurred in their case and as soon as their environment was not anymore with the Germans they came back to their initial and more negative attitudes towards them.

Worth mentioning about the sincerity of feelings and the ties which were bound in Bürgel, Fredericq's host family and some inhabitants of Bürgel kindly inquired about his well-being after his return to Belgium hoping also that the destructions were not too substantial.[180] There is no evidence of an answer from Fredericq whose diary did not refer anymore to Germany after the war. But we can assume that he was not annoyed with particular individuals – especially the down-to-earth inhabitants of Bürgel that he had described as *gemütlich* – but with German elites: the scholars, the politics and the military.

The same hypothesis is valid for Pirenne, and the collective condemnation of Germany that he carried out in his autobiographical sketch and in his official speeches in the aftermath, which have a tone of revenge.[181] These writings and public stances hide the fact that Pirenne made inwardly a distinction between the scholars who were involved in the war propaganda and the others, as shown in his diary and in his atti-

---

177 FD 13.3.1915: "kleingeestig, onwaardig, gevaarlijk voor de toekomstige wetenschapsbetrekkingen met Duitsland" [petty, indiscriminate, dangerous for the future scientific relationships with Germany].
178 *Académie Royale de Belgique. Bulletin de la Classe des Lettres et des Sciences morales et politiques*, 1919, 337.
179 *Ibid.*, 10.
180 See the letters inserted in his autobiography at the beginning of 1919.
181 See for instance Violante 2004, 207ff.

tude at the *Classe de Lettres* of the *Académie Royale de Belgique*. Illustrative of Pirenne's undifferentiated attitude is his speech held at the occasion of its reopening in the presence of the Royals Albert and Elisabeth, called *Le pangermanisme et la Belgique*.[182] Opposing the two Germanys, the liberal emanating from the *Aufklärung*, and the nationalistic, militaristic and racist one as a result of the unification by Prussia, Pirenne's anger is perceptible, particularly in the way in which he characterizes the subordination of German intellectuals to the State ideology as well as the German political goal of destroying the Belgian Nation-State based on two populations, the Flemish and the Walloons, in the name of an ethnic understanding of nationality.[183]

Pirenne's disillusion and anger lasted for some years. In 1923, no historian from the Central Powers participated in the first international congress of historical sciences held in Brussels under the presidency of Pirenne.[184] If he indeed denied the participation of the subscribers of the *Appeal* and of German and Austrian academies and universities, he was not opposed to the individual participation of the scholars who had not signed the *Appeal*, as shown in the correspondence between Pirenne and the Danish historian Aage Friis (1870–1949) who looked for a general reconciliation among scientists.[185] Contrary to what is generally assumed in the literature, Pirenne did not exclude collectively the German historians – they decided not to come as a sign of solidarity with the ones who were excluded –, but actually followed the rule that he had always observed during the war – his diary is the best evidence for his nuanced attitude towards the Germans –, making a distinction between the scholars who subordinated themselves to the politics and the others who kept a distance or were critical.

The demobilization in the second half of the twenties in the wake of the Locarno treaty, was supported by the creation of institutions such as the *Zentrale der Wahrheit* in Göttingen initiated by the economist and socialist theoretician Robert Wilbrandt (1875–1954), to which Nohl contributed to, in order to overcome the misunderstandings among the nations on the representations of the war. Pirenne seemed to have taken part to some meetings as attested by some letters of Nohl.[186]

Nonetheless, Pirenne's plea for the rebuilding of normal scientific relations between Belgium and Germany was first clearly expressed during the early 1930s in the correspondence with the historian Heinrich Sproemberg (1889–1966), specialist of the Netherlands, who had known Pirenne already before the Great War:

---

182 Pirenne 1919a.
183 In Fredericq's opinion, this speech was as remarkable as amazing: "merkwaardige rede van Pirenne over het vergiftigde pangermanisme" (FD 7.5.1919). [curious discourse of Pirenne upon the poisoned pangermanism].
184 Schöttler 2005, 510ff; Violante 2004, 281ff.
185 Violante 2004, 281ff.
186 Letters of Nohl from 19.01.1923 and from 11.09.1927 (Université libre de Bruxelles, Archives Henri Pirenne 26 PP: correspondance Henri Pirenne).

> "Je souhaite de tout mon cœur, croyez-le bien, que les relations scientifiques se rétablissent, telles qu'elles étaient avant la guerre entre travailleurs belges et travailleurs allemands."[187] [I hope with all my heart, believe it, that scientific relations are restored, as they were before the war between Belgian scholars and German scholars.]

In a subsequent letter, Pirenne expressed his joy of

> "[…] reprendre de plus en plus le contact avec l'Allemagne à laquelle je sais tout ce que je lui dois."[188] [to resume more and more contact with Germany to which I know all that I owe.]

As sketched before, Pirenne's attitude towards the Germans follows the temporality of the First World War's aftermath in Belgium.[189] It corresponds to a remobilization immediately after the war[190], which was followed by a 'demobilization', which occurred after the time of the Locarno Treaties (1925). As Pirenne died in 1935 and consequently did not participate to the general 'remobilization' against the Nazi Germany, he was nevertheless more politically conscious and attentive to signs of ideological changes among German scholars.[191]

9 Conclusion: diary writing, emotion regulation and cultural mobilization against the Germans

The journey that we proposed in this chapter by providing an insight into the diaries of the historians Fredericq and Pirenne reveals the evolutions of their attitude towards the Germans, which was not monolithic but very dependent on the context. The rejection of the Germans as invaders of Belgium and thus enemies changed into a more nuanced view making a distinction between the political and military authorities responsible for the war and the German population who increasingly suffered. Such a change in Fredericq's and Pirenne's opinions occurred only due to their captivity and particularly their reclusion in small German towns, where they lived next to the population. Their remobilization, e.g. the resurgence of their anger against Germany happened after their return to Belgium, noting the war destructions and devastations and mourning collectively the many losses in the families. Their attitude was also supported by the general postwar context of revenge against Germany, particularly high in Belgium and France.

The evolution in Fredericq's and Pirenne's attitude towards the Germans can be explained by the psychological rule of the proximity as the possibility to emotionally understand the point of view of others. Moreover, the ways in which they expressed their disappointment and anger by using harsh metaphors or resorting to humor are

---

187 Letter of Pirenne to Sproemberg, 11.3.1931 (Sproemberg 1971, 440).
188 Letter of Pirenne to Sproemberg, 31.5.1931 (Sproemberg 1971, 442).
189 See for instance Claisse, Lemoine (2004).
190 Such cultural remobilizations after the war were common. See Horne 2002b.
191 Letter of Pirenne to Sproemberg, 18.9.1933 (Sproemberg 1971, 443).

to be viewed as forms of emotion regulation. Finally, their intellectual activity during the war can be interpreted as a coping strategy in order to endure the war. Thus, three main psychological strategies were at stake in Fredericq's and Pirenne's attitude and acting during the war.

Unpublished Sources

Fredericq, P. (1869–1920). Dagboeken. University of Ghent, BHSL. HS.3704.
Fredericq, P. (1916–1918). Wegvoeringsdagboeken. University of Ghent, BHSL. HS.3708.
Fredericq, P. (1919). Autobiografie 1850–1919, met bijlagen, University of Ghent, BHSL. HS.3704.
Pirenne, H. (1914–1918). Journal de guerre. Private collection. Castle of Cernex (France).

References

Amara, M., Roland, H. (2004). *Gouverner en Belgique occupée. Oscar von der Lancken-Wakenitz-Rapports d'activité 1915–1918*. Bruxelles: P.I.E.-Peter Lang.
Baertsoen, M. (1922). *Gand sous l'occupation allemande. Notes d'un Gantois sur la guerre de 1914–1918,* Gent: Société anonyme de la presse libérale gantoise.
Cartellieri, A. (2014). *Tagebücher eines deutschen Historikers. Vom Kaiserreich bis in die Zweistaatlichkeit 1899–1953*. Steinbach, M. and Dathe U. (Eds). Munich: Oldenburg Verlag.
Claisse, S., Lemoine, T. (2005). Comment (se) sortir de la Grande Guerre? Regards sur quelques pays "vainqueurs": la Belgique, la France, la Grande-Bretagne. Paris: L'Harmattan.
Chickering, R (1993). *Karl Lamprecht: A German Academic Life (1856–1915)*. Atlantic Highlands, N. J.: Humanities Press.
Crawford, E (1992). *Nationalism and Internationalism in Science, 1880–1939. Four Studies of the Nobel Population*. Cambridge: Cambridge University Press.
Coppens, C. (1973). Bij een brief van Dr. Reismann-Grone. Paul Fredericq en het pangermanisme. *Wetenschappelijke Tijdingen*, 32, 216–226.
Coppens, C. (1990). *Paul Fredericq*. Gent: Liberaal Archief.
de Guchtenaere H., Lecointe G. (1919). *Les relations intellectuelles internationales d'après-guerre*, Brussels: Hayez.
de la Vallée Poussin, Ch., Lecointe, G., Massart, J. (1919). Conférence des Académies des sciences interalliées, tenue à Paris en 1918. Compte-rendu présenté à l'Académie des Sciences, des Lettres et des Beaux-Arts de Belgique. *Académie Royale de Belgique. Bulletin de la Classe des sciences*, 49–62.
de la Vallée Poussin, Ch., Lecointe, G., Massart, J. (1919). Conférence des Académies des sciences interalliées, tenue à Londres en 1918. Compte-rendu présenté à l'Académie des Sciences, des Lettres et des Beaux-Arts de Belgique. *Académie Royale de Belgique. Bulletin de la Classe des sciences*, 63–81.
De Schaepdrijver, S. (1997). *De groote Oorlog. Het koninkrijk België tijdens de Eerste Wereldoorlog*. Amsterdam/Antwerpen: Atlas.
De Schaepdrijver, S. (2000). La Belgique entre exaltation et rejet, 1914–1918. *Cahiers d'Histoire du temps présent*, 7, 17–49.

De Schaepdrijver, S. (2002). Occupation, Propaganda and the Idea of Belgium. In Roshwald, A. and Stites, R. (Eds), *European Culture in the Great War: The Arts, Entertainment, and Propaganda, 1914–1918*. Cambridge: Cambridge University Press, 267–294.

De Schaepdrijver, S. (2008). "We who are so Cosmopolitan": *The War Diary of Constance Graeffe, 1914–1915,* Brussels: Archives générales du Royaume.

De Schaepdrijver, S. (2010). Belgium. In Horne, J. (Ed.). *A Companion to World War I*. Chichester, U.K.; Malden: Wiley-Blackwell, 386–402.

De Schaepdrijver, S. (2011). "That Theory of Races": Henri Pirenne on the Unfinished Business of the Great War *Revue Belge d'Histoire Contemporaine*, 3–4, 533–552.

De Schaepdrijver, S. (2013). Populations under occupation. In Winter, J. (Ed.). T*he Cambridge history of the First World War. Civil society*, Cambridge: Cambridge University Press, vol. 3, 476–504.

De Schaepdrijver, S. (2014). Making Sense of the War (Belgium). In Daniel, U., Gatrell, P., Janz, O., Jones, H., Keene, J., Kramer, A., Nasson B. *1914-1918-online. International Encyclopedia of the First World War*. Berlin: Freie Universität Berlin. DOI: 10.15463/ie1418.10450.

De Schaepdrijver, S. and Proctor, T. M. (Eds) (2017). *An English Governess in the Great War. The Secret Brussels Diary of Mary Thorp*, Oxford: Oxford University Press.

Dmitriev, A. (Filler, A., transl.) (2002). La mobilisation intellectuelle. La communauté académique internationale et la Première Guerre mondiale. *Cahiers du monde russe*, 43, 4, 617–644.

Erdmann, K. D. (Nothnagle, A, transl.) (2005). *Towards a Global Community of Historians. The International Historical Congresses and the International Committee of Historical Sciences, 1898-2000.* New York/Oxford: Berghahn Books, 2005.

Frevert, U. (2009). Was haben Gefühle in der Geschichte zu suchen?. *Geschichte und Gesellschaft*, 35, 183–208.

Gheude, C. (1919). *Nos années terribles 1914–18*, Brussels: Lamberty.

Gille, L., Ooms, A., Delandsheere, P. (1919). *Cinquante Mois d'Occupation Allemande*. 4 vol. Brussels: Albert Dewit.

Hampe, K. (Reichert, F., Wolgast, E., Eds) (2004). *Kriegstagebuch 1914–1919*. Munich: Oldenburg Verlag.

Henwood, P., René-Bazin, P. (Eds) (2016). Écrire en guerre, 1914–1918. Des archives privées aux usages publics. Rennes: Presses universitaires de Rennes.

Hasquin, H. (2004). Henri Pirenne: un historien engagé. *Académie Royale de Belgique. Bulletin de la Classe des Lettres et des Sciences morales et politiques*, 6e série, 15, 85–109.

Hinz, U. (2004). Prisonniers. In Audoin-Rouzeau, S. and Becker, J.-J. (Eds), *Encyclopédie de la Grande Guerre 1914–18*. Montrouge: Bayard, 777–785.

Hocke, G. R. (1991). *Europäische Tagebücher aus vier Jahrhunderten*. Francfort/Main: Fischer Taschenbuch Verlag.

Horne, J. (2002a). Introduction. Démobilisations culturelles après la Grande Guerre. *14–18, Aujourd'hui, Today, Heute*, 5, 45–53.

Horne, J. (2002b). Locarno et la politique de démobilisation culturelle: 1925–1930. *Démobilisations culturelles après la Grande Guerre. 14–18, Aujourd'hui, Today, Heute*, 5, 53–87.

Horne, J. (2005). Belgian intellectuals and the German invasion, 1914–15. In Jaumain, S., Amara, M., Majerus, B., Vrints, A. (2005). *Une guerre totale? La Belgique dans la Première Guerre mondiale.- Nouvelles tendances de la recherche historique, Actes du colloque international organisé à l'ULB du 15 au 17 janvier 2003*. Brussels: Archives générales du Royaume, 391–404.

Iggers, G. (2002). Historians Confronted with the War. *Storia della Storiografia*, 42, 3–22.

Keymeulen, S., Tollebeek, J. (2011). *Henri Pirenne Historian. A life in Pictures*, Leuven: Lipsius.

Krumeich, G. (1997). Kriegsfront-Heimatfront. In Hirschfeld, G., Krumeich, G., Langewiesche, D., Ullmann, H.-P. (Eds) *Kriegserfahrungen. Studien zur Sozial- und Mentalitätsgeschichte des Ersten Weltkrieges.* Essen: Klartext Verlag, 12–19.

Loveling, V. (2013). *Oorlogsdagboeken: 1914–1918.* Van Peterghem, S. Stynen, L. with the collaboration of Van Raemdonck (Eds). Antwerpen: Manteau.

Luminet, O. (2013). *Psychologie des émotions. Nouvelles perspectives pour la cognition, la personnalité et la santé.* Brussels: De Boeck.

Lyon, B. (1966). The Letters of Henri Pirenne to Karl Lamprecht (1894–1915). *Bulletin de la Commission royale d'histoire*, 132, 161–231.

Lyon, B. (1971). *Henri Pirenne. An Intellectual Biography.* Ghent: Story-Scientia.

Lyon, B. and M. (1976). *The "Journal de guerre" of Henri Pirenne.* Amsterdam: North Holland Publishing Company.

Lyon, B., Pirenne, J.-H. (Eds) (1994). 'Réflexions d'un solitaire' by Henri Pirenne. *Bulletin de la Commission royale d'histoire,* 160, 143–257.

Lyon, B. (1997). Henri Pirenne's *Réflexions d'un solitaire* and his Re-evaluation of History. *Journal of Medieval History*, 23, 285–299.

Lyon, B. (1998). The War of 1914 and Henri Pirenne's Revision of his Methodology. In Tollebeek, J., Verbeeck, G., Verschaffel, T. (Eds). *De lectuur van het verleden. Opstellen over de geschiedenis van de gescheidschrijiving aangeboden aan Reginald de Schryver.* Leuven: Universitaire Pers, 507–516.

Max, P. (2006) *Journal de guerre de Paul Max. Notes d'un Bruxellois pendant l'occupation (1914–1918).* Majerus B., Soupart, S. (Eds). Brussels: Archives de la Ville de Bruxelles.

Nyrop, C. (1917). *L'arrestation des professeurs belges de l'Université de Gand: le droit contre la force.* Lausanne: Payot.

Pirenne, H. (1919a). Le pangermanisme et la Belgique. *Académie royale de Belgique. Bulletin de la Classe des Lettres et des Sciences morales et politiques,* 5e serie, 5, 341–373.

Pirenne, H. (1919b). Rapport de MM. Pirenne et Bidez sur la constitution de l'Union Académique Internationale. Séance du 3 novembre 1919. *Bull. Cl. Lettres....,* 5e serie, 5, 625–631.

Pirenne, H. (1920). Souvenirs de captivité en Allemagne (mars 1916-novembre 1918). *Revue des Deux Mondes*, 56, 540–560 et 831–858. Reedited in Devroey, J.-P., Knaepen, A. (Eds) (2014). *Histoire de l'Europe éditée d'après les carnets de captivité (1916–1918),* suivie des *Souvenirs de captivité.* Brussels: Éditions de l'Université de Bruxelles.

Pirenne, H. (1928). *La Belgique et la guerre mondiale.* Publications de la Dotation Carnegie pour la paix internationale. Paris: Les Presses universitaires de France; New Haven: Yale University Press.

Prochasson, C. (2004). Les intellectuels. In Audoin-Rouzeau, S. and Becker, J.-J. (Eds). *Encyclopédie de la Grande Guerre 1914–18.* Montrouge: Bayard, 665–676.

Rasmussen, A. (2004). Sciences et scientifiques. In Audoin-Rouzeau, S. and Becker, J.-J. (Eds). *Encyclopédie de la Grande Guerre 1914–18.* Montrouge: Bayard, 677–688.

Rasmussen, A. (2007). Réparer, réconcilier, oublier: enjeux et mythes de la démobilisation scientifique, 1918–1925. *Histoire@Politique*, 3, 1–13. DOI 10.3917/hp.003.0008

Reddy, W. (2009). Historical Research on the Self and Emotions. *Emotions Review*, 1, 302–315.

Reinbothe, R. (2010). L'exclusion des scientifiques allemands et de la langue allemande des congrès scientifiques internationaux après la Première Guerre mondiale. *Revue Germanique Internationale*, 12, 193–208.

Scheer, M. (2012). Are Emotions a Kind of Practice (and is that what makes them have a History)? A Bourdieuian Approach to Understanding Emotion. *History and Theory*, 51, 193–220.

Schöttler, P. (2004). Henri Pirennes Kritik an der deutschen Geschichtswissenschaft und seine Neubegründung des Komparatismus im Ersten Weltkrieg. *Sozial.Geschichte*, 19, 53–81.

Schöttler, P. (2005). Henri Pirenne face à l'Allemagne de l'après-guerre ou la (re)naissance du comparatisme en histoire. In Jaumain, S., Amara, M., Majerus, B., Vrints, A. (Eds). *Une guerre totale? La Belgique dans la Première Guerre mondiale.- Nouvelles tendances de la recherche historique, Actes du colloque international organisé à l'ULB du 15 au 17 janvier 2003.* Brussels: Archives générales du Royaume, 507–517.

Schröder-Gudehus, B. (1966). *Deutsche Wissenschaft und internationale Zusammenarbeit 1914-1928. Ein Beitrag zum Studium kultureller Beziehungen in politischen Krisenzeiten*, Genève: Dumaret et Golay.

Schröder-Gudehus, B. (1986). Pas de Locarno pour la science. La coopération scientifique internationale et la politique étrangère des États pendant l'entre-deux-guerres. *Relations internationales*, 46, 173–194.

Sproemberg, H. (1971). Pirenne und die deutsche Geschichtswissenschaft, in *id.* (Unger, M., Ed.), *Mittelalter und demokratische Geschichtsschreibung. Ausgewählte Abhandlungen*. Berlin: Akademie Verlag, 377–446.

Stern, F. (1994). Historians and the Great War. Private experience and Public Explication. *Yale Review*, 82, 34–54.

Theofilakis, F. (2016). De l'écriture en captivité à l'écriture captive: quand les prisonniers trompent l'encre… In René-Bazin, P. and Henwood, P. *Écrire en guerre 1914–1918. Des archives privées aux usages publics*. Rennes: Presses universitaires de Rennes, 57–70.

Thys, W. (Ed.) (2005). Ein *Landsturmmann* im Himmel: Flandern und der Erste Weltkrieg in den Briefen von *Herman Nohl* an seine Frau. Leipzig: Leipziger Universitätsverlag.

Tollebeek, J. (2008). *Fredericq & zonen. Een antropologie van de moderne geschiedwetenschap*. Amsterdam: Uitgeverij Bert Bakker.

Tollebeek, J. (2011). *Pirenne and Fredericq. Historiographical Ambitions Around 1900. Revue belge d'Histoire contemporaine*, 3–4, 383–409.

Tytgat, C. (1919). *Bruxelles sous la botte allemande – journal d'un journaliste*. Brussels: Charles Bulens.

Vanacker, D. (1991). *Het aktivistisch avontuur*, Ghent: Stichting Mens en Kultur,.

van Werveke, H. (1979). *Paul Fredericq in de spiegel van zijn dagboek*. Brussels: Koninklijke Academie voor Wetenschappen, Letteren en Schone Kunsten van België (Mededelingen van de Koninklijke Academie voor Wetenschappen, Letteren en Schone Kunsten van België. Klasse der Letteren, 41).

van Ypersele, L. (2004). Sortir de la guerre, sortir de l'occupation. Les violences populaires en Belgique au lendemain de la Première Guerre mondiale. *Vingtième Siècle. Revue d'histoire*, 83, 65–74.

Violante, C. (1987). Henri Pirenne e la grande guerra. *La cultura*, 25, 308–342.

Violante, C. (Dilcher, G. Ed.) (2004). *Das Ende der 'großen Illusion'. Ein europäischer Historiker im Spannungsfeld von Krieg und Nachkriegszeit, Henri Pirenne (1914–1923) – Zu einer Neulesung der 'Geschichte Europas'*. Berlin: Duncker & Humblot.

vom Brocke, B. (1985). Wissenschaft und Militarismus. Der Aufruf der 93 „An die Kulturwelt" und der Zusammenbruch der internationalen Gelehrtenrepublik im Ersten Weltkrieg. In Calder, W.M., Flashar, H., Linken, Th. (Eds), *Wilamowitz nach 50 Jahren*, Darmstadt: Wissenschaftliche Buchgesellschaft, 649–719.

von Ungern-Sternberg, J. and W. (2013²). *Der Aufruf „An die Kulturwelt!" Das Manifest der 93 und die Anfänge der Kriegspropaganda im Ersten Weltkrieg*. Francfort/Main: Peter Lang.

von Ungern-Sternberg, J. (2015). Les conséquences de la guerre sur la communauté scientifique en Europe. In Compagnon, A. (Ed.), *Autour de 1914-1918: nouvelles figures de la pensée. Sciences, arts et lettres*. Paris: Odile Jacob, 59–84.

Warland, G. (2004). L'*Histoire de l'Europe* d'Henri Pirenne: Genèse de l'œuvre et représentation en miroir de l'Allemagne et de la Belgique. *Textyles. Revue des Lettres belges de langue française*, 24, 38–51.

Warland, G. (2008). Avatars de la 'métahistoire' nationale et mise en récit de la Grande Guerre. Point de mire sur Henri Pirenne (1862–1935) et Ernest Lavisse (1842–1922). In Laserra A. M., Leclercq N., Quaghebeur M. (Eds), *Mémoires et antimémoires littéraires du XXᵉ siècle. La première guerre mondiale*. Vol. 2. Brussels: Peter Lang, 27–63.

Warland, G. (2011). Rezeption und Wahrnehmung der deutschen Geschichtswissenschaft bei belgischen ‚Epigonen': Paul Fredericq, Godefroid Kurth und Henri Pirenne. In Beyen, M., Draye, G., Roland, H. (Eds), *Deutschlandbilder in Belgien 1830–1940*. Münster/New York: Waxmann Verlag, 219–261.

Warland, G. (2014a). Pirenne, Henri. In Daniel, U., Gatrell, P., Janz, O., Jones, H., Keene, J., Kramer, A., Nasson B. *1914-1918-online. International Encyclopedia of the First World War*. Berlin: Freie Universität Berlin. DOI: 10.15463/ie1418.10090.

Warland, G. (2014b). Widersprüchliches Deutschland im Spiegel des geschichtswissenschaftlichen Diskurses in Belgien, Frankreich und den Niederlanden in den Jahren 1870–1920. In Dumoulin, M., Elvert, J., Schirmann, S. (Eds), *Encore ces chers Voisins. Le Benelux, L'Allemagne et la France aux XIXe et XXe siècles*. Stuttgart: Franz Steiner Verlag, 233–247.

Warland, G. (2016). Der deutsch-jüdische Historiker Martin Philippson (1846 bis 1916). Wissenschaftsvermittler zwischen Deutschland und Belgien. In Bischoff, S., Jahr, C. Mrowka T. and Thiel J. (Eds), *Belgica – terra incognita? Resultate und Perspektiven der Historischen Belgienforschung*, Münster/New York: Waxmann Verlag. Historische Belgienforschung, vol. 1, 56–67.

Warland, G. (2018a). Henri Pirenne, témoin fiable ou narrateur meurtri? De son *Journal de guerre* à ses *Souvenirs de captivité*. In van Ypersele, L., Warland, G., Amara M. (Eds), *Guerres mondiales et conflits contemporains*, 272, 51–64.

Warland, G. (2018b). Die *Académie Royale de Belgique* im Ersten Weltkrieg: Widerstand gegen die deutschen Besatzer. In Berg, M., Thiel, J. Weber D. (Eds), *Europäische Wissenschaftsakademien im „Krieg der Geister". Reden und Dokumente 1914 bis 1920*, Acta Historica Leopoldina, Stuttgart: Wissenschaftliche Verlagsgesellschaft, 209–238.

Wegner, L. (2014). Occupation during the War (Belgium and France). In Daniel, U., Gatrell, P., Janz, O., Jones, H., Keene, J., Kramer, A., Nasson, B. *1914-1918-online. International Encyclopedia of the First World War*. Berlin: Freie Universität Berlin. DOI: 10.15463/ie1418.10388.

Part II
Representations of the First World War in Belgium: Literature, Poetry, Cultural and Collective Memory

Part I

Myrthel Van Etterbeeck and Karla Vanraepenbusch[1]

War, Narratives and Memory: The Defence and Fall of the Belgian Fort Cities in the Cultural Memory of the First World War

1 Introduction

> "Andenne, Dinant, Tamines, our executed civilians, our burnt down homes, the red fights of Liège, Antwerp and the Yser, the bloodied corpses of our soldiers, the mothers without children, the children without father".[2]

With this enumeration of place names, the author Fernand-Hubert Grimauty drew a topography of war violence in Belgium, a neutral nation that had been invaded by German troops on the 4th of August 1914. The towns of Andenne, Dinant and Tamines soon became known as 'martyr towns', because of the atrocities that the German army engaged in against the local population, causing widespread death and destruction. With the second part of the list, Grimauty refers to the Belgian resistance at the 'fortified cities' of Liège and then Antwerp, where the Belgian army tried, in vain, to halt the invader. Nothing, however, seemed to be able to stop the invasion, until October 1914, when the Belgian army managed to halt the German advance at the Yser. This is where, for the next four years, the Belgians fought the Germans, while the Belgian territory was almost entirely occupied.[3]

The success of the concept of 'total war' in the recent historiography of the First World War has sparked a vivid interest in the war experience of civilian populations and in the extreme violence that they were confronted with.[4] While elements of the 'totalisation' of the war can be found world-wide[5], Belgium has been characterised as an emblematic case.[6] Historians have therefore paid ample attention to the mem-

---

1 Both authors contributed equally to this article. They would like to thank the following reviewers for their feedback: Elke Brems, Alain Colignon, Chantal Kesteloot, Olivier Klein, Laurence van Ypersele, Antoon Vrints, Geneviève Warland.
2 In French: "Andenne, Dinant, Tamines, nos civils fusillés, nos foyers incendiés, les rouges combats de Liège, d'Anvers et de l'Yser, les cadavres sanglants de nos soldats, les mères sans enfants, les enfants sans père." (Grimauty 1922, 55).
3 De Schaepdrijver 2002.
4 Winter and Prost 2005, 171–172.
5 Segesser 2014.
6 Benvindo and Majerus 2010, 127–148.

ory of the 'German atrocities' in the 'martyr towns'.[7] The memory of the attack and fall of the fort cities has been far less studied, even though these events did have a major impact on the lives of the inhabitants. Certainly, the battles at Antwerp and Liège claimed fewer civilian lives than the 'German atrocities' in the 'martyr towns'. But the impact of war violence cannot be solely assessed by the number of casualties. The Germans used a pioneering military strategy which purposefully targeted civilians, designed to pressure them into surrendering: the aerial bombing of cities.[8] Many thousands fled, those who remained lived under the constant threat of enemy fire until 'their' city fell into the hands of the German army. This marked the beginning of four years of occupation, during which their freedom of speech and movement was curtailed.[9] The events that took place at Antwerp and Liège in 1914 – bombardments, an invasion and an occupation – are all symptomatic of the 'totalisation' of war. Warfare unquestionably affected daily life and local populations. Since social psychologists note that such events are more susceptible to result in memory[10], it is relevant to examine whether the defence and fall of the fort cities left any traces in cultural memory.

The purpose of our study is to determine what kind of 'commemorative narratives' were produced about the battle of Liège and the siege of Antwerp. We borrowed this concept from Yael Zerubavel, a Jewish Studies scholar who argues that "each act of commemoration reproduces a commemorative narrative, a story about a particular past that accounts for this ritualized remembrance and provides a moral message for the group members".[11] With this concept, she draws attention to the process of narrativisation, in particular to the choices that a community makes when producing these narratives and to how they organise them. Suppressions and exaggerations are in fact, as Zerubavel has shown, standard procedures in the formation of a shared memory. In this chapter, we will analyse the 'commemorative narratives' that were produced about the fall of the fort cities, the choices that were made in the process of narrativisation, how the narratives of both cities differed and what that might mean.

We will examine literary works as well as monuments, commemorative plaques and street names. Confronting and comparing these two very different media of memory with one another presents the advantage of revealing how 'commemorative narratives' function and how they shape cultural memory. Memory Studies scholars Astrid Erll and Ann Rigney stress that, for a past event to become a part of cultural memory, a narrative not only has to be produced in media ('mediality'), but it has to be reproduced again and again. This can be done by producing the same narratives across different media platforms ('remediation') or through repetitive performances

---

7   Horne and Kramer 2001; De Schaepdrijver 2008, 194–207; Tixhon and Derez 2014.
8   Voldman 2002, 151–173.
9   De Schaepdrijver 2002, 116.
10 Pennebaker and Banasik 1997, 17.
11 Zerubavel 1995, 6.

along the same medium ('recursivity').[12] These constant reiterations allow people to become gradually more engaged with the past, as it creates a sense of immediacy. In short, there is no cultural memory formation without media, mediality, recursivity and remediation. Note that we understand the concept of 'cultural memory', developed by Jan and Aleida Assmann, in the terms proposed by Erll: as an umbrella concept that includes both social, material and cognitive dimensions. In contrast to Maurice Halbwachs' concept of 'collective memory', 'cultural memory' emphasises the importance of cultural processes in the creation of a shared memory.[13]

Our media-based approach has another advantage: it offers both a local, internal perspective (i.e. how is the war commemorated in/by the two cities) and a broader, external one (i.e. how are these events represented in the Belgian literature). The standard model in Memory Studies has been dominated by a nationalising perspective, as it centres on the constitutive role of memory in the construction of national identity and nation building, perhaps as a consequence of the immense influence of Pierre Nora's *Lieux de Mémoire* research project on the historiography of memory. An example of this approach is Yael Zerubavel's work on the invention of a new national tradition in Israeli memory.[14] Yet these scholars largely ignore the dynamic process of local, national and transnational influences in cultural memory formation.[15] Monuments, for example, should not solely be considered as expressions of cultural nationalism. They also transmit local sentiments and contribute to local identity formation, especially in Belgium, a nation with a decidedly urban culture and a political life characterised by a high degree of municipal autonomy.[16] Studying literary works as well as monuments, commemorative plaques and street names allows one to obtain a better insight into local, national, and to a lesser degree, international influences on 'commemorative narratives' of the First World War.

Since the formation of cultural memory is based on the 'mediation' of past experiences, we will first provide an overview of the events that took place in Liège and Antwerp during the invasion and then discuss the way in which these were 'mediated' in contemporary 'mass media'. The philosopher Jeffrey Andrew Barash has argued that 'mass media', particularly mass-produced images, facilitate public memory by simulating experience.[17] His research focuses on our own age, but the same process can also be detected during the First World War, a period when mass-produced and mass-circulated media such as journals, illustrated weeklies and postcards were booming. The narratives 'mediated' during the war through these 'mass media' deeply influenced the formation of cultural memory in other media ('remediation') during

---

12 Erll and Rigney 2009, 1–11; Rigney 2005, 20–21.
13 Erll 2008, 3–4.
14 Zerubavel 1995.
15 Beyen 2015, 1–23.
16 Van Ginderachter 2011, 110–130; Vannieuwenhuyze 2016, 197–217.
17 Barash 2016.

and after the war. In the third and fourth section of this paper, we will analyse the narratives in those other media, Belgian literature and material memory traces in urban space, respectively.

2 Wartime events and experiences

From 4 August 1914 onward, German troops invaded neutral Belgium in order to implement the Schlieffen-Moltke plan, a blueprint for victory against Germany's enemy France. For the Germans, a swift conquest of Liège was vital, since the city constituted a traffic node, connecting it to the rest of the country, as a kind of 'gate' into France. The Belgian army tried to halt the invader, even though it was too small and too ill-prepared for war to pose a real threat.[18] Entrenched in the forts built around Liège, the Belgian troops managed to repel the assailant during the first attacks on the 5th and 6th of August.[19] The Germans, however, did not just target the forts, but also the city itself. Liège was bombed, first, on the night of 5 to 6 August, by a zeppelin, then, during the following days, by heavy artillery, which resulted in significant material destructions and civilian casualties.[20] Intimidated, the military commander of the city surrendered on 7 August 1914. The Belgian troops, stationed in the forts, continued fighting, in vain it turned out, since the German army had, in the meantime, been reinforced with more troops and heavy artillery. Built at the end of the 19th century, the forts could not endure prolonged artillery fire, and one fort after the other fell. Loncin, the last one, fell on 15 August 1914, ten days after the beginning of the Battle of Liège.[21] For the inhabitants of Liège, now an occupied city, worse was yet to come. In the evening of the 20th of August, German soldiers lodged in the city centre thought they were being attacked by civilians ('*francs-tireurs*'). In retaliation, they set several buildings on fire and executed the men who lived there. In a single night, thirty houses were destroyed, and over sixty civilians died.[22]

As soon as the news of the fall of the forts of Liège had reached the capital, the royal family, the government and the army withdrew to the Belgian National Redoubt, the fortified city of Antwerp. But even there, they were not out of the range of the German army. In the night of 24/25 August 1914, a German zeppelin bombed the city centre, and while it missed the royal palace by a hair's breadth, the attack resulted in the city's first civilian casualties.[23] However, the Germans were interested neither in Antwerp nor in Belgium, and quickly focussed their attention back on the war with France. Thereupon, the Belgian army launched two rather successful sorties against

---

18 Bechet 2017.
19 Bechet 2014b, 135–146.
20 Nahoé 2014, 173–176.
21 Bechet 2014b, 146–155.
22 Bechet 2014a, 7–18.
23 Maes 2013, 49–53.

the Germans from the defensive position of Antwerp, because Albert I, king of the Belgians and commander-in-chief of the army, wished to prove his loyalty to Great Britain and France, the guarantors of his country's neutrality.[24] This kept several units of the German army occupied, so that they could not participate in the combats at the Marne, a battle eventually won by the French.[25] Exasperated, the German high command decided to lay siege to Antwerp. From 28 September 1914 onwards, the forts and the city were systematically bombed. It soon became clear that the fortified position, long deemed impregnable, would fall. The king, the government and the army subsequently crossed the river Scheldt and fled the city. As the Germans had not yet perceived their escape, they continued to bomb the city. In a quest to prevent further destructions, the city council surrendered on 9 October 1914, and Antwerp was thereupon invaded and occupied by German forces for the remainder of the war.[26]

3 Narratives mediated during the war

Both the Allies and the Central Powers were quick to proclaim victory at Liège, since Liège was the first large-scale battle fought during the First World War and the stakes were, subsequently, high. For the Germans, the fall of the city was a sure sign that their military strategy of a swift attack had worked well, and they considered Liège as the first of a series of victories to come.[27] The Allies also viewed the resistance of the forts as a victory, because they believed that it had delayed the German advance by several days, or even half a month, leading to the failure of the Schlieffen-Moltke plan. Already on 7 August 1914, the French president Poincaré awarded the *Légion d'honneur* to the city. From that moment on, the allied press wrote incessantly about 'the heroic defence of Liège', and the events soon took on mythical proportions. It was (falsely) alleged that the French had won the Battle of the Marne thanks to the delay caused by the Battle of Liège.[28] Even the 'neutral' American press was partial to the Belgian 'underdogs' defending themselves against an aggressive invader and judged

---

24 Haag 1990, 244–247.
25 von Hausen 1922, 179.
26 Maes 2013, 69–111.
27 Brüll 2014, 160–163.
28 Military historian Martin Van Creveld was the first to criticise and demystify the influence that the defence of Liège supposedly had on the outcome of the Battle of the Marne. He states that the troops forming the extreme right wing of the German army only began to fall behind schedule by 19 August (due to the fact that the supplies could not keep up the pace with the troops), which is several days AFTER the forts of Liège had fallen (Van Creveld 1977, 123). The Belgian military historian Henri Bernard confirmed that the German troops were still on schedule on 17 August 1914 (Bernard 1983, 67–68). For a more detailed deconstruction of the myth of the Battle of Liège, see Delhez 2013. We would like to thank Alain Colignon (CegeSoma) and Joost Vaesen (VUB) for helping us to find these references.

that the Belgians were fighting for a just cause.²⁹ The heroic defence of Liège became the keystone of a 'Brave Little Belgium' narrative that helped the Allies to legitimise their war effort.

Belgium adopted the myth of the heroic defence of Liège rather quickly, as it served two functions during the war: it strengthened the myth of Belgian heroism and therefore gave hope in times of hardship, while it also provided the Belgians with a moral template, an '*exemplum*', of how they should react when attacked by the enemy. Its success was largely facilitated by the existence of the 19th century romantic template of the heroic but unsuccessful resistance of Liège against Charles the Bold, Duke of Burgundy, in the 15th century. In 1914, right after Germany invaded Belgium, King Albert in fact referred to this episode from the medieval history of Liège as an appeal to his francophone army troops:

> "Remember, [...] Walloons of Liège, who are at this moment at the place of honour, the six hundred Franchimontois".³⁰

Supposedly, these Franchimontois had sacrificed their lives for the freedom of Liège. A decade before the war, in 1904, the episode had been the subject of a historical novel published by Henry Carton de Wiart, titled *La Cité ardente* (the fiery city), that was reissued during the war, in 1915.³¹ Carton de Wiart was the first to call Liège *la Cité ardente*, but the epithet became so popular and widespread during the war, that it came to refer both to the rebellion of the 15th century and to the city's resistance in 1914.³² In this way one narrative superimposes another, so that newly commemorated events and earlier memories reinforce one another.³³

The interchangeable narratives of '*la Cité ardente*', the heroic defence of Liège and 'Brave Little Belgium' do not seem to have been much affected by the sinister events that took place in Liège on the 20th August, 1914. Postcards representing the ravaged houses did circulate, but we can safely assume that these were part of the German propaganda effort, since they show German soldiers proudly posing. When the Belgian politician Pierre Nothomb listed, in 1915, all the "assassinated towns" of Belgium, he did not include Liège, and neither did the French historian Marius Vachon in his list of French and Belgian "martyr towns".³⁴ This might be explained by the fact that other cities had experienced much worse.³⁵ It was the 'sack of Louvain' that dom-

---

29 De Schaepdrijver 2009, 42–52.
30 In French: "Souvenez-vous, [...] Wallons de Liège, qui êtes en ce moment à l'honneur, des Six Cents Franchimontois" as quoted by La Meuse, 6 August 1914, 1.
31 The 1915 edition was published with a new preface by the French author Henry Bordeaux. This new introduction highlights that the fights at Liege have shown that the Belgians still possess the courage and spirit of sacrifice depicted in *La Cité ardente*.
32 Rottiers 1995a, 67–82; Rottiers 1995b, 343–377.
33 Rigney 2005, 19.
34 Nothomb 1915, Vachon 1915.
35 Tixhon and Derez 2014.

inated the front pages of the allied press, because the destruction of the university library, symbolising a civilised world that had fallen prey to the "Teutonic barbarians", was a powerful justification for the allied fighting.[36] The damages and massacres of Liège simply did not carry the same weight, neither in death toll nor symbolically. It seems, moreover, that the allied propaganda machine had been quite efficient in magnifying the resistance of the city, and that more sombre tonalities, distorting the dominant narrative, just did not fit in.

Although the two sorties from the fortified position of Antwerp had more of an influence on the outcome of the Battle of the Marne than the defence of Liège, the siege of Antwerp received significantly less attention in the international press. In August 1914, the fighting in Liège was at the centre of the action, partly because most of the belligerent nations were still in the midst of mobilising their troops, so that not much fighting took place elsewhere. Moreover, Liège had great symbolic importance as one of the first battles of the war, while a few weeks later, combat took place in two geographically separated fronts, both on the Eastern and Western Front. From then on, each Ally was fighting its own battles, and each nation's press focussed on the movements of its own troops.

Whenever the siege of Antwerp was mentioned, it was, above all, to strengthen a 'Poor Little Belgium' narrative that portrayed the country as a victim. The photographs published in the illustrated weeklies showed a city in ruins. Considered as objective proof of the destruction of Antwerp's rich cultural heritage, these photographs implicitly accused the Germans of a barbarian act, and thereby justified the allied war effort.[37] This 'Poor Little Belgium' narrative proved far more effective in mobilising the international public opinion than that of 'Brave Little Belgium'. The more so, since the siege of Antwerp had not presented the same simple 'success story' as Liège; the city had not 'held out', but had surrendered. The Belgian refugee press as well as tracts distributed in the city went as far as accusing the city councillors of treason. Part of the confusion stems from the fact that the Belgian government refrained from taking a position; they only endorsed the city council's decision to surrender in March 1915.[38]

---

36 van Ypersele 2013, 111–126.
37 Henneman 2014, 180; Tollebeek and Van Assche 2014, 80–138.
38 Wils 2014, 59–74; Van Alstein 1999–2000, 209–223.

4 Cultural memory: literature

Every medium will (re-)construct the past according to its own means, thus influencing the kind of memory it produces.[39] Through narrative, literature can "put us in touch with the past [...] and envisage its future [...] as the future that it still was for the historical agents."[40] In other words stories can offer a glimpse into the past from the perspective of an individual, which delivers an intimate and emotionally charged view on the events. Yet, stories can also be used to impose control upon the past, through the reiteration of well-known patterns and templates from culture and history, highly disruptive contingent events such as war can be transformed into meaningful narratives thus integrating them into fabric of history.[41]

For this study we selected 55 prose works about the First World War. First, we sought a (relative) balance between the share of Dutch and French language novels (33/23) and between the civilian and military perspective.[42] Secondly, we wished to cover the entire period, not every year had to be represented but no large gaps should be present. Finally, we took genre and ideological background into account to insure the diversity of the selection. The corpus thus includes: diaries and (semi-)memoirs as well as works of fiction, ranging from overtly (Flemish) nationalist works and humoristic novels to more nuanced, literary texts. After searching the texts for significant references to the battle of Liège and the siege of Antwerp,[43] we retained 13 francophone and 21 Flemish works written between 1914 and 1939.[44] We found that the cities appear most frequently in works published during the war and in the 1920's. Their share diminishes in the 1930's. Of the 14 works published in the 1930's only 5 contained significant references to either Liège or Antwerp. This might be partly due to the smaller number of soldiers' accounts, who are more likely to linger on the war of movement, and the diversification of the subject matter in remaining war novels. Whatever the reason, it makes it difficult to address the evolution in the depiction of

---

39 Erll 2008, 389.
40 Grethlein 2013, 16.
41 Erll 2009, 114.
42 This is an estimate based on the experiences of the authors during the war. We found that the majority of those who served in the army in our corpus depicted life in the army whereas those who fled or spent the war in occupied Belgium focused mainly on civilian life.
43 We searched the texts for keywords such as Antwerp, Liège and alternative designations like *Scheldestad* or *cité ardente*, the names of individual forts and the historical figures connected to the events. The high number of texts that had to be discarded is not surprising if one considers that not all war novels deal with the beginning of war nor do all give an overview of wartime events.
44 We had already read 19 of these books from cover to cover before embarking on this research, of the others I read parts. This allowed us to get a better view of the position and meaning of the discourse surrounding Liège and Antwerp in relation to other elements in the story. A basic familiarity with the novels also prevents that the passages are taken out of context.

the cities in depth.⁴⁵ Besides time, proximity proved to be an especially important determining factor. The chances that Liège or Antwerp are discussed in detail rise significantly when the narrative is either situated in the surroundings of one of the cities or when the main character/author has fought at or visited them during the war. This indicates that war fiction is often informed by personal memories. Consequently, Liège is mentioned slightly more in francophone writings, while Antwerp is more popular in Flemish books. Notwithstanding this trend, two thirds of the books include both cities.

4.1 The afterlife of 'Brave Little Belgium' in literature

In early and distinctly nationalist novels the conflict appears to be unambiguous. The actions at Liège and Antwerp are placed in a highly simplified narrative wherein the small but brave Belgian troops engage in battle against a numerically superior force. The German soldiers are vilified and the invasion itself is depicted as a natural catastrophe. In 1914 G. Raal (pseudonym of Lode Opdebeek) envisions the enemy forces as a flood; the Belgian troops break its waves but cannot stop it entirely.⁴⁶ Following the same logic, the Belgian army is described as a throng of bees⁴⁷, Liège as a nut which proves hard to crack, and Antwerp as a porcupine.⁴⁸ These metaphors are meant to emphasise that the much smaller Belgian army does everything in its power to make the invasion as difficult and unpleasant as possible for the assailants. The eventual success of Germany is not due to the inherent qualities of its soldiers. Novels often stress that "it was the German artillery which would secure victory"⁴⁹ at Liège and Antwerp, which further underlines the moral dichotomy between the brave Belgian forces and the German army relying on underhanded methods, superior numbers and firepower.

The presence of this 'Brave Little Belgium' trope may be most visible in patriotic novels written during the war, and in its immediate aftermath when feelings were running high, but its general outline lives on, especially in soldiers' accounts. Throughout the interwar period, Antwerp and Liège will consistently appear side by side in summary descriptions of the first months of war, often joined by a third fort city, Na-

---

45 Another potential difficulty is that some soldiers' accounts are based on wartime notes or diaries but only published years after the war. We therefore thought it wise to avoid generalisations about the evolution of the depiction in literature beyond the most obvious ones.
46 Raal 1914, 140.
47 Raal 1914, 140.
48 Grimauty 1915, 166.
49 In Dutch: "'t Was de Duitsche artillerie, die de zege zou behalen" (Hans 1919b, 184). See also Raal 1914.

mur, and the Yser.⁵⁰ This indicates that these cities occupy a privileged and emblematic position in the tale of Belgium's heroic resistance. Their centrality is highlighted in the novel *De blijde kruisvaart* (The joyful crusade).⁵¹ About halfway through the narrative, soldiers decide to stage a play, *The swansong of the pin helms,* a humorous patriotic rendition of recent events, consisting of four acts: I. The battle of Liege, II. The fall of Antwerp, III. The battle of the Yser and IV. The trenches. Each of the key episodes of the beginning of the war is present: The unexpectedly strong resistance at Liege and Antwerp, Belgium's "last hope", as one novel puts it⁵², the fall of Antwerp and the retreat to the Yser where the German army is finally brought to a halt. The players' characters chiefly bear humorous names, but we also find a Jan Breydel and a lad of Flanders, connecting current events to episodes in Belgium's illustrious past when a minority heroically defended its freedom against a stronger force.⁵³ Tellingly, the play is never completely performed since the amateur playwright loses the final act of the script. The performance thus ends with the battle of the Yser, also the natural conclusion of the first stage of war.⁵⁴

The success of the 'Brave Little Belgium' narrative is partly due to its correspondence to one of the most powerful leitmotifs in Belgium's historical self-image, namely 'the myth of foreign domination', the belief that the little State had laboured, struggled and fought under foreign dominations for 18 centuries before casting off the yoke in 1830 and winning its fervently wished-for independence.⁵⁵ James Wertsch would refer to this story as a schematic template "from which several copies (i.e. specific narratives) can be generated".⁵⁶ In our case, the schematic narrative 'from foreign domination to freedom and independence', easily facilitates the Brave (and also Poor) Little Belgium tropes with the added bonus that it indirectly alluded to the inevitability of future victory.

4.2 The representation of Liège

However, there turns out to be a considerable difference between the actual representation of the events at Liège and at Antwerp. Overall, the depiction of Liège, cast during the war as the emblem of Belgium's heroic resistance, is surprisingly unequiv-

---

50 Amongst others: Vermeulen 1918; Hans 1919; Loveling 2005 [1914–1918]; De Wilde 1919; Grimauty 1919 & 1922; Corvillain 1923; Tasnier 1928 and Schoup 1932.
51 Francken [1916] 1919.
52 Grimauty 1915, 93.
53 Fritz Francken (pseudonym of Frederik Clijmans, 1893–1969) was a flamingant author best known for his war poetry and prose. In this novel the author shows himself a supporter of the Flemish cause within the framework of Belgium.
54 van Ypersele 2006, 280–282.
55 Verschaffel 1998, 147; Stengers 1981.
56 Wertsch 2007, 29.

ocal and static. It does not change substantially throughout the interwar period. Works of all kinds of plumage, in terms of genre and political persuasion, stress the importance of the first real confrontation with the enemy:

> "We are entering into war! And Liège is where it begins",[57]

exclaims a young girl fearfully in Abraham Hans' rather tendentious,[58] Flemish, novel *Het beleg van Antwerpen* (The siege of Antwerp). Whereas Louis Tasnier includes a letter from the king to general Leman in his military memoir *Notes d'un combattant de la campagne* (Notes of a combatant of the campaign), stating that:

> "In the titanic struggle ahead, you are honoured, since you are the frontrunners. The world is looking at you with fixed eyes".[59]

The defence of Liège has an air of exceptionality, sacrality, even among soldiers:

> "Our men regard their comrades who have seen fire at Liège with respect",[60]

writes the army doctor Max Deauville (pseudonym of Maurice Duwez). Less than a week after the events took place, a combatant already assures Deauville that the days at Liège would be forever engraved in his memory as something great and terrible.

The actions of the army at Liège vindicate Belgium's and Liège's self-image, feeding off and into the narrative of a continuous struggle for freedom, integral to the city's identity. Both Flemish Auctor[61] (pseudonym of Jan Bruylants, 1921) and Francophone Tasnier (1928) stress that the town's defence is the embodiment of the Belgian rejection of the German ultimatum. Liège is where Belgium shows its true colours. The Catholic and patriotic Martial Lekeux makes the most explicit allusions to the town's history. According to him, the war awoke the city's inner nature:

> "Ah! Liège with a flaming heart! You remained the fiery city (Cité ardente) of old with your noble ire! Your blood has not cooled since the folly of the Franchimontois! Here again it spills, and pours in great waves over the hills during the fights of salvation".[62]

---

57 Hans 1919b, 19.
58 A tendentious novel seeks to promote a particular cause or point of view.
59 In French: "Dans la lutte gigantesque qui s'annonce, vous êtes à l'honneur puisque vous êtes au premier rang. Le monde a les yeux fixés sur vous" (Tasnier 1928, 15). Robert De Wilde, also a soldier, echoes this statement in his memoir: "À nous l'honneur de la première rencontre" („To us the honour of the first contact/encounter") (1918).
60 In French: "Nos hommes regardent leurs camarades qui ont vu le feu à Liège avec un certain respect" (Deauville 1917, 21–22).
61 Auctor writes in Dutch: "Toen kwam, als een donderslag bij helderen hemel, de vraag van Duitschland om door België te mogen trekken en 's anderendaags de oorlogsverklaring en het doordringen op Belgisch grondgebied… En het geschut van de Luiker forten werd met het antwoord gelast…" (1921, 84).
62 In French: "Ah! Liège au cœur de feu! Comme tu es bien restée la vieille cité ardente aux colères généreuses! Ton sang n'a pas tiédi depuis les folies de Franchimont! Voici que de

In the logic of the narrative, the willingness to live and die for something larger than oneself demonstrated at Liège is the central lesson of war. To Lekeux, war redeemed and elevated a people lost in selfishness. In the same register, Hans tells his readers that the troops at Liège fought "for king and the people, for the small violated country, for honour and justice."[63] The elevated language of sacrifice and heroism and the reliance on non-debatable terms like justice and honour and grand abstractions is typical of nationalist texts and propaganda. Elizabeth Marsland remarks that this vocabulary is used to bolster belief in "the complex of myths associated with patriotic heroism".[64] It is therefore worthy of note, albeit not surprising, that it often appears in connection with Liège.

Of course, not all novels adhere to this template. Jean Tousseul (1933), Abel Torcy (1919) and Henri Davignon (1919) draw the attention of the reader to the (misleading) influence of the newspapers and their high-minded language on the perception of the Belgian civilians:

> "The adventure of Liege" writes Davignon, "seems an image from a legend [...] everyone spoke of heroism and victory. But no one represented nor evoked the reality of war, its horror and danger".[65]

They denounce the inflated language of the reports, but simultaneously reproduce parts of it to praise the behaviour and the actions of the soldiers, thus steering clear of any fundamental criticism.

Likewise, we find no substantial criticism on the conduct of the army. General Leman is presented by all parties as the uncontested hero of Liège who exemplifies the Belgian spirit of war. The attention is focussed foremost on his dedication to duty and his decision to remain at his post until the bitter end.[66] Only two francophone soldiers' accounts in our corpus depart (however slightly) from the beaten path. De Wilde (1918) and Tasnier (1928) describe how a party of German soldiers penetrated the general's headquarters in Liège by posing as Englishmen. Tasnier concludes that, since the city was compromised, the general had no choice but to withdraw his troops and that defending the forts under these circumstances was nothing less than heroic.

---

nouveau il coule, et, à grands flots, jaillit sur les hauteurs dans les combats de salut" (Lekeux 1922, 24).

63 In Dutch: "Te Luik streden zijn makkers voor koning en volk, voor 't kleine, geschonden vaderland, voor eer en recht" (Hans 1915, 58).

64 Marsland 1991, 4.

65 In French: "L'aventure de Liège apparaissait de loin comme une image légendaire. [...] tout parlait d'héroïsme de victoire et de gloire. Mais personne ne pressentait, ni n'évoquait la réalité de la guerre, son horreur et son danger" (Davignon 1919, 149).

66 The positive image of general Leman was furthered by circumstances, partly of his own making. In the immediate aftermath of the battle, he insisted that the report on the events mention that he never surrendered but was taken prisoner while unconscious. He also died fairly quickly after the war, in 1920, which further solidified his reputation as a hero.

Ironically, from a modern reader's perspective, this passage is the only clue that there ever was criticism of Leman's decision to retreat from the city. Note, that both De Wilde and Tasnier were soldiers who were present at Liège, suggesting that the event never made it into cultural memory.

Given the numerical superiority of the enemy, there is no shame in the eventual defeat. In Lekeux's novel the soldiers' wounds and exhaustion become emblems of "a great victory".[67] It was their stubborn resistance that foiled the German plan:

> a "speedy advance was impossible now. Liège had cost many men and much time".[68]

In line with the international press, four novels explicitly mention that the events at Liège were instrumental to the French victory at the Marne. In contrast, the atrocities carried out in the city are but rarely mentioned. De Wilde notes that there are "plenty of atrocities committed in the environment of Liège"[69] as do Hans (1919b) and Jean Tousseul (1933), but none say anything about the situation in the city itself. Similarly, we find no trace of the zeppelin attack in either francophone or Flemish writings. The strong focus on the military component silences all other voices and what emerges is an uncomplicated narrative of heroism in the face of a stronger enemy.

4.3 The representation of Antwerp

The discourse surrounding the fall of Antwerp is far more complex. Its depiction is not encased in a strong media framework as Liège's is which leaves more ground for personal memories and interpretations. This does not mean that the military aspect is absent in literature, far from it. Unlike international media, who present Antwerp purely as a victim, Belgian novels and memoirs also pay attention to its opposition to the German troops. Three authors stress that the Belgian resistance stopped the Germans from fully concentrating on France.[70] Although:

> "The faith of Namur and Liège had proven that no vesting in existence could withstand Krupp's big Bertha"[71], "Preparations are made everywhere for a rigorous resistance".[72]

---

67 Lekeux 1922, 44.
68 Hans 1915, 97.
69 In French: "plein des atrocités commises dans les environs de Liège" (De Wilde 1918, 48).
70 One francophone (Grimauty 1915) and two Flemish (Hans 1919a; Auctor 1921) works state this explicitly in reference to Antwerp.
71 In Dutch: "Het lot van Luik en Namen heeft eens en voor altijd aangetoond, dat er geen enkele bestaande vesting bestand is tegen Krupp's vesting-artillerie" (Hans 1919a, 37). De Wilde uses the same argument to foreshadow the inevitable fall of Antwerp (De Wilde 1918, 95).
72 In French: "On se prépare partout à une rigoureuse résistance" (De Wilde 1918, 95).

But in the end, the so called impregnable fortifications of Antwerp succumbed to the steel kisses of big Bertha.[73]

It is here that the shoe pinches; at Liege no one (initially) believed that the Belgians could stop the enemy troops, but Antwerp was touted as being unassailable. The news of its swift fall couldn't be presented as a victory; it was nothing less than a disappointment. Even the most pessimistic, writes Edward Vermeulen, thought that it would roughly hold out eight months.[74] When writing about Antwerp it is practically commonplace to include the "so called safety of Antwerp".[75] However, different authors will attach different meanings to its swift fall. In his 1915 novel, the ultra-patriotic Fernand-Hubert Grimauty is laudatory about Antwerp and defends the actions of the army leadership and the government, writing that he honestly believes they took the best course of action in difficult circumstances. He admits that he, like all Belgians, had been blinded by his almost inborn faith in its impregnability but does not take it any further.[76] Moderate Flemish authors Stijn Streuvels and Fritz Francken seem to lay part of the blame on the shoulders of Antwerp itself by alluding to Antwerp's pride and its inhabitants' misplaced confidence.[77] Lekeux, with his single-minded focus on sacrifice, is less concerned with the fall itself than with the conduct of the army. He finds the decision to retreat to the Netherlands despicable. And he is not the only one to deliver criticism of the upper echelons of the army. On October 13, 1914 Streuvels notes:

> "it used to be rumoured that our officers were a bad lot, now it is said out loud".[78]

That Antwerp was surrendered by the *civilian* administration created an additional obstacle. Flamingant Hans emphatically defends the course of action taken, but he is one of the few to do so.[79]

Simultaneously, authors report a growing awareness of the selective and unreliable nature of both the press and official communications. They were willing to believe in Belgium's good luck at Liège but by the time the siege of Antwerp arrived, many profess to have learned their lesson. Even the forgiving and mild Hilarion Thans re-

---

73 Francken 1919, 5.
74 In Dutch: "Antwerpen, dat sommigen oninneembaar verklaarden en dat de zwartziensten aanzagen als ten minste eene maand of acht to moeten wederstaan en dat nauwelijks eenige dagen weerstond" (Vermeulen 1934, 138).
75 De Backer 1934, 15.
76 Grimauty 1915, 47, 50.
77 Streuvels 23 September 1914; Francken 1919, 3.
78 In Dutch: "Vroeger reeds werd er gefluisterd dat onze officieren niet deugden; nu wordt het luidop gezegd."
79 In his novel *The siege of Antwerp* the municipal authorities are willing to sacrifice all that is required but now the army has left they wonder: "should they let Antwerp be shelled until it was completely destroyed? What was the military goal? What was the use of this resistance?" (Hans 1919b, 215).

marks that the coverage of the events at "Liege made him suspicious with regard to the optimistic army related news in our papers".[80] Streuvels is more severe, scant days before Antwerp's fall, he comments upon the discourse surrounding Liège:

> "once again it strikes me how cleverly the notices by the military authorities are compiled. One must weigh every word to grasp its true meaning [...] Les forts tiennent toujours! They write, succinctly and cheerfully; who would find fault with that and think it should be: tous les forts tiennent!?"[81]

Streuvels, like Hilarion Thans and Virginie Loveling, seems less willing to trust what he reads about Antwerp and more inclined to make up his own mind.

This sense of failure and deception is a complicating factor for the creation of a shared cultural memory. The Flamingant novelist Hans (1919b) recounts that soldiers who had fought bravely at Liège were locked away in Antwerp to keep the truth from getting out whereas myths about Antwerp and Liège were stimulated. But his novel also raises the question of whether this might have been a necessary strategy to keep the inhabitants from panicking. Jan Gustaaf Schoup (1932) answers this negatively in his socialist novel. To him the inhabitants of Antwerp (and society at large) have been systematically and habitually deceived by a political system entrenched by militarism.

In the end, there is no consensus in Belgian literature about how to interpret the siege and fall of Antwerp. Instead the works show us a multitude of different perspectives, some of which tie in with the image of 'Brave little Belgium' while others do not. The variety becomes even greater when we include the literary depiction of the impact of warfare on civilian life. Although this side of the story is less fraught with difficulties: passages about civilians mostly mirror the 'Poor Little Belgium' narrative also found in international media. They show readers the tragedy of war and are meant to facilitate emotions of pity and compassion. Hans, for instance, interrupts his narrative, traverses the boundaries between fact and fiction, to recount his own recollection of the bombardment lingering lengthily on his emotional responses:

> "Terrible, horrendous, devastating, horrible! Our Antwerp, burning! [...] Wilfully set on fire [...] flames over Antwerp the city of commerce, art and the capital of our Flemish movement! [...] I feel it, I cannot find the words to convey my full impression..."[82]

In the aftermath of the battle, diarists Stijn Streuvels and Virginie Loveling, both well-respected Flemish novelists, focus on the material and symbolic damage wreaked

---

80 Thans [1925] 1937, 163.
81 Streuvels 5 October, 1914.
82 In Dutch: "Vreeselijk, verschrikkelijk, ontzettend, gruwelijk! Ons Antwerpen in brand! [...] vlammen boven Antwerpen stad van handel kunst, hoofdstad onzer Vlaamsche Beweging. [...] Ik gevoel het, ik kan de woorden niet vinden om mijn vollen indruk weer te geven...Ik zie telkens en telkens weer die vuurzee, die laaiende, lekkende vlammen..." (Hans 1915, 181–182).

upon the city. They observe that the normally bustling harbour is unnaturally still after the invasion:

> "the wind blows through vacant spaces"[83], "there are no sails, no masts, no coming and going of workers at the docks"[84], in fact "(t)here is little movement"; "it's dead, desolate, deserted".[85]

Everywhere in the city, Loveling witnesses the signs of destruction left by the bombs. But the single most oppressing symbol of the foreign domination might be the presence of a German flag flying on the top of the tower of the Cathedral of Our Lady, which "remind(s) the population of the heavy pressure of the occupation".[86] It gives a "terribly sad impression".[87] What these passages have in common is that they disseminate an image of Antwerp as an (innocent) victim, virtuously suffering. Hans makes this position explicit by introducing a sleeping beauty motif:

> "Antwerp sleeps until the Belgian soldier wakes it again. And then… ha… then the carillon [of the aforementioned cathedral] will play…!"[88]

The strongest emotions are saved for the depiction of civilian suffering. The infamous zeppelin attack which targeted citizens is invoked by Raal as proof of German barbarity.[89] By purposely focussing on the impact of the bombardment on civilians, Lekeux strives to achieve the same results:

> "the entire south end – thousands of buildings – is destroyed. Entire streets crumble under the deluge of shells. The roads are swarming with fleeing people."

He zooms in and describes a woman, her clothes ripped to pieces, tearing at her hair, sobbing, screaming, shrilly, desperately, for her lost child:

> "My child! My child! My baby!"[90]

Refugees, frightened of the bombs and on the run from the approaching German army, are likewise regularly described in great detail, inviting the reader to empathise with the victims and judge those who caused it.[91]

---

83   Loveling 13 August 1915.
84   Loveling 13 August 1915.
85   Streuvels 8/9–14 August 1915, 466.
86   Streuvels 8/9–14 August 1915, 466.
87   Loveling 13 August 1915.
88   Hans 1919, 233.
89   Raal 1914, 125.
90   In French: "Tout le quartier sud – des milliers de maisons – est détruit. Des rues entières s'écroulent sous un déluge d'obus. Un immense nuage monte de la cité: Anvers brûle. […] myn kind! myn kindje! myn kindjelief!" (Lekeux 1922, 04).
91   The larger question of whether one should stay in Belgium or flee is a point of tension in Belgian war literature, with regard to Antwerp some accounts (e. g.: Hans 1919b and Baekelmans 1918) mention that a true native should never abandon his city.

5 Cultural memory: memorials and street names

Cities have been described, by historians Stefan Goebel and Derek Keene, as "sites of heightened anticipation, dense experience and concentrated commemoration of military conflict".[92] Geographers have highlighted that they "serve as powerful symbols and repositories of memory".[93] Just like literary works, the memorials, commemorative plaques and street names form a text that can be read, a 'city-text'. What distinguishes these material memory traces from other media, such as literary works, is precisely their spatial dimension: they occupy a specific place in the (quasi-)public space.[94] It is this link between material culture and place that allows the retrieval of memories, as material memory traces anchor past events and the absent dead in the urban space.[95] In line with these observations, we will investigate if the fall of the fort cities led indeed to the formation of a cultural memory in urban space. Our purpose is to 'read' the 'city-text' and to discover how the fortified cities commemorated their fall during the interwar period.

Reading the 'city-text' is, however, challenging, since commemorative narratives are constantly reconstructed in urban space, just like urban space itself is continually reproduced. We therefore focussed our attention on the production of these narratives. This does not only require a focus on the narratives themselves and on the processes of narrativisation, but also on those agents who discursively produced urban space. For the formation of cultural memory is not only the result of narrativisation and recursivity, but also depends on the agency of political and civic actors that select the narratives, a process that Erll and Rigney call the "social performance" of narratives in the public arena.[96] As a consequence, two subtopics are at stake: public memory policies (or lack thereof) of public governments and civil society memory activism. Although it should be understood that the boundaries between both forms of agency can sometimes be rather vague.

---

92 Goebel and Keene 2011, 1.
93 Rose-Redwood *et al.* 2009, 162.
94 Carr *et al.* propose the following definition of 'public space': "Public space is the stage upon which the drama of communal life unfolds. The streets, squares, and parks of a city give form to the ebb and flow of human exchange. These dynamic spaces are an essential counterpart to the more settled places and routines of work and home life, providing the channels for movement, the nodes of communication and the common grounds for play and relaxation" (Carr *et al.* 1992, 3). Note that the public and private realms of space are socially constructed, and that they can be contested (Giesking and Mangold 2014, 183–186).
95 Winter and Sivan 1999, 37.
96 Erll and Rigney 2009, 9.

5.1 Public Memory Policies as a Means to Remember or Forget the Past

The discursive frameworks in which commemorative narratives can be produced and can operate in urban space depend largely on public policy decision-making. Public governments wish to exercise control over these narratives, because they are aware that these do not just have a commemorative function: they also convey political messages.

> "Cultural leaders orchestrate commemorative events to calm anxiety about change or political events, eliminate citizen indifference toward official concerns, promote exemplary patterns of citizen behavior, and stress citizen duties over rights",

observed John Bodnar.[97] In Belgian cities, those in control of the discursive production of urban space were the city councils. They always had had, more so than in the neighbouring countries, a high degree of political autonomy and decision-making power.[98] After the war, when the central government actively discouraged municipalities to build war memorials for financial reasons, the majority of local authorities blatantly ignored their request.[99] Hence, we will examine if and to what extent the city councils of Antwerp and Liège acted as memory agents, what kind of commemorative narratives they produced and what kind of political messages these conveyed.

It should be noted, first of all, that the city council of Liège was a very active memory agent. Shortly after the Armistice, in December 1918, it donated 250,000 Belgian francs to erect a Monument for the National Defence[100], a sum that was, given the difficult economic context of post-war reconstruction, relatively high. This initiative demonstrates both the urgency and the will of the local authorities to consolidate the myth of the defence of Liège in stone. Designed as a 90-meter-high "belfry of victory", it was meant to dominate the city centre. Each floor would be constructed in a different architectural style, from the base in Romanesque style, up to the bell chamber in Empire style. The belfry thus served as a symbolical timeline that referred to the golden age when the city was still the capital of the Prince-Bishopric of Liège. In this timeline, Liège's resistance in 1914 was envisaged as the culmination of a long history of local struggles for freedom.[101] Thus, the defence of Liège was integrated into a larger

---

97   Bodnar 1992, 15.
98   Van Ginderachter 2011, 110–130.
99   Claisse 2013, 146–152.
100   Colignon 1999, 217–244.
101   "La page d'histoire que nous avons vécue en 1914 est-elle autre chose que le couronnement d'une histoire de 10 siècles de luttes pour la liberté? La pierre et le bronze devront donc rappeler l'histoire de Liège, la lutte de ses Métiers contre les princes, la paix de Fexhe, la résistance aux ducs de Bourgogne, 1789, 1830. Nous y chanterons le triomphe du Droit, notre amour de la Liberté […]", quote from a letter of J.-M. Remouchamps to Gaston Grégoire, dated 24 Mai 1919, Musée de la Vie wallonne, catalogue 3A.4, n. 36.933, as quoted by Colignon 1999, 225.

triumphant, but mostly local, narrative of continuous struggle for freedom against a foreign oppressor, as a local take on the national 'myth of foreign domination'.[102] The "belfry of victory" clearly meant to strengthen local pride and identity, yet it was never built, because the costs proved higher than anticipated.

Also in December 1918, the city council of Liège introduced several street names that referred explicitly to the Battle of Liège. One street was literally called "Boulevard des Défenseurs de Liège", while the others were named after the military commanders and army regiments that had defended the forts, or after the forts themselves.[103] Commemorative street naming can be a powerful vehicle to introduce specific narratives of the past into the public sphere and into the present. It is a political act, often closely related to local and national identity formation.[104] And location matters: the places where the streets are situated have a significant impact on the narrative that they communicate.[105] In Liège, almost all of these street names were located outside the city centre, often close to military compounds, or sometimes in the neighbourhood where one of the commanders was born or had lived. So even though the city council showed a strong interest in commemorating the Battle of Liège, the street names were generally not located where they would have been most visible, in the city centre.[106] One has to consider, however, that the city council planned to erect the "belfry of victory" on the market square in the heart of the city. The street names, conversely, connected the narrative of the heroic defence in 1914 with the city's status as a place of military quartering, and thus also with the Belgian army. In this way, they implicitly supported a narrative that represented Liège as a military outpost guarding the nation in the past as well as in the present.

Almost a decade later, in 1926, the city council of Liège erected a war memorial at Robermont, its main municipal cemetery. Even though Robermont was located at the outskirts of the city, it occupied an important place within the symbolic urban space, since municipal cemeteries are the "obverse" or "intemporal image" of the city of the living, and the allied war[107] dead, buried in a separate honorary lot, were manifestly

---

102 Blaas 2002, 155.
103 Boulevard des Défenseurs de Liège, Place du Général Leman, Rue du Général Bertrand, Rue Général Collyns, Rue Général Jacques de Dixmude, Rue Commandant Duchesne, Rue du Commandant Marchand, Rue Commandant Victor Naessens, Rue Commandant Speecen, Rue du Fort de Pontisse, Rue du Fort de Loncin, Boulevard du 12ᵉ de Ligne, Boulevard du 14ᵉ de Ligne.
104 Rose-Redwood *et al.* 2018, 1–24.
105 Azaryahu and Foote 2008, 179–194.
106 The exception was the street named after Commandant Marchand, closer to the city centre than the other names, because he had been killed by German soldiers at the headquarter of the Belgian army, that was situated, at that time, in the city centre.
107 Ariès 1974, 74.

considered as an elite group.[108] The memorial was built on that same lot, right in front of the graves of the war heroes. It depicts a female figure personifying "an acknowledging Humanity bowing before the heroes who fell for the people's freedom"[109], followed by a long funeral procession. Inscriptions quote the words of General Leman, the hero of Liège, pronounced at the beginning of the war,[110] and the victory speech of Marshal Foch.[111] These inscriptions implied that, by doing their duty, the Belgian army and the inhabitants of Liège had made a significant contribution to the interallied victory in what could only be described as a 'just war', fought for the noble cause of freedom. This political message echoed the speech held by the French President Raymond Poincaré, on 24 July 1919, the day when he personally handed over the *Légion d'honneur* to the city of Liège. In his speech, Poincaré praised the Belgian soldiers and the inhabitants of Liège for "having not hesitated to do their duty", and he even went as far as connecting the myths of Liège and Verdun, two places of heroic resistance against the German aggressor, concluding that "both had paid a worthy tribute to justice and freedom".[112] Consequently, the inscriptions on the memorial demonstrate how certain words and ideas connected to the Battle of Liège, for example that the heroic resistance at Liège had advanced a just war fought for freedom, were continually reproduced in media of memory. This process of consistent 'remediation' and

---

108 Note that there were also German soldiers buried in this municipal cemetery, but their graves were separated from those of the Allies, and they had their own monument, built during the occupation of the city. For more information on how the local authorities dealt with the funerary heritage of the 'enemy', see Vanraepenbusch and Havermans 2016, 1–20.

109 In French: "L'Humanité reconnaissante s'incline [sic] devant les héros tombés pour la liberté des peuples" as quoted by the local newspaper La Meuse 31 octobre 1922, 5.

110 The inscription read: "LA GRANDE ALLEMAGNE ENVAHIT NOTRE TERRITOIRE / APRÈS UN ULTIMATUM QUI CONSTITUE UN OUTRAGE. LA / PETITE BELGIQUE A RELEVÉ FIÈREMENT LE GANT. L'AR-/MÉE VA FAIRE SON DEVOIR. LA POPULATION DE LIÈGE AC-/COMPLIRA LE SIEN. SON ARDENT PATRIOTISME EN RÉPOND. VIVE LE ROI, COMMANDANT EN CHEF DE l'ARMÉE! / VIVE LA BELGIQUE INDÉPENDANTE! Lieutenant Général Gouverneur militaire de Liège, Leman. 4 août 1914".

111 The inscription read: "APRÈS AVOIR RÉSOLUMENT ARRÊTÉ L'ENNEMI, VOUS / L'AVEZ, PENDANT DES MOIS, AVEC UNE FOI ET UNE ÉNERGIE / INLASSABLES, ATTAQUÉ SANS RÉPIT. VOUS AVEZ GAGNÉ LA / PLUS GRANDE BATAILLE DE L'HISTOIRE ET SAUVÉ LA CAU-/SE LA PLUS SACRÉE: LA LIBERTÉ DU MONDE. SOYEZ FIERS; / D'UNE GLOIRE IMMORTELLE VOUS AVEZ PARÉ VOS DRA-/PEAUX; LA POSTÉRITÉ VOUS GARDE SA RECONNAISSANCE. Le Maréchal de France commandant en chef des armées alliées, Foch. 19 novembre 1918".

112 In French: "Cette splendide épopée n'est pas seulement celle du Général Leman. Elle est celle du soldat belge. Elle est celle de la ville de Liège. Au mois d'août 1914, aucun de vous n'a hésité sur son devoir [...]. De même que Liège avait dit à l'Allemagne: 'Arrête-toi, je le veux. Attends que la Belgique et la France soient prêtes!', de même Verdun lui a signifié: 'Tu ne passeras pas!'. [...] Toutes deux ont bien mérité de la justice et de la liberté" as quoted by *Le Petit Parisien* 25 juillet 1919, 3.

'recursivity' contributed to the coherence and ultimately also to the durability of the commemorative narrative over time.

During the inauguration ceremony of the war memorial at Robermont, attended by representatives of all the former Allied nations, Emile Digneffe,[113] Burgomaster of Liège, gave a speech that can be interpreted as a 'topos of history as a teacher'[114]: he alluded to the horrible events that had taken place in Liège during the war to warn the allies about their slacking attitude against a former enemy who, in his eyes, remained a threat to be reckoned with.[115] Given the general political climate of cultural demobilisation that reigned in 1926[116], one year after the peace treaty of Locarno had been signed, and a month after Germany had been admitted to the League of Nations, this speech was a political act to preserve the immediate post-war order, "an inter-allied culture of victory that was slowly dissolving".[117] The Burgomaster (re)presented Liège as an outpost guarding the nation and even the world, both in the past, the present and the future, against a former 'enemy'. His position was in fact representative of the stance that most Francophone Belgians took during the interwar period.[118] It shows that cultural demobilisation and reconciliation were part of a non-straightforward process that happened according to different temporalities in different regions.

In contrast to Liège, the city council of Antwerp was a rather passive memory agent, though not completely absent from the scene. Hardly a month after the signing of the Armistice, Burgomaster Jan De Vos[119] had declared that the names of the locals who fell during the war, including the victims of the siege of the city, would be set in stone.[120] Yet such a memorial was never built. The city council did place a small monument at the municipal cemetery Schoonselhof, but it was, paradoxically, meant as a temporary reminder of its decision to erect a more significant monument in the fu-

---

113 Emile Digneffe (1858–1937) was a member of the liberal party. During the First World War, he was deported to Germany after having accused the German occupiers of using food supplies that were meant to feed the Belgian population.
114 Forchtner 2016, 41–76.
115 In French: "la froide raison nous force à nous dire, que les jours d'épreuves ne sont pas encore révolus pour nous, que notre horizon n'est point encore éclairci, puisque le peuple qui nous valut ces effroyables malheurs, bien que vaincu par nos armées, il y a 8 ans, n'a pas encore désarmé", quoted from the inauguration speech of the liberal Burgomaster Émile Digneffe (1858–1937). Ville de Liège & Province de Liège, *Liste des Héros Liégeois morts pour la Patrie 1914-1918. Monument érigé à Robermont à la mémoire des héros alliés morts pour la patrie*. Bruxelles: Imprimerie Janssens, Leunis & Havet, 1926, 5.
116 Horne 2002, 45–53.
117 Eichenberg & Newman 2013, 12.
118 van Ypersele 2014a, 138–143.
119 Jan De Vos (1844–1932) was a member of the liberal party.
120 Felix Archief, 1398 #241, *Bulletin communal, second semestre – 1918*. Anvers: Imprimerie E. Secelle, s.d., 23–23. Procès-verbal de la séance publique du conseil communal, 9 décembre 1918.

ture.¹²¹ The counsellors also (re)named a dozen streets to commemorate the First World War, especially those that had referred to Germany or that had simply sounded too German.¹²² These new street names not only served to commemorate the war, but also to 'reclaim' urban space after the invasion and occupation of the city, since they were mainly situated in the neighbourhoods where German immigrants had lived before the outbreak of the war. This obviously also happened in Liège: the University Square was, for example, renamed "Place du Vingt Août" to commemorate the date, 20 August 1914, when German soldiers had burned down the houses on the square and had executed several civilians. Yet in Antwerp, the street names either honoured the Belgian war heroes and the Allies, or commemorated the war-damaged cities at the front and the martyr towns. Apparently, the local authorities did not wish to remember (or be reminded of) local war experiences such as the fall of the city, and the role that they had played in surrendering it.

A much more ambitious monument was finally inaugurated a decade later in the city centre of Antwerp. It was qualified, by those who had it built, as "completely Antwerpian",¹²³ because it had been financed "by Antwerpian people from all walks of life",¹²⁴ to commemorate "our Heroes".¹²⁵ Collective unity and solidarity indeed formed the monument's key political message. King Albert was represented in the middle, flanked by a group of fighting soldiers and by a deported man and his grieving family. These scenes were traditional representations of the Belgian war experience that typically depicted military heroism and civilian martyrdom as equivalent expressions of the greatness of the fatherland.¹²⁶ The equestrian statue of King Albert dominating the memorial endowed the dead with patriotic meaning, all the more so since it was highly unusual to portray a living monarch through a statue, even one as popular as the

---

121 The inscription read: "TER HERINNERING AAN / DE BESLISSING VAN / 27 JANUARI 1919 VAN HET GEMEENTEBESTUUR EEN / WAARDIG GEDENKTEEKEN / TE ZULLEN DOEN OPRICHTEN", and in French: "EN COMMÉMORATION / DE LA DÉCISION PRISE LE / 27 JANVIER 1919 / PAR LE CONSEIL COMMU- / NAL DE FAIRE ÉRIGER UN / MONUMENT EN l'HON-/NEUR DES FUSILLÉS, DES / SOLDATS BELGES ET / CEUX DES ALLIÉS EN-/TERRÉS AU SCHOONSELHOF".

122 On 17 December 1918, the city council of Antwerp took the decision to change the Albert von Barystraat into Jan Blockxstraat; on 10 January 1919 Coburgstraat into Ieperstraat; on 20 June 1919 Hochstetterstraat into Borzestraat (after a request of the inhabitants of the street); on 22 December 1919 Lubeckkaai into Nieuwpoortkaai, Hamburgkaai into Oostendekaai, Bremerkaai into Veurnekaai, on 29 February 1920 Keulsestraat into Dinantstraat; on 29 November 1920 Saksenstraat into Dendermondestraat, Oostenrijkschestraat into Visestraat.

123 In Dutch: "ten volle Antwerpsch", in *Het Handelsblad van Antwerpen*, 22 april 1930, 1.

124 In Dutch: "van wege alle de standen en rangen der Antwerpsche bevolking", in *Het Handelsblad van Antwerpen*, 22 april 1930, 1.

125 In Dutch: "aan onze Helden", in *Het Handelsblad van Antwerpen*, 22 april 1930, 1.

126 van Ypersele 2014b.

knight-king.[127] Its patriotic message was further strengthened by the inauguration ceremony, which took place in 1930, the year of the nation's centenary anniversary, and was attended by the royal family.

The initiative to build this war memorial came not from the city council but from a local patriotic association (*Ligue du Souvenir 'Nooit vergeten'*), and the agency of the *Ligue* is essential to understand its political message. Well-known in the early 1920s for its profound patriotic and anti-German attitude, the *Ligue* did soften its combative tone considerably in the 1930s, probably because the cultural demobilisation after the signing of the Locarno Pact had been rather more successful in Flanders.[128] The *Ligue* did, however, not let go completely of memories of wartime heroism and sufferings, as it still described its goal in 1933 as "keeping the Belgian national spirit alive and developing it, by glorifying our heroes and martyrs, by remembering the committed crimes and our shared sorrows".[129] During the memorial's inauguration ceremony, a representative of the *Ligue* held a speech that was quite similar, though perhaps less explicit and more diplomatic in tone, to the one held in Liège by Burgomaster Émile Digneffe, insisting that the Antwerp monument had to serve as a 'topos of history as a teacher' so that the nation would always be prepared to "prevent the horrible past from repeating itself".[130] Uttered in 1930, more than a decade after the end of the war, this position seems strange, but it does make sense when looking at the organisation's membership, consisting mainly of French-speaking *bourgeois,*[131] who were ideologically closer to French-speaking liberal politicians such as Digneffe than to Flemish politicians. Not only had these bourgeois lost much of their political power in Antwerp after the elections of 1921, but they were also confronted with the political rise of the Flemish Movement, which probably made them nostalgic for the wartime government and sentiments of national unity. Since the new Burgomaster, flamingant

---

127 van Ypersele 2006, 262–268.
128 van Ypersele 2014a, 138–143.
129 In Dutch: "De Belgische nationale geest levendig houden en ontwikkelen, door de verheerlijking onzer helden en martelaren, door de herinnering aan de bedrevene misdaden en het gemeenschappelijk ontstane leed, dat is zijn Vaderland dienen en het voor de toekomst versterken. Dit is het programma van 'Nooit vergeten'", in *Bond voor Aandenken – Ligue du Souvenir 'Nooit vergeten' Antwerpen – Anvers,* 11 november 1933, s.p.
130 In Dutch: "Het denkmaal dat onze medeburgers voortaan, hier op deze plaats zullen groeten, zal dus niet alleen de rampen der schrikkelijke dagen herinneren. Het zal er tevens toe bijdragen, aan allen die bijdragen, aan allen die deelmaken van onze Belgische gemeenschap een kalm doorzicht in te boezemen, evenals het nemen van bereneerde voorzorgen, alsook werkdadige en mannelijke besluiten van aard om de hernieuwing dier afgrijselijkheden te vermijden", in *Bond voor Aandenken – Ligue du Souvenir 'Nooit vergeten' Antwerpen – Anvers,* 11 november 1933, s.p.
131 A membership list can be found in *Ligue du Souvenir 'Nooit vergeten', Rapport (octobre 1922).*

Frans Van Cauwelaert,[132] showed little interest in war remembrance, there was a vacuum left for the *Ligue* to fill as they deemed fit.

5.2 Civil society memory activism as a means of adjusting official narratives

Notwithstanding the control that local authorities have over the official narratives that are told in public space, this does not mean that individuals, neighbourhoods and civic groups do not also have agency. In democracies, cultural memory formation in urban space is not simply imposed in a top-down manner, but negotiated within and between many different elite and non-elite groups. Historians Jay Winter and Emmanuel Sivan argue that collective remembrance should be considered as "the outcome of agency, as the product of individuals and groups who come together, not at the behest of the state or any of its subsidiary organizations, but because they have to speak out".[133] Their argument can also be applied to the First World War and the interwar period, when many individuals sharing similar war experiences formed their own associations. Some of these engaged in memory activism, erecting their own war memorial in public space, expressing their own commemorative narratives alongside the official ones. In this section, we will examine civil society memory activism concerning the invasion and the fall of the fort cities, and the tensions that might have existed between these initiatives and official narratives.

In Antwerp and even more so in Liège, many fraternal veterans' organisations wished to honour the army brigades and regiments that had defended the fort cities in 1914 by building regimental memorials. These memorials were generally inaugurated quite late, around 1930,[134] probably because of the surge in patriotism that accompanied the nation's centenary anniversary in 1930, and because many regiments celebrated their own hundredth anniversary in the early 1930's.[135] Almost all of these monuments were erected in or just outside the military compounds where the regiments had been stationed in 1914. Those situated within the compounds served to strengthen the bonds of fraternal unity, since they mainly commemorated the regi-

---

132 Frans Van Cauwelaert did reiterate, from time to time, the promise inscribed on the first temporary monument at Schoonselhof, to erect a second war memorial at the municipal cemetery, but this promise was never kept. See for example *Gazet van Antwerpen*, 9 februari 1925, 3 & *Het Handelsblad van Antwerpen*, 22 april 1930, 2.
133 Winter and Sivan 1999, 9.
134 In Liège, two commemorative plaques had been placed in 1919 (the 12nd line infantry regiment) and in 1937 (the motorcyclists of the 3rd army division), respectively. All regimental monuments, in Antwerp and Liège, were, without exception, erected in the period 1929–1931.
135 When the 2nd artillery regiment celebrated its centenary anniversary, it placed a commemorative plaque for Cavalier Fonck, see *La Meuse*, 27 octobre 1930, 2. The monument of the 12th line infantry regiment was erected when the regiment celebrated its hundredth anniversary in 1931, see *La Meuse*, 25–26 avril 1931, 2.

ment's war dead, while those located extra muros glorified their involvement in the war to the outside world. It is noteworthy that, in the military memory of the First World War, participation in the battle of Liège and the siege of Antwerp were both considered in a positive light. The monument of the 12th line infantry regiment in Liège, for example, carried an inscription enumerating the battles it had heroically fought: Antwerp and Liège appear next to the front city Dixmude and (the) Yser.[136] This implies that both fort cities formed an integral part of the military narrative of the First World War in Belgium, a narrative that closely followed the same official Belgian nationalist discourse that we also found in literary works.

In Antwerp, several homeowners placed plaques on the facades of their house to commemorate its destruction during the bombardments of 1914 and/or its reconstruction afterwards.[137] One of these was placed during the war, and its inscription read: "Destroyed by war fire and in reality lost, though as a phoenix risen from its ashes".[138] The phoenix motif refers, of course, to the house, but it might also have referred to the city itself or even to the nation. In that case, the plaque would have presented a subtle form of symbolic resistance against the German occupiers, warning them that the destruction of the city/nation would precede its triumphant resurrection. Another plaque stated: "Here stood, before the bombing of 1914, the home of David Teniers, artist 1610–1690".[139] David Teniers was, like Rubens, an artist of the so-called Antwerp baroque school that had flourished in Antwerp's 'golden age' and that largely defines its identity, up until today, as the *'métropole des arts'*.[140] The plaque, accusing the Germans of destroying the city's rich cultural heritage, thus served as a tangible proof of the German nation's descent into barbarism, just like the many photographs of ruins had done during the war. Both plaques expressed, in fact, the recurrent motive of an innocent city fallen victim to a barbaric fighting machine, which formed an essential element of the 'Poor Little Belgium' narrative. Far from being anecdotal, these plaques demonstrate, just like the Belgian literature did, that the fall

---

136 The full inscription reads: Liège – Anvers – Dixmude – Yser (on the left side of the monument) and Merckem – Stadenberg – La Lys (on the right side). These battle honours were also embroidered in gold on the regiment's colours.

137 It is difficult to know how many of these plaques have been placed and the specifics of their instalment and content, since these private initiatives 'from below' were rarely registered in official sources or in the press, and they did not always survive as new house-owners might not have wanted to keep them.

138 In Dutch: "Door 't oorlogsvuur vernield en in den grond verloren, doch als de feniks weer uit d'eigen asch herboren", *La Métropole d'Anvers*, 20 juin 1916, 3. This commemorative plaque was placed at the Kasteelpleinstraat 24 in Antwerp. The house still exists, but the plaque has disappeared.

139 In Dutch: "Op deze plaats stond voor de beschieting van 1914, het woonhuis van David Teniers, kunstschilder 1610–1690". This plaque still exists and can be found at Lombardenvest 63.

140 Deseure *et al.* 2011, 179–210; Croon 2003, 19–83.

of Antwerp was rather expressed in diverse personalised memories than in a unified 'top down' memory.

The same motive of the innocent fallen city can also be found in another war memorial. In 1921, the head pastor of the Antwerp cathedral celebrated the fiftieth anniversary of his ordination with the installation of a new chapel.[141] Despite being dedicated to Our Lady of Peace, this chapel was not a pacifist memorial: during the jubilee festivities, the pastor explicitly honoured the Belgian military commanders who had fought in the war.[142] The altarpiece showed a Madonna with Child, surrounded by King Albert and Queen Elisabeth, represented respectively as knight-king and queen-nurse, and their patron saints, as well as the jubilee, pastor Cleynhens, and Cardinal Mercier, holding the pastoral letter in which he had, during the war, openly criticised the German occupation of Belgium. Five small paintings placed underneath showed the devastated regions of Belgium: Antwerp (in flames) in the middle, the martyr towns Leuven and Dinant on the left, and the front town of Ypres on the right.[143] This altarpiece visibly integrated the local war experience of the bombardment of the city in 1914 into the national narratives of 'Poor Little Belgium' (the devastated regions) and of 'Brave Little Belgium' (the king, queen and cardinal as symbols of national resistance). Situated in the cathedral, this altarpiece occupied a prominent place in the symbolic heart of the city.

Similar civic initiatives valorising the local war experience can also be found in Liège. On 24 August 1924, a local patriotic association inaugurated a plaque at the University Square that commemorated the horrible events that took place on the night of 20 August 1914, when "the Germans have, without provocation, burned 20 houses and executed 17 people".[144] During his inauguration speech, the municipal councillor Louis Fraigneux warned the audience "about our ex-enemies, and the threat that they still pose",[145] which is quite remarkable since the diplomatic relations between Belgium and Germany were slowly thawing at that time. In October 1924,

---

141 Jubelfeest van Mgr. Cleyhens, in *Gazet van Antwerpen*, 24 augustus 1921, 2.
142 Priester Cleynhens jubileert, in *Het Handelsblad van Antwerpen*, 29 september 1921, 1.
143 De Koningin van de Vrede bij Jozef Janssens, in *Het Handelsblad van Antwerpen*, 4 december 1923, 1.
144 The inscription read: "XX AOÛT 1914 / SUR CETTE PLACE / DANS LA NUIT DU / 20 AOÛT 1914 / LES ALLEMANDS / ONT, SANS PROVOCATION / BRÛLÉ 20 MAISONS ET / FUSILLÉ 17 PERSONNES. / CE MÉMORIAL A ÉTÉ ÉRIGÉ / PAR SOUSCRIPTION PUBLIQUE / ET EST DÛ À L'INITIATIVE DU CERCLE LES XXI – SOUVENIR LIÉGEOIS".
145 The liberal municipal councilor Louis Jean Fraigneux (1863–1938) as quoted by *La Meuse*, 26 août 1924, 1: "On voit actuellement en ville des affiches où se lit, en lettres énormes: 'Guerre à la guerre!'. N'est-ce pas le vœu de tout le monde? Mais nous devons tenir compte de la mentalité de nos ex-ennemis et continuer à prendre toutes nos précautions pour éviter le retour des heures sanglantes".

another plaque with a similar inscription and also paid for by public subscription was placed on the facade of a house located in the folksy neighbourhood Outremeuse.[146]

This does not mean that there would have been some sort of a divide between 'top-down' and 'bottom-up' cultural memory in Liège. The city council did not completely ignore the memory of the German atrocities. In December 1918, it had changed, as we mentioned before, the name of the University Square to "Place du Vingt Août" to commemorate the date when these tragic events had taken place.[147] But this one street name simply pales in comparison with the dozens of street names commemorating the defence of Liège. It was clear that the city council was more interested in connecting the city's reputation with the 'Brave Little Belgium' narrative than with the 'Poor Little Belgium' narrative. At the same time, the local population did admire the military heroes who had defended Liège. General Bertrand, for example, was given a statue in 1934 by the inhabitants of Outremeuse, although he had never even lived there.[148] So, bottom-up initiatives do not, in the case of Liège, express a 'counter-memory' challenging or even opposing official commemorative narratives.[149]

6 Conclusion

Our case study on the cultural memory of the fall of the fort cities in 1914 illustrates both the feasibility and the necessity of interdisciplinary research in memory studies. Coming from (not too) different academic backgrounds (history and literary studies) and working with (quite) different 'media' (material memory traces and literary works), crossing these disciplinary boundaries allowed us to confirm the importance of narrativisation in the formation of cultural memory. Our research indicates that narratives were formed early on, in wartime 'mass media', and that they were subsequently 'mediated' and 'remediated' in other 'media', such as the Belgian literature and the material memory traces in urban space. Shared theoretical framework and concepts, developed by memory studies scholars Astrid Erll and Ann Rigney, proved crucial in bridging these disciplinary boundaries. Cultural memory is indeed constructed through 'mediation', 'remediation' and 'recursivity', as the case of Liège proves. The narrative of the brave resistance, which quickly came to dominate contemporary 'mass media', drew strength from national and local frames of identity.

---

146 *La Meuse,* 21 octobre 1924, 1.
147 *Bulletin administratif de la Ville de Liège 1918,* 30 décembre 1918, 285.
148 Archives de la Commission royale des Monuments, Sites et Fouilles, Dépôt Ville de Liège, Boîte 3, Dossier Lieutenant Général Bertrand.
149 Yael Zerubavel defines 'counter-memory' as an "alternative commemorative narrative that directly opposes the master commemorative narrative, operating under and against its hegemony […]. As the term implies, counter-memory is essentially oppositional and stands in hostile and subversive relation to collective memory" (Zerubavel 1995, 10–11).

Both the myth of foreign domination and the local depiction of the city as *la Cité ardente* offered powerful memorial models, while the award of the French *Légion d'honneur* provided external validation of the city's self-image. In the war's aftermath, these memories were consolidated as both local authorities and inhabitants became active agents of memory. Monuments, speeches and street names proved to be effective tools of identity politics and the wartime events were seen as an expression, or even culmination, of local history and identity. This 'heroic clarity' was achieved at the cost of deliberate omissions. "The price of communality", writes Rigney, "is a loss of literal accuracy and hence of the plenitude of highly personalized memory".[150] In the case of Liège, the emphasis on the brave resistance swept the memory of the 'German atrocities' to the side-line.

At Antwerp, the reverse happened: the siege and subsequent fall of the city never acquired a definitive meaning; instead, several perspectives vied for attention. The 'mass media' pushed the 'Poor Little Belgium' angle and ignored the Belgian army's sorties from Antwerp as a contribution to the inter-allied war effort. Along the same lines, bottom-up initiatives in the city presented Antwerp as an innocent victim of war by putting up plaques and constructing local memorials. But Antwerp was not only presented as a victim. Belgian literature and regimental monuments listed Antwerp alongside Liège and the Yser, emblems of Belgium's resistance, and praised the resistance of the Belgian troops in Antwerp. Antwerp's role as a low point in the narrative of the national war experience makes structural sense in the story but was problematic for Antwerp. The supposedly impregnable city's swift fall and its surrender by the civilian administration evoked conflicting emotions. Moreover failure, unlike victimisation, does not make for a strong source of identification. Failure has the potential to fragment identity[151] and requires far more demanding memory work than the heroic victim status that Liège cultivated.[152] In the absence of a strong master narrative during the war, like the one that existed in Liège the representations of Antwerp's admittedly complicated war history never achieved unity. The heritage of the war remained fragmented and was thereby more likely to be forgotten.

References

Primary (mentioned in the text, details of my copies)

Carton de Wiart, H. (1904). *La Cité ardente*. Paris: Perrin.
Davignon, H. (1919). *Jan Swalue*. Paris: Plon.
Deauville, M. (1917). *Jusqu'à l'Yser*. Paris: Calmann-Lévy.
De Wilde, R. (1918). *De Liège à l'Yser. Mon journal de campagne*. Paris: Plon.

---

150   Rigney 2009, 15.
151   Fortchtner 2016, 205.
152   Fortchtner 2016, 101.

Francken, F. (1919) *De blijde kruisvaart.* Antwerpen: Gust Janssens.
Grimauty, F. H. (1915). *Six mois de guerre en Belgique par un soldat belge.* Paris: Perrin et Cie.
Hans, A. (1919a). *Aan de IJzer.* Antwerpen: L. Opdebeek.
Hans, A. (1919b). *Het beleg van Antwerpen of de liefde van Louise.* Kontich: B. H. Hans.
Hans, A. (1915). *Voor de vrijheid.* 's-Hertogenbosch: Berger.
Lekeux, M. (1922). *Mes cloîtres dans la tempête.* Paris: Plon.
Loveling, V. (2005). *Virginie Lovelings oorlogsdagboek [1914-1918].* KANTL/Universiteitsbibliotheek Gent. [https://lib.ugent.be/fulltxt/RUG01/000/924/065/BIB-G-025872_2005_0001_AC.pdf].
Nothomb, P. (1915). *Les barbares en Belgique.* Paris: Perrin.
Raal, G. (1914). *Soldatentypen uit den Grooten Oorlog.* Antwerpen: L. Opdebeek.
Streuvels, S. (1979). *In oorlogstijd. Het volledige dagboek van de Eerste Wereldoorlog.* Brugge/Nijmegen: Orion/B. Gottmer.
Tasnier, L. (1928). *Notes d'un combattant de la campagne 1914-1918.* Bruxelles: Vanderlinden.
Thans, H. (1937). *Onder de wolk.* Mechelen: Sint Franciscus Drukkerij.
Torcy, A. (1919). *Les civils. L'exode.* Bruxelles: Oscar Lamberty.
Tousseul, J. (1933). *La rafale.* Bruxelles: Les éditions de Belgique.
Schoup, J. G. (1932). *In Vlaanderen heb ik gedood!* Rotterdam: W. L. & J. Brusse N.V.
Vachon, M. (1915). *Les villes martyres de France et de Belgique.* Paris: Payot & Cie.
Van Hausen, M. (1922). *Souvenirs de la Campagne de la Marne en 1914.* Paris: Payot & Cie.
Vermeulen, E. (1934). *Dagboek van een banneling.* J. Lannoo: Tielt.

Secondary

Ariès, P. (1974). *Western Attitudes to Death: From the Middle Ages to the Present.* Baltimore/London: The John Hopkins University Press.
Assmann, A. (2008). Transformations between History and Memory. *Social Research*, 75 (1), 49-72.
Azaryahu, M., Foote, K. (2008). Historical Space as Narrative Medium. On the Configuration of Spatial Narratives of Time at Historical Sites. *GeoJournal*, 73 (3), 179-194.
Barash, J. A. (2016). *Collective Memory and the Historical Past.* Chicago/London: The University of Chicago Press.
Bechet, C. (2014a). Les massacres du 20 août 1914 à Liège. *Bulletin du CLHAM,* 137, 7-18.
Bechet, C. (2014b). La défense de Liège. In Maréchal, C. & Schloss, C. (Eds), *1914-1918 Vivre la guerre à Liège et en Wallonie.* Liège: Éditions du Perron, 135-146.
Bechet, C. (2017). Pre-war Military Planning (Belgium). In U. Daniel *et al.* (Eds), *1914-1918-online. International Encyclopedia of the First World War.* Berlin: Freie Universität Berlin, 2017-01-08. DOI: 10.15463/ie1418.10339.
Benvindo, B., Majerus, B. (2010). Belgien zwischen 1914 und 1918: ein Labor für den totalen Krieg. In Bauerkämper, A. & Julien, E. (Eds), *Durchhalten! Krieg und Gesellschaft im Vergleich 1914-1918.* Göttingen: Vandenhoeck & Ruprecht, 127-148.
Bernard, H. (1983). *L'an 14 et la campagne des illusions.* Bruxelles: La Renaissance du Livre.
Beyen, M. (2015). Introduction: Local, National, Transnational Memories: A Triangular Perspective. In Beyen, M. & Deseure, B. (Eds), *Local Memories in a Nationalizing and Globalizing World.* Basingstoke: Palgrave Macmillan, 1-23.

Blaas, P. B. M. (2002). Het romantische verhaal. In Tollebeek, J. et al. (Eds), *De palimpsest. Geschiedschrijving in de Nederlanden 1500–2000.* Hilversum: Uitgeverij Verloren, 143–158.

Bodnar, J. (1992). *Remaking America: Public Memory, Commemoration and Patriotism in the Twentieth Century.* Princeton: Princeton University Press.

Brüll, C. (2014). La prise de Liège. In Maréchal, C. & Schloss, C. (Eds), *1914–1918 Vivre la guerre à Liège et en Wallonie.* Liège: Éditions du Perron, 160–163.

Carr, S. et al. (1992). *Public Space.* Cambridge: Cambridge University Press.

Claisse, S. (2013). *Du soldat inconnu aux monuments commémoratifs belges de la guerre 14–18.* Bruxelles: Académie royale de Belgique.

Colignon, A. (1999). Le 'beffroi de la victoire': un lieu de mémoire belgo-wallon avorté. In Courtois, L. & Pirotte, J. (Eds), *Entre toponymie et utopie. Les lieux de mémoire wallonne.* Louvain-la-Neuve: Fondation Wallonne Pierre-Marie et Jean François Humblet, 217–244.

Croon, B. (2003). Toe-eigeningsstrategieën bij stedelijke en nationale identiteitsvorming in de kunst-en handelsmetropool Antwerpen: de negentiende-eeuwse Rubenscultus. *Volkskunde,* 104, 19–83.

Delhez, J.-C. (2013). *Douze mythes de l'année 1914.* Paris: Economica.

De Schaepdrijver, S. (2002). *De Groote Oorlog. Het koninkrijk België tijdens de Eerste Wereldoorlog.* Amsterdam: Olympos.

De Schaepdrijver, S. (2008). Gemartelde steden en verwoeste gewesten. Twee legaten van 1914–1918. In Tollebeek, J. (Ed.), *België, een parcours van herinnering. Plaatsen van tweedracht, crisis en nostalgie.* Amsterdam: Uitgeverij Bert Bakker, 194–207.

De Schaepdrijver, S. (2009). Liège en 1914 et l'opinion publique américaine. *Bulletin du CLAHM,* 10 (5), 42–52.

Deseure, B. et al. (2011). Rubensmania. De complexe constructie van cultuur in heden en verleden. In Bertels, I. et al. (Eds), *Antwerpen. Biografie van een stad.* Antwerpen: De Bezige Bij, 179–210.

Eichenberg, J. & Newman, J. P. (2013). Introduction: The Great War and Veterans' Internationalism, In Eichenberg, J. & Newman, J. P. (Eds), *The Great War and Veterans' Internationalism.* Basingstoke: Palgrave Macmillan, 1–15.

Erll, A. (2008). Cultural Memory Studies: An Introduction. In Erll, A. & Nünning, A. (Eds), *Cultural Memory Studies. An International and Interdisciplinary Handbook.* Berlin: De Gruyter, 1–15.

Erll, A. (2008). Literature, Film, and the Mediality of Cultural Memory. In Erll, A. & Nünning, A. (Eds), *Cultural Memory Studies. An International and Interdisciplinary Handbook.* Berlin: De Gruyter, 389–398.

Erll, A. & Rigney, A. (2009). Introduction: Cultural Memory and its Dynamics. In Erll, A. & Rigney, A. (Eds), *Mediation, Remediation and the Dynamics of Cultural Memory.* Berlin: De Gruyter, 1–11.

Forchtner, B. (2016). *Lessons from the Past? Memory, Narrativity and Subjectivity.* Basingstoke: Palgrave Macmillan.

Gieseking, J. J. & Mangold W. (2014). *The People, Place and Space Reader.* New York/London: Routledge.

Goebel, S. & Keene, D. (2011). Towards a Metropolitan History of Total War: An Introduction. In Goebel, S. & Keene, D. (Eds), *Cities into Battlefields. Metropolitan Scenarios, Experiences and Commemorations of Total War.* Farnham: Ashgate, 1–46.

Grethlein, J. (2013). *Experience and teleology in ancient historiography: "futures past" from Herodotus to Augustine.* Cambridge: Cambridge University Press.

Haag, H. (1990). *Le comte Charles de Broqueville, Ministre d'État, et les luttes pour le pouvoir (1910–1940)*. Bruxelles: Éditions Nauwelaerts.

Henneman, I. (2014). *Shooting Range: Photography & the Great War*. Antwerpen: FotoMuseum.

Horne, J. & Kramer, A. (2001). *German Atrocities, 1914: a History of Denial*. New Haven/London: Yale University Press.

Horne, J. (2002). Démobilisations culturelles après la Grande Guerre. *14–18: Aujourd'hui, Today, Heute*, 45–53.

Jorgensen, M. & Phillips, L. (2002). *Discourse analysis as theory and method*. London: Sage Publications.

Maes, T. G. (2013). *Antwerpen 1914. Bolwerk van België tijdens de Eerste Wereldoorlog*. Antwerpen: Houtekiet.

Marsland, E. (1991). *The nation's Cause. French, English and German Poetry of the First World War*. London: Routledge.

Nahoé, D. (2014). La population liégeoise face aux soldats allemands en août 1914. In Maréchal, C. & Schloss, C. (Eds), *1914–1918 Vivre la guerre à Liège et en Wallonie*. Liège: Éditions du Perron, 173–176.

Pennebaker, J. W. & Banasik, B. L. (1997). On the Creation and Maintenance of Collective Memories: History as Social Psychology. In Pennebaker, J. W. *et al*. (Eds), *Collective Memories of Political Events. Social Psychology Perspectives*. Mahwah: Lawrence Erlbaum Associates, 3–20.

Rigney, A. (2005). Plenitude, Scarcity and the Circulation of Cultural Memory. *Journal of European Studies*, 35 (1), 11–28.

Rigney, A. (2001). *Imperfect Histories: the Elusive Past of Romantic Historicism*. Ithaca/London: Cornell University Press.

Rigney, A. (2008). The Dynamics of Remembrance: Texts between Monumentality and Morphing. In Erll, A. & Nünning, A. (Eds), *Cultural Memory Studies. An International and Interdisciplinary Handbook*. Berlin: De Gruyter, 345–353.

Rose-Redwood, R. *et al*. (2008). Collective Memory and the Politics of Urban Space: An Introduction. *GeoJournal*, 73, 161–164.

Rose-Redwood, R. *et al*. (2018). The Urban Streetscape as Political Cosmos. In Rose-Redwood, R. *et al*. (Eds), *The Political Life of Urban Streetscapes*. London/New York: Routledge, 1–24.

Rottiers, S. (1995a). L'honneur des Six Cents Franchimontois. In Morelli, A. (Ed.), *Les grands mythes de l'histoire de Belgique, de Flandre et de Wallonie*. Bruxelles: Éditions Vie Ouvrière, 67–82.

Rottiers, S. (1995b). Six cents patriotes en quête d'auteurs. Historicité et littérarité des Six Cents Franchimontois: étude d'un cas de figure, La Cité ardente de Henri Carton de Wiart. *Revue belge de philologie et d'histoire*, 73 (2), 343–377.

Segesser, D. M. (2014). Controversy: Total War. In Daniel, U. *et al*. (Eds), *1914-1918-online. International Encyclopedia of the First World War*. Berlin: Freie Universität Berlin. DOI: 10.15463/ie1418.10315.

Stengers, J. (1981). Le mythe des dominations étrangères dans l'historiographie belge. *Revue belge de Philologie et d'Histoire*, 95 (2), 382–401.

Tixhon, A. & Derez, M. (2014). *Villes martyres, Belgique, août-septembre 1914: Visé, Aarschot, Andenne, Tamines, Dinant, Leuven, Dendermonde*. Namur: Presses universitaires de Namur.

Tollebeek, J. & Van Assche, E. (2014). *Ravage. Kunst en cultuur in tijden van conflict*. Brussels: Mercatorfonds.

Van Alstein, M. (1999–2000). *Belegerde Stad. Het Antwerps Stadsbestuur 4 augustus – 10 oktober 1914,* unpublished master thesis, Ghent: Ghent University.

Van Creveld, M. (1977). *Supplying War. Logistics from Wallenstein to Patton.* Cambridge: Cambridge University Press.

Van Ginderachter, M. (2011). An Urban Civilization: The Case of Municipal Autonomy in Belgian History 1830–1914. In Whyte, W. H. & Zimmer, O. (Eds), *Nationalism and the Reshaping of Urban Communities in Europe, 1848–1914.* Basingstoke: Palgrave Macmillan, 110–130.

Vannieuwenhuyze, K. (2016). De productie van een politieke stedelijke ruimte. Het Antwerpse stadsbestuur en de aanleg en ontwikkeling van de Leopoldlei en haar omgeving, 1857–1876. *Tijdschrift voor Geschiedenis,* 129 (2), 197–217.

Vanraepenbusch, K. & Havermans A.-M., (2016). Omgaan met het erfgoed van de 'vijand'. Duitse WO1-monumenten op stedelijke begraafplaatsen in België. *Volkskunde,* 117 (1), 1–20.

van Ypersele, L. (2006). *Le Roi Albert: histoire d'un mythe.* Bruxelles: Éditions Labor.

van Ypersele, L. (2013). Patrimoine et propagande. Le cas de la destruction de Louvain en août 1914. In Nivet, P. (Ed.), *Guerre et patrimoine artistique à l'époque contemporaine.* Amiens: Encrage Édition, 111–126.

van Ypersele, L. (2014a). The Great War in Belgian Memories: From Unanimity to Divergence. In Sumartojo, S. & Wellings, B. (Eds), *Nation, Memory and Great War Commemoration. Mobilizing the Past in Europe, Australia and New Zealand.* Oxford/Bern: Peter Lang, 138–143.

van Ypersele, L. (2014b). Commemoration, Cult of the Fallen (Belgium). In Daniel, U. et al. (Eds), *1914–1918 online. International Encyclopedia of the First World War.* Berlin: Freie Universität Berlin. DOI: 10.15463/ie1418.10313.

Verschaffel, T. (1998). Leren sterven voor het vaderland. Historische drama's in het negentiende-eeuwse België. *BMGN,* 113 (2), 145–176.

Voldman, D. (2002). Les populations civiles, enjeux du bombardement des villes (1914–1945). In Audoin-Rouzeau, S. et al. (Eds), *La violence de guerre 1914–1945.* Bruxelles: Éditions Complexes, 151–173.

Werstch, J. V. (2007). National Narratives and the Conservative Nature of Collective Memory. *Neohelicon,* 34 (2), 23–33.

Wils, L. (2014) *Onverfranst, onverduitst? Flamenpolitik, Activisme, Frontbeweging.* Kalmthout: Pelckmans.

Winter, J. & Prost, A. (2005). *The Great War in History. Debates and Controversies, 1914 to the Present.* Cambridge: Cambridge University Press.

Winter, J. & Sivan, E. (1999). Setting the Framework. In Winter, J. & Sivan, E. (Eds), *War and Remembrance in the Twentieth Century.* Cambridge: Cambridge University Press, 6–39.

Wodak R. et al. (1999). *The Discursive Construction of National Identity.* Edinburgh: Edinburgh University Press.

Wodak R. (2001). The Discourse-Historical Approach. In Wodak, R. & Meyer, M. (Eds), *Methods of Critical Discourse Theory.* London: Sage Publications, 63–94.

Zerubavel, Y. (1995). *Recovered Roots: Collective Memory and the Making of Israeli National Traditions.* Chicago/London: The University of Chicago Press.

Annex 1

Complete corpus literature (The final selection is underlined)

Fraipont, A. (1921). *Instantanés: notes d'un fantassin*. Bruxelles: Albert Dewit.
André, F. (1931). *Les affamés*. Paris: Librairie Valois.
<u>Auctor. (1921). *Tijl Uilenspiegel aan het front en onder de Duitschers*. Antwerpen: L. Opdebeek</u>
<u>Baekelmans, L. (1918). *Meneer Snepvangers*. Amsterdam: Van Kampen.</u>
Bonjean, A. (1938) *La vieille Barnabé*. Bruxelles: La Renaissance du Livre.
Broeckaert, A. (1930). *Roomdale's jonge lieden in de verzoeking en de beproeving*. Brugge: Excelsior.
Burniaux, Constant. (1930). *Les désarmés*. Bruxelles: La Renaissance du Livre.
<u>Buysse, C. (1917). *Van een verloren zomer*. Bussum: C. A. J. Van Dishoeck.</u>
Buysse, C. (1917). *Uit de bron*. Gent: Van Rysselberghe en Rombout.
<u>Claes, E. (1919). *Oorlogsnovellen*. Leiden: Vlaamsche Boekenhalle.</u>
<u>Claes, E. (1919). *Namen 1914*. Antwerpen: L. Opdebeek.</u>
Claes, E. (1923). *De vulgaire geschiedenis van Charelke Dop*. Blaricum: De Waelburgh.
<u>Corvillain, Marcel. (1923). *C'était le bon temps*. Bruxelles: A. Leempoel.</u>
<u>Davignon, H. (1919). *Jan Swalue*. Paris: Plon.</u>
<u>de Backer, F. (1934). *Longinus*. Arnhem: Van Loghum Slaterus.</u>
de Croÿ, M. (1933). *Souvenirs de la princesse Marie de Croy: le martyre des pays envahis 1914–1918*. Paris: Plon.
de Croÿ, M. (1932). *War memories*. London: Macmillian and Co.
<u>De Wilde, R. (1918). *De Liège à l'Yser: mon journal de campagne*. Paris: Plon.</u>
Deauville, M. (1917). *Jusqu'à l'Yser*. Paris: Calman-Lévy.
Deauville, M. (1922). *La boue de Flandres*. Bruxelles: Ed. Maurice Lamartin.
Droogstoppel, J. (1914). *Uit den Duitsche bandietenkrijg. Verhaal uit den omtrek van Mechelen*. Amsterdam: Boek- en Handelsdrukkerij.
<u>Francken, F. (1919) *De blijde kruisvaart*. Antwerpen: Gust Janssens.</u>
Grimauty, F. H. (1915). *Six mois de guerre en Belgique par un soldat belge*. Paris: Perrin et Cie.
Grimauty, F. H. (1922) *Les six derniers mois de guerre en Belgique*. Paris: Perrin et Cie.
<u>Hans, A. (1919a). *Aan de IJzer*. Antwerpen: L. Opdebeek.</u>
<u>Hans, A. (1919b). *Het beleg van Antwerpen of de liefde van Louise*. Kontich: B.H. Hans.</u>
<u>Hans, A. (1915). *Voor de vrijheid*. 's-Hertogenbosch: Berger.</u>
<u>Hans, A. (1919). *'t Maagdeke van Meessen*. Antwerpen: Vlaamsche Boekhandel.</u>
<u>Kenis, P. (1919). *De wonderlijke avonturen van Cies Slameur Gentsch koetsier en soldaat*. Gent: St-Michielsdrukkerij.</u>
<u>Lefèbvre, H. (1918). *Journal d'un fantassin*. Bruxelles: Lebègue.</u>
<u>Lekeux, M. (1922). *Mes cloîtres dans la tempête*. Paris: Plon.</u>
Lekeux, M. (1931). *Passeurs d'hommes: le drame de la frontière 1914–1915*. Paris: Saint-Michel.
Linze, G. (1936). *Les enfants bombardés*. Bruxelles: La Renaissance du Livre.
<u>Loveling, V. (2005). *Virginie Lovelings oorlogdagboek [1914–1918]*. KANTL/Universiteitsbibliotheek Gent. [https://lib.ugent.be/fulltxt/RUG01/000/924/065/BIB-G-025872_2005_0001_AC.pdf].</u>
Mathy, C. (1933). *La trahison de Judas*. Bruxelles: Ed. de Belgique.
Meert, L. (1924). *De nood van 't land*. Amsterdam: Maatschappij voor Goede en Goedkope Lectuur.

Paessens, A. (1935). *Leo Koecke*. Aarschot: Tuerlinckx-Boeyé.

Proumen, H. J. (1921). *Les transplantés chez Albion*. Paris/Bruxelles: Librairie Moderne.

Raal, G. (1914). *Soldatentypen uit den Grooten Oorlog*. Antwerpen: L. Opdebeek.

Sabbe, M. (1915). *In 't gedrang. Vertellingen uit den oorlog*. Bussum: Van Dishoeck.

Schoup, J. G. (1932). *In Vlaanderen heb ik gedood!* Rotterdam: W. L. & J. Brusse N.V.

Simons, J. (1921). *Verhalen van een kannonier*. Brussel: Ons Vaderland.

Simons, J. (1927). *Eer Vlaanderen vergaat*. Brussel: Gudrun.

Streuvels, S. (1979). *In oorlogstijd. Het volledige dagboek van de Eerste Wereldoorlog*. Brugge/Nijmegen: Orion/B. Gottmer.

Tasnier, L. (1928). *Notes d'un combattant de la campagne 1914–1918*. Brussels: Vanderlinden.

Teirlinck, H. (1920) *De nieuwe Uilenspiegel in tien boeken. Of de jongste incarnatie van den scharlaken Thijl*. Amsterdam: Maatschappij voor goede en goedkoope lectuur.

Thans, H. (1921). *Mijn oorlog*. Mechelen: Sint Franciscus Drukkerij.

Thans, H. (1937). *Onder de wolk*. Mechelen: Sint Franciscus Drukkerij.

Thiry, M. (1927). *Passage à Kiew*. Bruxelles: Edition de la renaissance d'occident.

Torcy, A. (1919). *Les civils I: L'exode*. Bruxelles: Oscar Lamberty.

Tousseul, J. (1933). *La rafale*. Bruxelles: Les éditions de Belgique.

Van Rumbeke, V. L. (1929). *Sennelager. Drie jaar in 'n Duitsch concentratiekamp*. Amsterdam: Stella.

Vermeulen, E. (1934). *Dagboek van een banneling*. Tielt: J. Lannoo.

Voos de Gisthelles, G. (1939). *Le retour de M. Latouche*. Bruxelles: Vanderlinden.

Zielens, L. (1935). *Nu begint het leven*. Amsterdam: Elsevier.

Elke Brems, Reine Meylaerts, Pierre Bouchat, Olivier Klein

Dulce et decorum est: Reading First World War Poetry

1 Introduction

The First World War led to the production of a wide array of literary texts, throughout Europe and worldwide. According to Geert Buelens '(t)he culture of war that characterized the First World War (…) was, to a large extent, a literary culture, and more specifically a poetic culture'.[1] Paul Fussell first explored the idea of the Great War as a literary war in his seminal work The Great War and Modern Memory and it has since gained a lot of acclaim. The written and especially artistic renditions helped to perpetuate the afterlives of these events, and transfer them from what Aleida and Jan Assmann call communicative memory into cultural memory.[2]

Contrary to what you might expect, a lot of WWI literature was anti-patriotic and more so as the war advanced and after it was finished. Feelings of horror and disgust were predominant. Famous literary texts like Barbusse's *Le Feu, Journal d'une escouade* (1916) and Remarque's *Im Westen nichts Neues* (1929) revealed the moral bankruptcy of western society. In Belgium, a mass of literary texts and especially poetry was produced during and shortly after the First World War, but it has almost all been forgotten. According to Buelens this has to do with the lack of unity in Belgian war memory. Literature couldn't be used patriotically to support the Belgian State as it did e.g. in Great Britain, because during the war the Belgian State had shown itself failing.

Furthermore, there is a widespread claim, since the 1920's and still supported now, that Flanders, the Dutch-speaking part of Belgium, has no war literature.[3] Hardly any literary text, be it a novel or a poem, has entered Dutch-speaking Belgian

---

1 'De oorlogscultuur die de Eerste Wereldoorlog kenmerkte (…) in hoge mate een literaire en meer in het bijzonder een poëtische cultuur.' (Buelens 2008, 301).
2 The communicative and the cultural memory are both forms of collective memory, the more common term originally introduced by Maurice Halbwachs. See Assmann 1992 and 1999.
3 This claim was first made by Filip De Pillecyn in 1920 in the journal *Vlaamsche Arbeid*. With regards to francophone Belgian war literature Madeleine Frédéric wrote in 2002 that those novels are 'still too often unknown, not only abroad, but even in Belgium' (la production romanesque est encore trop souvent méconnue, non seulement à l'étranger, mais même en Belgique) (Frédéric 2005, 579). When discussing francophone war literature, critics and scholars usually don't distinguish between French and francophone Belgian literature.

cultural memory. A famous exception in the realm of poetry is Paul Van Ostaijen's volume *Bezette Stad*. It was translated into English as *Occupied City* by David Colmer in 2016, in the revival of First World War literature worldwide. In Flanders, the centenary of the First World War has seen efforts to reenter old literary texts into Flemish cultural memory by publishing new editions of older texts (e. g. war diaries, think of *The Passchendaele Year* by Achiel Van Walleghem), by making literary texts available online (think of the diary of the writer Virginie Loveling), by producing new literary texts that deal with the First World War (think of e. g. the internationally successful *Oorlog en Terpentijn* (*War and Turpentine* by Stefan Hertmans), or by translating foreign war literature (old and new).

Our chapter aims at looking into the reading of WWI poetry in Belgium, in particular to the poems of the so-called War Poets translated into Dutch by the Belgian author Tom Lanoye. If war literature helps us to preserve or even construct the cultural memory of the First World War, what is its effect on the readers? How do they interpret and read war literature one hundred years later? We will focus on three types of readers: the translator, the critic and the student. We will thus approach the topic from the viewpoint of three different disciplines: literary studies, translation studies and psychology.

We will rely on reception studies as a general framework. Reception is a term that, since its introduction in literary studies in the 1960s, has shifted the focus from the text and the author to the reader. The bottom line is that a text has no meaning without the contribution of the reader. The reader in this article is studied in three different manifestations: the *translator* as reader, the *professional reader* (the critic) and the *occasional reader* (here: the students in our classroom). In the first part we will study the reception of the original poems by the translator, Tom Lanoye in his book *Niemands Land*. What is his reading/interpretation of the War Poets? How does he appropriate them, how does he 'use' them? This part is situated in the field of Translation Studies. In the second part we look at how literary critics in the Flemish and Dutch press received *Niemands Land*. Using discourse analysis as a method, we will analyze the critics' interpretation of the poems. This part can be situated within Literary Studies. The third part will concentrate on occasional readers. How do they receive Lanoye's translation, and more in particular: how does reading these poems influence their attitude towards peace and war? Given the role played by World War I in the emergence of a global pacifist movement, and, more specifically, the contribution of literature to this movement[4], we will indeed be particularly (but not exclusively) interested in the relation between exposure to World War I related poems and pacifism. This third part will take the form of a psychology experiment, using questionnaires to measure the effect of the war poems on a reader's emotions, his or her patriotism and attitudes towards pacifism. From a disciplinary viewpoint, the third part is to be situ-

---

4 See White 2008.

ated within the field of social psychology and will rely on a quantitative analysis of questionnaire surveys.

By combining Translation Studies, Literary Studies and Psychology this paper wants to give a better understanding of how First World War Poetry is read by three different types of readers after one hundred years. It also aims at examining whether an interdisciplinary approach can teach us more about reading as a research object and about the (im)possibillity of combining approaches.

2 The translator

A special case of filling the gap in Flemish cultural memory is the new translation of the British War Poets into Dutch[5] by the Flemish author Tom Lanoye.[6] Their poems are considered as part of the canon of WWI literature, belonging to the cultural memory of not only the UK but of Western Europe as a whole. Lanoye made efforts to infiltrate them into Flemish cultural memory particularly (e.g. by his translation strategies, see below).

In 2002 and 2004 he published two volumes of translated international war poetry, collected in a single volume in 2014, during the boom of the literary commemoration of the beginning of the First World War. In *Niemands Land* Lanoye translated poems by the English War Poets, such as Siegfried Sassoon, Wilfred Owen, Ivor Gurney and Rupert Brooke. It contains mainly traditional poetry, whereas the second volume contains more experimental or avant-garde poetry, with a range of modernist poets writing about WWI, using a distorted dissonant poetic form to express the horrors of war, such as Trakl, Marinetti, Stramm, Ungaretti, but also Majakovski and Apollinaire. Lanoye still tours with a performance based on the poems from his two volumes and reaches theatre audiences all over Flanders and The Netherlands.

In this article we will focus on the first volume, *Niemands Land* (No Man's Land). The publisher, Prometheus, informed us that the book had only one edition with a print run of 9000 copies, sold both in Flanders and The Netherlands. Since an average collection of poetry has a print run of a few hundred, *Niemands Land*'s print run is rather impressive. Translated poetry especially sells very badly. Lanoye's collection is also very widespread if we look at Flemish library catalogues.[7]

---

5   Flemish is not a language, it refers to a region in Belgium (Flanders), where Dutch is spoken.
6   Tom Lanoye (*1958) is a Belgian novelist, poet, columnist, screenwriter and playwright. He is one of the most widely read and honoured authors in the Dutch-speaking language area who lives and works in Antwerp and Cape Town (South Africa). His literary work has been published and/or performed in over fifteen languages. Lanoye started out as an *enfant terrible*, but has become an established writer, and even a cultural entrepreneur. His company is called L.A.N.O.Y.E. nv. He is famous and even notorious for branding himself, for putting himself on the market as a producer of cultural goods.
7   The 2014 collection had a print run of 1000 copies.

In the introduction to the 2014 volume, Lanoye calls his work a literary shadow play. This can be interpreted in two ways: Lanoye's translation of the poems as the shadow of the original poems or the original poems as the shadow of Lanoye's poetic undertaking. One could call it a shadow play with an imaginary author. In an interview Lanoye states:

> "Yet I adapt poems of the War Poets, who wrote from the trenches, as if there were a namesake of mine in the trenches that wrote one big poetry volume in which he cried out his despair. Hence the anachronisms. (…) I want to give us a small literary legacy through which the First World War – and with it all the wars – finds a place in our shared history."[8]

In the media, Lanoye has had plenty of opportunity to explain why he has translated war poetry. He shares the opinion that Dutch-speaking Belgium has no war poetry and 'therefore' no cultural memory of the war. Lanoye sees it as his task to give Flanders exactly that: a cultural memory of the war, so that it can come to terms with its past. As Kasten says, Lanoye has declared the existing corpus of British war poetry no man's land, and by translating them has claimed them for the Flemish literary tradition and Flanders cultural memory.[9]

Lanoye calls Belgians wonderfully antipatriotic and declares that patriotism means nothing to him. His choice of poems to translate is by no means patriotic, according to him. He finds it odd that one of the most nationalistic conflicts ever was fought on a narrow piece of land, called no man's land (in this respect, it needs to be stressed that Lanoye is a left-wing public figure).[10]

Lanoye says he wants to achieve his goal by pretending to be a poet-soldier in the trenches. Formulating it like that, it almost seems as if Lanoye writes as an author, not as a translator. His view complies with Alvstad's concept of the 'translation pact': we read the translation as an original. 'There is a dominant sociocultural convention according to which translated texts are read as if they were produced solely by the author'.[11] In the framework of this article, there is no room for discussing the translated character of Lanoye's volume or to discuss the author-translator persona of Lanoye. Let it suffice to say that Tom Lanoye translates one hundred year old war poetry by several authors in his singular voice (of an imagined protagonist). He changes British place and proper names to Flemish ones; he uses Flemish expressions and idiomatic phrases. This is a form of 'memory transfer': British war poets are transferred through translation to Flemish war memory and to the 21st century.

---

8   'Toch bewerk ik gedichten van de *War Poets*, die schreven vanuit de loopgraven, alsof er een naamgenoot van mij in de loopgraven zat die één grote bundel schreef waarin hij zijn wanhoop uitschreeuwde. Vandaar de anachronismen. (…) Ik wil ons een kleine literaire erfenis geven waardoor de Eerste Wereldoorlog – en daarmee alle oorlogen – een plek vindt in onze gezamenlijke geschiedenis.' (Luyten 2001).
9   Kasten 2011, 87.
10 See Luyten 2001.
11 Alvstad 2014, 217.

Rigney mentions that "(c)entral to the role of literature as a medium of collective memory-making (…) is its ability to cross existing cultural borders and to provide an imaginative template for articulating values and defining identities."[12] This corresponds to Erll's notion of 'travelling memory', relating to 'the fact that in the production of cultural memory, people, media, mnemonic forms, contents, and practices are in constant, unceasing motion'.[13] In her conceptual framework, translators, and in this case, Lanoye can be called a 'carrier of memory', someone with a specific agenda (in this case filling a gap in Flemish cultural memory). Erll thinks researchers should "pay close attention to the various ways in which traveling memory is localized (…). (They) should ask how translocal mnemonic forms and practices are translated and integrated into local repertoires; (…) how contents of memory are continually hybridized."[14] Lanoye definitely hybridizes the British War Poets.

To spread a pacifistic message was not one of Lanoye's concerns. On the contrary: he claims he is not a pacifist: "I don't believe there will ever be a time without war (…) everything we value wouldn't have been there without bloodshed."[15] This dilemma, cruel and moving as it is, is exactly what he found (read) in the British War Poets.

3 The critics

Let us now look from the angle of literary studies at how literary critics in the Flemish and Dutch press received *Niemands Land*. Using discourse analysis as a method, we will analyze these professional readers' interpretation of the poems. We analyzed the Flemish and Dutch reviews of Lanoye's volume[16] to see whether there were links to patriotism, whether emotional reactions were mentioned and whether there were any comments on the poems and their relation to cultural memory.

If we look at the reviews of Lanoye's volume, we notice that his poems are perceived as emotional. Flemish literary scholar Dirk De Geest says that it is impossible not to be moved by them.[17] The Flemish poetry critic Carl De Strycker sums up the emotions the volume evokes: despair, doubt, fear and despondency.[18] The Dutch crit-

---

12 Rigney 2012, 6.
13 Erll 2012, 12.
14 Erll 2012, 14–15.
15 'Ik geloof niet dat er ooit een periode komt waarin er geen oorlog zal zijn (…) alles wat wij van waarde achten er niet zou gekomen zijn zonder bloedvergieten' (Luyten 2012).
16 We found six reviews of *Niemands Land* and added one review of the volume *Overkant*, because the reviewer also discusses *Niemands Land* there. We also added one review of the presentation of *Niemands Land* at the Menin Gate. To find the reviews we searched the databases Literom, GoPress and BNTL.
17 'Wie deze gedichten leest, kan onmogelijk onbewogen blijven' (De Geest 2003).
18 'De wanhoop, de twijfel, de angst, de moedeloosheid: ze worden allemaal opgeroepen' (De Strycker 2005).

ic Guus Middag simply says the war must have been terrible and it makes him feel miserable.[19] The Dutch literary scholar Jos Joosten comments on how Lanoye has in a way translated the emotional stake of the original poems. He says Lanoye has toned down the often too big words of the original poems, exactly like the black-and-white photographs of pompous war monuments by photographer Michiel Hendryckx that accompany the poems tone down the feelings of bombast into something more intimate:

> "Thus, his (…) adaptations run parallel with Hendryckx' photographic work in the collection: the bombast of the most often pompous commemorative monuments becomes almost intimate thanks to his subtle, rigid black-and-white photo technique, and in this manner the photographer resuscitates the once-intended feeling of grief and mourning".[20]

The emotions of grief and mourning expressed a century ago in the war monuments are 'translated' by the photographer into more contemporary expressions of those same emotions, so that when we see them we can feel the same emotions people did a century ago. The same effect is reached, according to Joosten, by Lanoye's poetry translations: in order to reach the same emotional goals as e.g. Sassoon and Owens in their time, Lanoye has to use a different, less bombastic register.

With regard to the state of Flemish cultural memory, the reviewers comment on the fact that Lanoye has made the poems his own, that his translations are in fact adaptations. He has transferred them to his own idiom and he has transferred them to 21st century Flanders. London and the Thames become Ghent and the river Leie, the Highland fling becomes the Horlepiep, the mustard mentioned is now replaced by the local brand 'de Kroon' ('the crown', which happens to be Lanoye's father's favorite mustard) etc. De Geest sees this poetry as a new, enriching and integral part of Dutch literature.[21] That means he doesn't regard them as English poems anymore, but as Dutch poems (De Strycker also speaks about 'Flemish poems'). Typically, cultures are more likely to receive cultural products from across their borders when there are literary vacuums.[22] In this case the literary vacuum is to be defined as the lack of literary heritage and cultural memory that is concerned with the First World War (or at least a perceived lack thereof). Translation can help to fill such a gap. You could say that in the eyes of a critic like De Geest, Lanoye has succeeded in his effort to transplant a travelling memory to Flanders, or rather, to Dutch literature and to contribute to its

---

19 'Het moet (…) verschrikkelijk zijn geweest', 'Groote Oorlog, Mooi Boek, maar wel om beroerd van te worden' (Middag 2002).
20 'Daarmee lopen zijn overige bewerkingen mooi parallel met Hendryckx' fotowerk in de bundel: de bombast van de veelal pompeuze herdenkingsmonumenten krijgt door zijn subtiele, strakke zwart-wit fototechniek haast iets intiems en zo reanimeert de fotograaf als het ware het ooit beoogde gevoel van verdriet en rouw' (Joosten 2002).
21 'dat Lanoye de Nederlandse literatuur met een aantal overtuigende teksten heeft verrijkt' (De Geest 2003).
22 Even-Zohar 1990.

cultural memory. The Dutch critic Middag also acknowledges the fact that Flanders has now been given the poetry it lacked for one hundred years. However, he doesn't seem to perceive this 'vervlaamsing' ('flemishizing') as only positive. He calls it Lanoye's 'urge to annex' other author's poems, significantly using a military metaphor. He particularly mentions Lanoye's translation of Robert Nichols' poem *The Assault*, which Lanoye turns Flemish by translating it in the style of Van Ostaijen (mentioned above), thus creating a polyphonic new poem featuring three voices: Nichols, Van Ostaijen and Lanoye. Other critics too have criticized the fact that Lanoye makes the poems his own, and that he seems to have little respect for 'the original'. In fact, these critics criticize the creation of cultural memory through translation as a form of annexation. The Flemish journalist Tom Rummens does not use the metaphor of annexation but the well-known, and more positive, metaphor of palimpsest. He even calls Lanoye's translations a form of cultural jealousy. But he sees the result as mainly positive, especially because Lanoye has managed to link these 100 year old poems to what is happening now. Rummens refers to the presentation of the volume at the Menin Gate in Ypres where Lanoye made the link with Blair and Bush and the Iraq War:

> "The Great War may be a closed episode, its meaning has such a universal dimension that every generation, every human being has to turn it into its own story again. This book helps in doing that."[23]

Joosten has a more nuanced view on the success of the travelling memory. He thinks Lanoye's poetry is so good that it clearly shows that this poetry (the original) is in fact dead, that it has a jargon and a sentimentality that is no longer topical.[24] This corresponds to Erll's idea that mnemonic objects (like poetry) need to be invested with new meaning (and thus hybridized) to remain relevant.

The topic of patriotism seems to be largely absent from the reviews. If it is mentioned it is ridiculed. For example, Joosten compares the stance of some of the poems to 'the stupid heroism of American comic book artists after 11 September'.[25] He doesn't seem to acknowledge the fact that the poems are largely anti-patriotic, or rather, even in their anti-patriotism he reads a connection to the concept of fatherland (even if it is criticized) that seems ridiculous (though not outdated). This link is, of course, still clearly present in the poems, denouncing the idea of fatherland also means taking it as a theme. Middag reads the poems as resisting the morale that it is good and sweet (*dulce et decorum*) to die for the fatherland. The title *Niemands Land*

---

23 'De Groote Oorlog mag dan een afgesloten episode zijn, de betekenis ervan heeft zo'n universele dimensie dat elke generatie, elk mens er weer zijn eigen verhaal van moet maken. Dit boek helpt daarbij' (Rummens 2002).

24 'juist Lanoyes geslaagde poging om de oude gedichten tot leven te schrijven, toont aan hoe dood deze poëzie in feite is, met een jargon, een humanitair realisme, een sentimentaliteit ook en eendimensionaliteit die niet van deze tijd is' (Joosten 2002).

25 De stompzinnige heroïek van de Amerikaanse comicbook-tekenaars na 11 september (Joosten 2002).

(No Man's Land) seems to be significant in this respect. It opposes the concept of fatherland. As De Geest says: 'This "No Man's Land" is a country where no one feels at home, but that concerns us all'.[26] The title also seems a comment on the 'Britishness' of the war poets, meaning poetry is not bound to a nation or a 'land' but can travel through e. g. translation and thus be meaningful for others.

Even more absent is the topic of pacifism. We know Lanoye had no pacifistic intentions (indeed, his entire oeuvre shows his fascination for war), and the critics certainly do not try to read that in to the book. 'No more war' is no theme in the reviews.

4   The students

Moving away from the reader-reviewer, this third approach to reception assumes a focus on 'occasional readers' and makes use of data collection methods such as questionnaires and interviews. In the present instance, we relied on questionnaire surveys. These included questions calling for participants to express their opinion on rating scales. One example of such a question could be:

To what extent do you experience the following emotions when you think of WWI soldiers?

Admiration   Not all ☐ ☐ ☐ ☐ ☐ ☐ Very Much

Pity   Not all ☐ ☐ ☐ ☐ ☐ ☐ Very Much

These ratings are subsequently coded as numbers, e. g., somebody who ticks the leftmost square above would receive a "1" for admiration. Scores on several items can be combined into a single "scale" (e. g. averaged) if a statistical analysis (called reliability analysis) offers sufficient evidence that they measure the same construct. One can then examine the relations between these ratings and other variables. This approach makes it possible to translate psychological constructs such as attitudes or emotions into numerical scales.

In this approach, we limited ourselves to two of Lanoye's poems, considering that poetry is usually read in small portions by 'real readers'. The two poems are *In Vlaamse velden*, a translation of John McCrae's *In Flanders Fields*, and *Tegenaanval*, a translation of Siegfried Sassoon's *Counter-Attack*. The first one is *the* iconic WW I poem and that is also why we chose it for our experiment. Most readers will immediately recognize it as a poem about the First World War. Moreover, it is not difficult to grasp or interpret as it is straightforward. The speaker is a first person plural ('we') and there is an explicit appeal to the reader ('you'), thus asking for the involvement of the reader, another reason to choose this poem. It is situated in Flanders so there is no relocation necessary in the translation. Lanoye uses puns and alliterations to give a lighter

---

26   'Dit "Niemands Land" is een land waar niemand thuis is, maar dat ons tegelijk allen aanbelangt' (De Geest 2003).

tone to the poem. Those stylistic features typically ground the poem in the Dutch language because they are so language-bound. One example of such a pun is the translation of 'poppies grow', namely 'klappen rozen open' (literally 'roses fold open'). In Dutch 'poppies' are 'klaprozen' (literally 'folding roses'), so Lanoye broke open the word 'klaprozen' (poppies) into a noun (rozen, 'roses') and a verb (klappen, 'fold'). Another example is the use of the homonyms 'kust' ('kisses') and 'kust' ('coast'). Puns are often considered untranslatable as they ground a text into one specific language; they actually foreground the language (the form) instead of the meaning. When he translates 'We (…) saw sunset glow' by 'De zon zagen wij zakken', a Flemish reader will not only notice the z-alliteration but also the reference to a well-known children's song. Intertextual references like that, of course, also put the poem in a certain cultural frame, here a Flemish frame, which makes it easier for the audience to identify with. The second poem is a longer poem, and was chosen because of its gruesome realism. It draws a horrible picture of the rotting corpses in the trenches and of the meaningless death of one particular soldier. It tells the story of the soldier in the third person ('he'), as he is observed by 'us'. There is no explicit appeal to 'you', but the details ('naked sodden buttocks', 'plastering slime') ensure the reader's involvement and attention. Lanoye even heightens the gruesomeness by e. g. translating the 'butchered frantic gestures of the dead' by 'verminkte, krankzinnige gebarentaal van *verse* doden' (the *fresh* dead). By replacing some of the cultural specific elements that might puzzle a Flemish reader ('Lewis guns' by 'mitrailleurs' e. g.), Lanoye explicitly has a Flemish reader in mind. And again, he makes ample use of alliterations to fully stress the Dutch language of his poems.

To examine the impact of World War I poetry on emotions and attitudes such as pacifism and patriotism, as well as on creating cultural memory, we organized a listening experiment. We asked a drama teacher to read the two poems to 91 freshmen students in literature at the University of Leuven, of which we selected 85 who reported being Belgian and of Belgian ancestry (and 83 whose mother tongue was Dutch). The students were more or less all of the same age (average of 19 years) and shared an interest in literature. The reading was audiotaped. Three months prior to the listening experiment, we had administered a questionnaire assessing several psychological variables, such as their level of pacifism, their attachment to Belgium, their emotions towards World War I soldiers. After the reading, we asked them what emotions they felt during the reading of the poem and inquired again about the variables previously assessed. For example, we asked them to report "what was the maximal intensity of emotion they felt during the listening of the poems"[27] on a scale (see below), where they had to tick the bullet that best represents the intensity of their emotions. The bullets are then coded from 1 to 10.

---

27   Questions pertained to the two poems without distinguishing them.

Total absence of emotion									Greatest emotion in my life
O	O	O	O	O	O	O	O	O	O

On that scale, we find that students vastly differ in the intensity of emotions they experienced with an average of 5.4 (see Figure 1). When we asked them how much they liked the poems (1 = not at all, 10 = very much), a very similar pattern emerged (the mean is 5.15). And indeed, the two ratings were correlated at .48, which reflects a medium to strong correlation.[28]

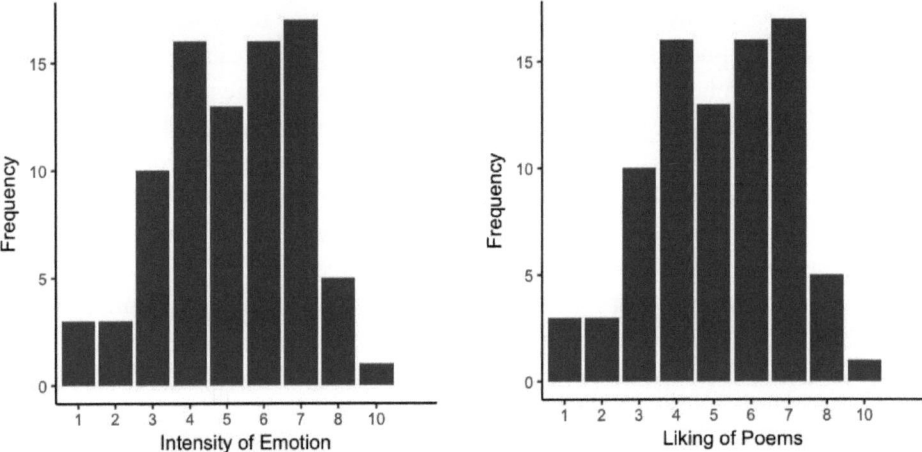

Figure 1: Reactions to the listening of the poems

We were particularly interested in the emotions associated with exposure to these poems as arguably one of the possible functions of poetry is to convey and elicit emotions, and we were wondering whether a century after the First World War, poems could convey emotions about this experience to contemporary audiences. Hence, we also submitted a list of different emotions and asked them to express how much they experienced each of them when listening to the poems (1 = Not at all, 7 = Extremely). We focused on emotions associated with the war experience. These included emotions that conveyed a sense of elevation (admiration, pride, respect), emotions associated with the victimization of soldiers (pity, empathy, sympathy, sorrow) and finally emotions expressing a negative reaction to war itself (anger, disgust). We also included indifference, a plausible (lack of) reaction a hundred years after the fact. As can be seen in Figure 2, the most intense emotions are respect, pity, empathy, sympathy and sorrow. All of these emotions are negative and we do not find any of the "elevating"

---

28   See Cohen 1988.

emotions that could be associated with a heroic vision of war in this "top 5". By contrast, the main emotions convey a sense of proximity towards those who experienced this war as if the poems led readers to empathize with their plight.

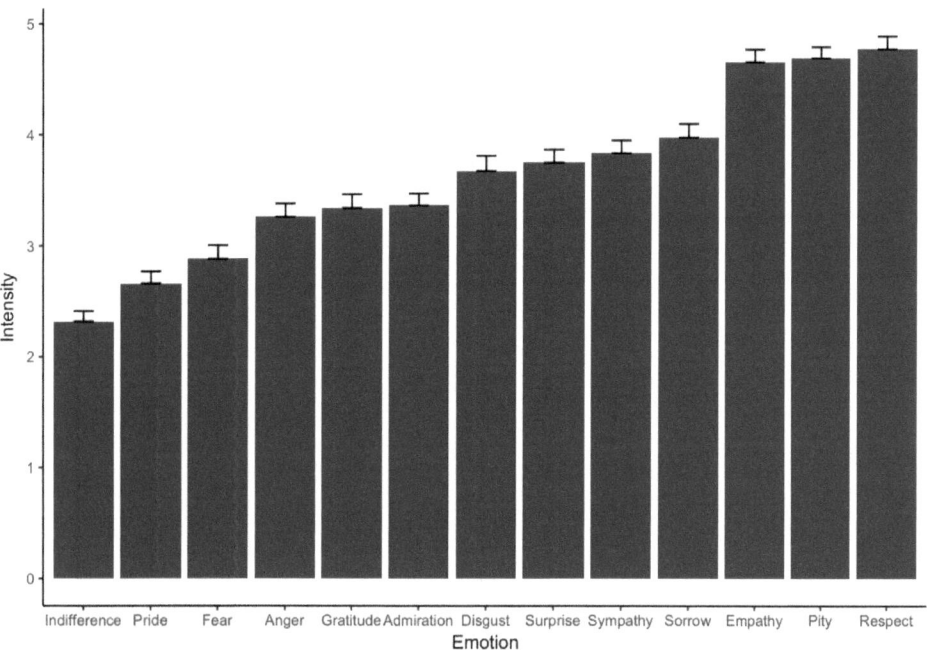

Note: error bars are standard errors.

Figure 2: Mean intensity of reported emotions when listening to two WWI-related poems

4.1 Effect on pacifist attitudes

Having identified the main emotions experienced when listening to the poems, the first question we sought to answer was whether reading such poems influenced the endorsement of pacifist attitudes. To address this question, we measured two dimensions of pacifist attitudes using a well-validated scale[29]: attitudes towards peace on the one hand, and attitudes towards war on the other. For example, one item from the peace subscale read "We must devote all our energy to securing peace throughout the world", whereas an item from the war subscale was "War breeds disrespect for human life." These are indeed distinct notions (although they are correlated, r = -.45). For example, people can value peace while considering war to be an acceptable outcome in some circumstances. Not surprisingly, attitudes towards peace were much more favorable than attitudes towards war (means of 5.38 and 2.74 on scales from 1 to 7).

---

29 Bizumic *et al.* 2013, Van der Linden et al. 2017.

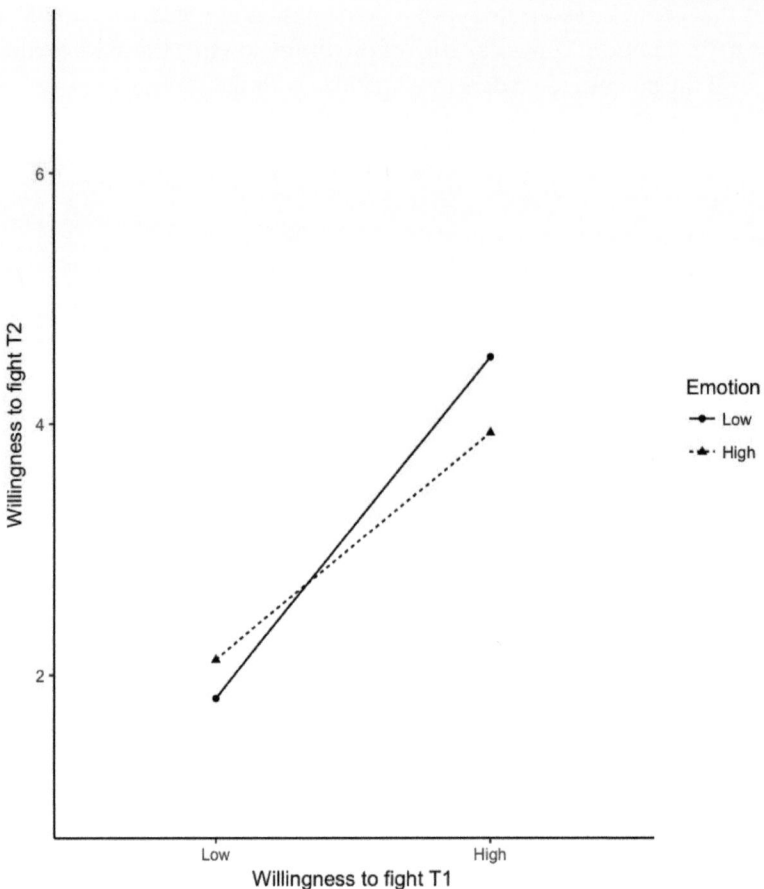

Figure 3: Willingness to fight for one's country at time 2 as a function of willingness to fight for one's country at time 1 and level of emotional intensity experienced during the listening of the poems

But, overall, we did not find any change in students' attitude towards either peace or war between time 1 and time 2. It seems therefore that the poems did not induce an overall tendency to endorse more positive attitudes.

Next we sought to examine whether, although there was no overall effect of listening to the poems on attitudes, experiencing emotions during the reading of the poems affected such attitudes. In other words, all being otherwise equal, are people who experience emotions when listening to poems also more likely to endorse pacifist attitudes subsequently? Indeed, experiencing emotions was associated with a positive change in attitudes towards peace.[30] However, the intensity of emotions experienced

---

30 $\beta = .21$. We also examined whether specific emotions may be differentially associated with increases (or decreases) in pacifism. No such effect was found.

during the reading of the poems had no effect on the scale measuring attitudes towards war.

We also asked participants whether they would be willing to fight on behalf of their country in case of war. This is an interesting measure because it taps directly into their disposition to act on their beliefs and not only on their attitudes. The mean response on this scale (3.07 on a scale from 1 = "not ready at all" to 7 = "totally ready") did not overall change as a function of the reading of the poems. However, we found an interesting (although only marginally significant) tendency. Obviously, students who were willing to fight before listening to the poems tended to be more willing to fight after the reading of the poems (and vice versa). This is shown in Figure 3, where the "right side" is higher than the "left side". However, this consistency between attitudes before and after reading the poems was weaker among students who experienced strong emotions as shown by the dotted line in Figure 3 being less steep. More precisely, among students who were more willing to fight at time 1, those who experienced a high level of emotional intensity were less willing to fight at time 2 than those who experienced a lower level of emotional intensity.[31]

4.2 Effect on attachment to the country

Through his book, Tom Lanoye hoped to induce a Flemish cultural memory. National memory is intimately associated with collective identity, as it provides meaning and substance to this identity by anchoring it in the past.[32] A legitimate question arises: Does listening to these poems affect in any way the students' attachment to their national identity? To respond to this question, we used a scale developed to measure such attachment to one's nation.[33] The eight questions, which do not refer to a specific country, are like the following "I love my country", "Being a citizen of my country is an important part of my identity", etc. on scales from "don't agree at all" (1) to "totally agree" (7). We averaged responses on the eight items. We found indeed that participants reported a slightly higher attachment to their country after ($M = 4.13$) than before ($M = 3.93$) listening to the poem.[34] Given, however, that the items did not specify "Belgium" as the focal country, it is possible that some participants thought of other "entities", such as Flanders, when responding to this question.

---

31   $\beta = .85$ for people who score 1 SD above the mean in emotionality, $\beta = .57$ for those who score 1 SD below the mean in emotionality.
32   Licata, Klein & Gély 2007.
33   Roccas, Klar & Liviatan 2006.
34   Using a linear mixed model, $t(1,90) = 1.83, p = .07$.

4.3 Effect on emotions towards soldiers

Next, we sought to examine the emotions our listeners experienced towards the soldiers who fought during World War I as a function of listening to the poems. We first examined the mean level of endorsement of these emotions across the two time periods. The order of the emotions is very similar to what was observed regarding the listening of the poems: respect, empathy, pity, admiration and sympathy are the strongest emotions. Interestingly, although The First World War may seem like an ancient event, indifference is the "emotion" (if it can be seen as such) that is the least endorsed by the participants. Similarly, they did not experience very negative emotions such as disgust, anger and fear. Thus, the attitude towards the soldiers seems to be dominated by respect, combined with a pity for their plight, which seems to resonate quite well with the content of the poems. Again, this suggests a sense of proximity with the soldiers.

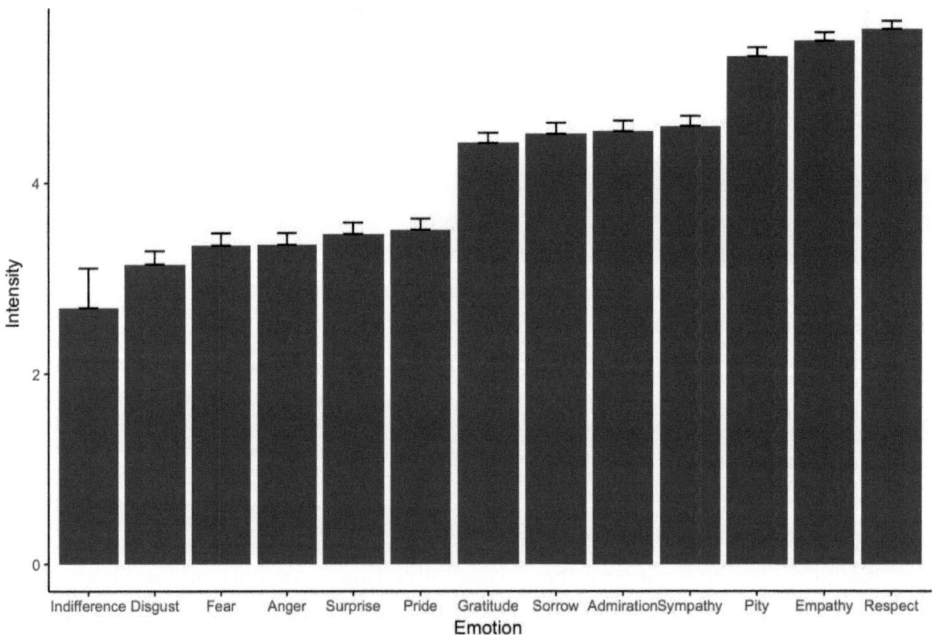

Figure 4: Mean Levels of Emotions Felt Towards WWI Soldiers

Next, we sought to examine whether the emotions varied as a function of exposure to the poems. To respond to this question, we first divided the emotions into two main categories, based on the correlations between these variables.[35] The first category combines five positive emotions: admiration, empathy, pride, respect, sympathy. The

---

35 This was done via a statistical technique known as principal components analysis, using here three factors and Varimax rotation.

second combines four more negative emotions (fear, anger, disgust)[36] as well as surprise. When comparing the means on these variables, we found that only the positive emotions varied with a *decrease*[37] (from 4.86 to 4.66) in such emotions after exposure to the poems, compared to before. To understand which emotions drove this effect, we examined them individually. Remarkably, for the six positive emotions, we found a decrease in only two: empathy and sympathy[38], as shown in Figure 5. This may seem quite surprising given that we would expect the poems to increase, rather than decrease, such emotions.

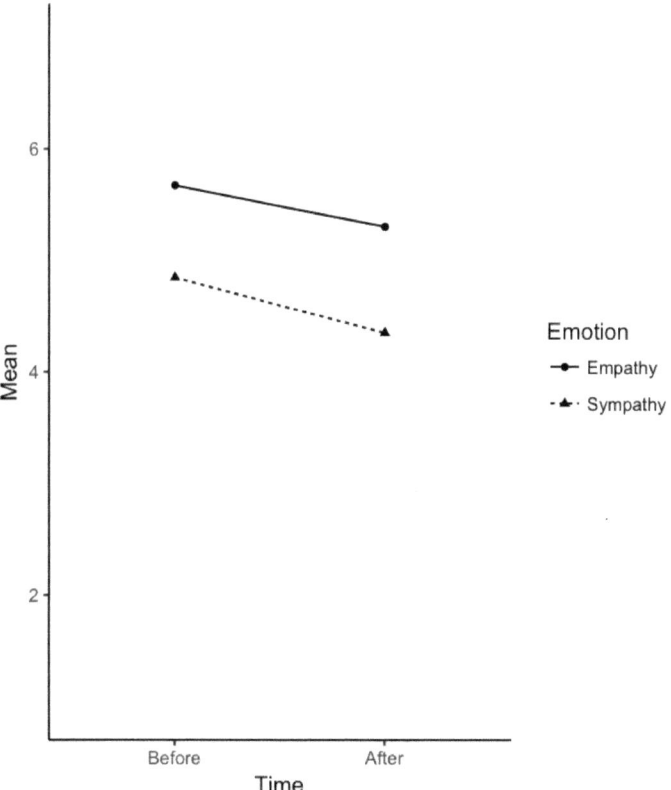

Figure 5: Change in empathy and sympathy from time 1 to time 2

Having considered these quantitative analyses, we can highlight a few findings. First, a large portion of these students in literature at the University of Leuven report experiencing emotions when listening to these poems evoking a century-old event. This

---

36 Three emotions: sorrow, pity and indifference could not be fit into this model.
37 $t(88.6) = -2.11, p = .037$ using LMM.
38 $t(88.9) = 2.5, p = .008$ for empathy & $t(88.9) = -3.17, p = .002$ for sympathy using LMM.

testifies to the capacity of Lanoye's hybrid translation to invest the poems with new meaning and make them relevant again for the 21st century reader. The most intensely experienced emotions (respect, sympathy, sorrow …) are positive and reflect a sense of proximity and empathy that corresponds well with the emotions they report feeling towards the soldiers themselves. In other words, the poems seem to convey the emotions that the participants spontaneously felt towards WWI soldiers. This may be, of course, because these emotions are heavily connected to culturally shared representations of the First World War. Commemorations of the Great War, be they through collective gatherings, or through the media, are in this regard occasions to communally experience these emotions.[39] These may have fostered "communities of shared emotional experiences" to paraphrase the concept of "interpretive communities". These then provide a lens to appraise the poems, which may also serve to confirm and bolster such emotions.

We also find, and this may be the most remarkable result of these analyses, that this emotional intensity tends to be associated with more pacifist attitudes, which coheres with the cultural significance of these poems. Interestingly, this is compatible with a (slightly) greater attachment to their country after listening to the poem, which suggests that pacifism and national identity can coexist. Why this is the case is difficult to answer. One possibility is that listening to the poems makes Word War I salient, and hence the status of Belgium as a party to the conflict salient. Another unexpected finding resides in the decrease in empathy and sympathy for the soldiers after listening to the poems. As these are some of the emotions that these poems, which precisely deal with soldiers' experience, may seem to evoke most readily, this may seem surprising. One possible interpretation of this finding is that of a contrast effect: to the extent that they felt more empathy towards the individual soldiers, whose unique experience is described in the poem, they may have felt slightly *less empathy* towards other soldiers. In other words, the empathy felt towards the soldiers portrayed in the poems may lead them to perceive their feelings towards other soldiers as somewhat less intense.

Finally, it would be useful to examine in further research whether the effects we have uncovered here can be generalized for other populations, especially British students. Does the greater emphasis placed on the memory of World War I in the UK (but also Canada, Australia and New Zealand) make the listening of such poems more potent than in Belgium, where such memory has been much less salient until the recent commemorations?

---

39 Paez *et al.* 2015.

5 Conclusion

In this chapter, we examined how poems about the First World War that are a century old could travel in time through different manifestations of readership: the words of a translator and their receptions by professional critics and undergraduate students. We discovered the critics' nuanced and complex appraisals of Tom Lanoye's enterprise, but also their sometimes diverging interpretations of the same work. In any case, both the reception by the translator and by the critics make the poems part of Flemish cultural memory and are (deeply) influenced by different types of (positive and negative) emotions evoked by the memory of World War I. In the last part, we relied on a very different audience (students in literature, rather than literary critics). This focus on a more general public is important to grasp the current reception of these poems. In doing so, we used a very different methodology informed by a more quantitative orientation. This approach seeks to establish causal relationships between variables indicative of psychological constructs. The use of such divergent approaches reflects our distinct epistemological backgrounds (translation studies and literary studies vs. experimental social psychology). This more quantitative approach did not allow us to capture the rich and nuanced interpretations of the poems that had surfaced in the previous parts. Also, as it tends to focus on average tendencies, it does not offer an opportunity to capture possible disagreements or variability in such appraisals.

By contrast, however, this multidisciplinary approach enabled us to touch upon the actual effect of these poems on our audiences' psychological states. Overall, the impacts we detected were of relatively small magnitude, which is to be expected given the small scope of our 'intervention'. But they nevertheless revealed remarkable interactions between the public's psychological state and their reactions to the poems. Especially, they highlight that high emotionality, associated with the hearing of these poems, seems to be associated with pacifism and a lower willingness to fight. Or, in other words, insofar as they could resonate with the audience's emotions, they were effective in influencing their stance towards peace and war. That they are so effective in inducing such attitudes, even 100 years later, may explain why, in the aftermath of World War I, they have become emblems of pacifism.

As an *exercice de style* in combining different epistemological approaches, the present chapter may seem like an unfinished enterprise. In our view, the main limitation of the present work resides in the absence of a middle ground between the two approaches. A 'bridge' would have been offered by preceding the quantitative appraisal with more qualitative work with the students on their appraisal of the poems and the emotions and attitudes they associated with it. While such findings could have been more easily compared to the reception of the poems by professional critics, it could also have informed the construction of the questionnaire. Thus, in the future, it would be useful to move from a mere multidisciplinary perspective, which involves appraising the same object from different disciplinary angles, to an *interdisciplinary or even transdisciplinary* approach that tries to go past, and aims at transcending, disciplinary boundaries.[40] From a methodological perspective, such an approach could make use of a "mixed methods" perspective that seeks to articulate qualitative and quantitative data as a coherent whole.[41]

Nonetheless, at this time, we are confident that it opens stimulating avenues for further research on this topic. If anything, we hope it will stimulate more dialogue between translation studies, literary studies and social psychology.

References

Alvstad, C. (2014). The Translation Pact. *Language and Literature, 23* (3), 270–284.
Assmann, J. (1992). *Das kulturelle Gedächtnis. Schrift, Erinnerung und politische Identität in frühen Hochkulturen.* München: Beck.
Assmann, A. (1999). *Erinnerungsräume. Formen und Wandlungen des kulturellen Gedächtnisses.* München: Beck.
Bizumic, B., Stubager, R., Mellon, S., Van der Linden, N., Iyer, R. & Jones, B. M. (2013). On the (in) Compatibility of Attitudes toward Peace and War. *Political Psychology, 34* (5), 673–693.
Brems, E. & Ramos Pinto, S. (2013). Reception and Translation. In Gambier, Y. & Van Doorslaer, L. (Eds), *Handbook of Translation Studies*. Amsterdam: John Benjamins, 142–147.
Brems, E., Ceuppens, J., Toremans, T. & Mus, F. (2017). Waterloo. Special Issue of *Interférences littéraires 20.*
Buelens, G. (2008). *Europa Europa! Over de dichters van de Grote Oorlog.* Amsterdam: Ambo.
Choi, B. C. K. & Pak, A. W. (2006). Multidisciplinarity, Interdisciplinarity and Transdisciplinarity in Health Research, Services, Education and Policy: 1. Definitions, Objectives, and Evidence of Effectiveness. *Clinical and Investigative Medicine, 29* (6), 351–364.
Cohen, J. (1988). *Statistical Power Analysis for the Behavioral Sciences* (2nd edition). Hillsdale, NJ: Erlbaum.
De Geest, D. (2003). Niemands land: gedichten uit de Groote Oorlog. *Leesidee*, 1-02-03.
De Strycker, C. (2005). Overkant: moderne verzen uit de Groote Oorlog. *De Leeswolf*, 1-4-05.
Erll, A. (2011). Travelling Memory. *Parallax, 17* (4), 4–18.
Even-Zohar, I. (1990). The Position of Translated Literature within the Literary Polysystem. *Poetics Today, 11* (1), 45–51.
Frédéric, M. (2005). Femmes et enfants dans la guerre: le regard des récits de fiction. In Jaumain, S., Amara, M., Majerus, B. & Vrints, A. *Une guerre totale? La Belgique dans la première guerre mondiale. Nouvelles tendances de la recherche historique.* Bruxelles: Archives générales du Royaume, 579–595.
Joosten, J. (2002). Gereanimeerde rouw. Tom Lanoyes 'Gedichten uit de Groote Oorlog'. *De Standaard*, 3-10-02.
Kasten, M. J. A. (2011). Vertaalslag in niemands land: Tom Lanoye en de poëzie uit de Groote Oorlog. In Houppermans, J. J. M., Jacobs, J. G. A. M. & Kruk, R. (Eds), *Déjà vu; herhaling in literatuur en kunst.* Leiden: Leiden University Press, 71–91.
Lanoye, T. (2002). *Niemands Land. Gedichten uit de Groote Oorlog.* Amsterdam: Prometheus.

---

40   See Choi & Pak 2006.
41   Hesse-Biber, Rodriguez & Frost 2015.

Lanoye, T. (2014). *Niemands Land/Overkant. Gedichten uit de Groote Oorlog*. Amsterdam: Prometheus.

Leemans, E. (2002). Van de doden weten we wat we weten: Tom Lanoye, Michiel Hendryckx en Dooreman in 'Niemands land'. *Poëziekrant, 26* (6), 8–15.

Leerssen, J. (2006). *National Thought in Europe. A Cultural History*. Amsterdam: Amsterdam University Press.

Licata, L., Klein, O. & Gély, R. (2007). Mémoire des conflits, conflits de mémoires: une approche psychosociale et philosophique du rôle de la mémoire collective dans les processus de réconciliation intergroupe. *Social Science Information, 46* (4), 563–589.

Luyten, A. (2001). Vlamingen hebben littekens, geen geheugen (interview). *De Standaard*, 31-10-01.

Middag, G. (2002). Broertje Lood is zo lief. *NRC Handelsblad*, 01-10-02.

Páez, D., Rimé, B., Basabe, N., Wlodarczyk, A. & Zumeta, L. (2015). Psychosocial effects of perceived emotional synchrony in collective gatherings. *Journal of Personality and Social Psychology, 108* (5), 711–729.

Reynebeau, M. (2004) Het kan nooit te ver gaan (interview). *De Standaard*, 4-11-04.

Rigney, A. (2012). *The Afterlives of Walter Scott. Memory on the Move*. Oxford: Oxford University Press.

Roccas, S., Klar, Y. & Liviatan, I. (2006). The paradox of group-based guilt: Modes of national identification, conflict vehemence, and reactions to the in-group's moral violations. *Journal of Personality and Social Psychology, 91* (4), 698–711.

Rummens, T. (2002). Getuigenis uit verleden met aanspraak op heden. *De Morgen*, 17-9-02.

Van der Linden, N., Leys, C., Klein, O. & Bouchat, P. (2017). Are attitudes toward peace and war the two sides of the same coin? Evidence to the contrary from a French validation of the Attitudes Toward Peace and War Scale. *PloS one, 12* (9), e0184001

Vantyghem, P. (2002). Het Niemandsland voorbij. *De Standaard*, 14-2-02.

White, R. (2008). *Pacifism and English Literature: Minstrels of Peace*. Basingstoke: Palgrave Macmillan.

In Flanders Fields

In Flanders fields the poppies blow
Between the crosses, row on row,
That mark our place; and in the sky
The larks, still bravely singing, fly
Scarce heard amid the guns below.

We are the Dead. Short days ago
We lived, felt dawn, saw sunset glow,
Loved and were loved, and now we lie
In Flanders fields.

Take up our quarrel with the foe:
To you from failing hands we throw
The torch; be yours to hold it high.
If ye break faith with us who die
We shall not sleep, though poppies grow
In Flanders fields.

John Mc Crae

In Vlaamse velden

In Vlaamse velden klappen rozen open
Tussen witte kruisjes, rij op rij,
Die onze plaats hier merken, wijl in 't zwerk
De leeuweriken fluitend werken, onverhoord
Verstomd door het gebulder op de grond.

Wij zijn de Doden. Zo-even leefden wij.
Wij dronken dauw. De zon zagen wij zakken.
Wij kusten en werden gekust. Nu rusten wij
In Vlaamse velden voor de Vlaamse kust.

Toe: trekt gij ons krakeel aan met de vijand.
Aan u passeren wij, met zwakke hand, de fakkel.
Houd hem hoog. Weest gíj de helden. Laat de doden
Die wij zijn niet stikken of wij vinden slaap noch
Vrede – ook al klappen zoveel rozen open
In zovele Vlaamse velden.

Tom Lanoye

Counter-Attack

We'd gained our first objective hours before
While dawn broke like a face with blinking eyes,
Pallid, unshaved and thirsty, blind with smoke.
Things seemed all right at first. We held their line,
With bombers posted, Lewis guns well placed,
And clink of shovels deepening the shallow trench.
The place was rotten with dead; green clumsy legs
High-booted, sprawled and grovelled along the saps
And trunks, face downward, in the sucking mud,
Wallowed like trodden sand-bags loosely filled;
And naked sodden buttocks, mats of hair,
Bulged, clotted heads slept in the plastering slime.
And then the rain began, – the jolly old rain!

A yawning soldier knelt against the bank,
Staring across the morning blear with fog;
He wondered when the Allemands would get busy;
And then, of course, they started with five-nines
Traversing, sure as fate, and never a dud.
Mute in the clamour of shells he watched them burst
Spouting dark earth and wire with gusts from hell,
While posturing giants dissolved in drifts of smoke.
He crouched and flinched, dizzy with galloping fear,
Sick for escape, – loathing the strangled horror
And butchered, frantic gestures of the dead.

An officer came blundering down the trench:
'Stand-to and man the fire-step!' On he went…
Gasping and bawling, 'Fire- step…counter-attack!'
Then the haze lifted. Bombing on the right
Down the old sap: machine-guns on the left;
And stumbling figures looming out in front.
'O Christ, they're coming at us!' Bullets spat,
And he remembered his rifle…rapid fire…

And started blazing wildly…then a bang
Crumpled and spun him sideways, knocked him out
To grunt and wriggle: none heeded him; he choked
And fought the flapping veils of smothering gloom,
Lost in a blurred confusion of yells and groans…
Down, and down, and down, he sank and drowned,
Bleeding to death. The counter-attack had failed.

Siegfried Sassoon

Tegenaanval

Ons eerste doel al urenlang veroverd als
De ochtend zich vertoont: een smoel met varkensoogjes –
Bleek, dorstig, ongeschoren en verblind door smoor.
Alles onder controle, eerst: wij in hun stellingen,
Ons zwaar geschut gereed, de mitrailleurs gericht,
Klinkklank van spades die een noodtranchee verdiepen.
(Vergeven van de lijken; plompe groene benen,
Gelaarsd; verspreid, verzwolgen deels, in sappes en
In kokers; tronies neer – de modder zuigt eraan;
Vertrapt, verdraaid, als slect gevulde zakken zand;
Spiernaakte, opgezwollen konten; plukken haar op
dikkoppen, klonterend, slapend in klittend slijm.
Dan gutst de regen neer. De goede oude regen.)

Een geeuwende piot leunt tegen het talud,
Staart overdwars de mistig vage morgen in
En vraagt zich af wanneer de mof eraan begint –
Die dan, natuurlijk, prompt eraan begint. Vijf-negens
Klieven tevoorschijn, reken maar! Met nooit één blindganger
Erbij. Verstomd door hun geraas ziet hij ze exploderen,
Zwart zand en draad opspuwend, geisers uit de hel:
Wat zich onneembaar voordeed, spat uiteen in rook.
Hij gooit zich plat, door zijn op hol slaande paniek
Verdoofd, haast brakend, smachtend naar ontsnapping, kruipend,
Wég van die gruwelijke wurggreep: de verminkte,
Krankzinnige gebarentaal van verse doden.

Een officier komt aangestrompeld door de loopgraaf:
'Sta op! Beman de borstwering!' Zo loopt hij door,
Hijgend en blaffend: 'Op! Klaar voor de tegenaanval!'
Dan trekt de nevel weg. Bombardementen op
De oude sappe, rechts. Fel mitrailleurvuur, links.
Pal vóór: opeens een rij van struikelende schimmen.
'Mijn God, ze komen op ons af!' Er fluiten kogels
En hij herinnert zich plots zijn geweer… En snelvuur…
Als gek schiet hij in 't wilde weg, totdat een knal
Hem samendrukt, terzijde smijt en vloert. Hij kermt
En kronkelt nog. Geen mens slaat acht op hem. Hij vecht
Tegen de sluiers van zijn stikkend lot, wegzakkend
In een misbaar, vervagend, van gekreun en kreten.
Omlaag, omlaag, omlaag zinkt hij. Tot hij verdrinkt.
Gans leeggebloed. De tegenaanval is mislukt.

Tom Lanoye

Valérie Rosoux, Pierre Bouchat, Olivier Klein

Retelling the War to Give a Chance to Peace. A Comparative Analysis of Great War Memories

"Ici aussi, les gens ont cru qu'ils pourraient échapper à leur histoire, ils se sont aimés, ils ont eu des enfants, mais soudain ils se sont souvenus qu'ils avaient des raisons de se craindre, de trembler à la vue de l'autre."[1]

1 Introduction

The First World War was a major historical event. The world's first truly global conflict ushered in a new era, an era of industrialized warfare. Millions of combatants were thrown into the heat of battle, while the majority of civilian populations participated more or less directly in the war effort. By the end of the conflict, between 15 and 18.4 million people had been killed and nearly 24 million soldiers wounded.[2] Certain areas were completely devastated by years of fighting. National borders shifted dramatically, leading to new demographic challenges. The industrial landscape underwent profound changes due to the specialization of the war industry. Finally, the generation gaps caused by the loss of human life permanently modified the political, economic and social organization of many countries.

The importance of these events is such that, a century later, the Great War remains one of the most significant events in all representations of history. For example, when social psychologist James Liu and his colleagues asked participants from six Western and six Asian countries to name the seven most significant events in world history, the Great War was the second most cited event in eleven of the twelve samples.[3]

Although global in scope, this conflict has affected Europe in a specific way. It was, after all, European rivalries that led to the outbreak of war and it was on the European continent where the first and major battles took place. Although most European nations committed themselves to one side or the other, their experience of the war differed significantly. Some countries were occupied while others managed to preserve their territorial integrity. Some populations suffered terrible losses while

---

1 Duroy 2012, 189.
2 Audoin-Rouzeau & Becker 2000.
3 Liu *et al.* 2005.

others survived relatively unscathed. Some countries experienced radical territorial and political changes, while there was little change to the status quo in others.

A century later, as the last witnesses of the war disappeared, and the events of 1914–1918 were followed by equally – if not more – tragic episodes, the question of how to remember and represent the Great War remains. The century of totalitarianism and industrial scale slaughter was also the century of European construction. In the aftermath of the Second World War, a handful of European countries gambled on pooling their coal and steel production together. This economic and increasingly political integration was achieved with the explicit aim of making it impossible for war to be waged between the member states of the European Union. Some might disagree with such an assertion, pointing to the seemingly intractable Cyprus conflict or the succession of crises linked to the economy, immigration or foreign policy. Others may point to the rise of rhetoric concerned with waging 'war on terrorism'. Yet, no one can deny that an armed conflict between Member States of the European Union seems further away than ever before. Such a dramatic shift from war to more or less peaceful cohabitation between European States deserves close analysis.

How could these countries, some of whom had defined themselves as hereditary enemies, manage memories as conflicting and confrontational as those of the Great War? Has their rapprochement been based in part on a progressive and common reading of the past? Does this rapprochement imply a substantial change in the collective memory of the groups involved? Thanks to the work of Maurice Halbwachs (1877–1945)[4] and Marie-Claire Lavabre[5], we know that the notion of collective memory is based on the interaction between public narratives of the past (whether presented by official representatives or historians) and individual memories (experienced and/or transmitted by the population). It is therefore useful to consider the articulation of the social and psychological components of collective memory in the long term. For example, what is the impact of public narratives of the past on individual memories? Have these narratives had any impact on the shifting relations between former belligerents?

These questions formed the basis of a wide-ranging survey by questionnaire, developed in the framework of a European COST project called *IS1205: Social Psychological Dynamics of Historical Representations in the Enlarged European Union*. The purpose of the survey was to examine current representations of the First World War in nineteen countries (see below). The results obtained make it possible to reflect on the evolution of representations of the past and, by extension, on the representations of the other, and ultimately on the representations of one's own group.

This chapter is divided into three main sections. The first considers a widely shared hypothesis in the field of international or intercommunity conflict resolution. The hypothesis is as follows: the sustainable transformation of the relationships be-

---

4   Halbwachs 1925, 1950.
5   Lavabre 1994, 2001.

tween former enemies implies a gradual modification of narratives of the past. As we will see, Paul Ricœur (1913–2005) and Jean-Marc Ferry highly emphasized the importance of this type of evolution, often described as a 'memory work'. The second section describes the most significant results of the survey. It attempts to understand respondents' representations of the Great War in three respects: their country's responsibility for the outbreak of the war, the degree of violence of their own soldiers and enemy soldiers, and finally the suffering endured and inflicted throughout the war. The third section proposes an interpretation of these results based on the initial hypothesis that stresses the importance of the memory work. The analysis focuses mainly on two groups of states with clearly different profiles, with France and Germany in one group and Serbia and Bosnia-Herzegovina in the other. The Belgian case is then discussed following this comparison.

The comparison of these two groups of states makes it possible to reflect on two particular memory dimensions. The first is strategic. It concerns the purpose of references to the past, whether these references are official or individual: do they manufacture otherness or do they seek to promote the normalization of relations with others? The second dimension is temporal. When are official representatives and citizens of a state ready to revise the representations of an embarrassing past? What is the most appropriate time scale? Is it a question of years, decades or generations?

2 Telling the past in another way

The starting point of the research is based on a general observation: political science is characterized by a wealth of publications devoted to the importance and political uses of the past, whether in a local, national or international context.[6] There is also a large body of literature on the need for memory work to promote the transformation of relations between former enemies (see below). These studies advance a particular epistemological perspective. They take into account how political actors portray the past. In doing so, they show that these portrayals do not result from scientific descriptions, but from specific representations. The following analysis therefore seeks to complement the model of rational decision-making by taking into account actors' perceptions and interpretations. The studies carried out so far show that it is not only the events themselves, but also – and above all – the representation of these events that influence decision-making.[7]

---

6   See Foong Khong 1992; Langenbacher & Shain 2010; May 1975; Rosoux 2001.
7   See Assman & Conrad 2010; Bell 2010.

2.1 The elaboration of a pluralistic narrative

In the aftermath of a war, the question that arises is not only "what happened?", but also – and above all – "what to do with the past?" Of course, the *facts* of the past cannot be altered. No one can undo or alter what has been done. But, as Paul Ricœur argues, the meaning of what happened "is never completely set in stone" either.[8] How can we then recount the past when its meaning continues to divide people? How can we revive memories without nourishing desires for revenge? There is a consensus among authors and practitioners on the need to settle past disputes. Beyond a somewhat binary distinction between memory *or* forgetfulness – often presented as opposites – is it not above all a question of considering how to remember *and* forget in order to move on? From this alternative perspective we must make sense out of the meaning given to events in order to live *with* memory, rather than living without it, or against it.[9]

For Ricœur, this approach to memory is fundamental because it is about "healing, and not just understanding".[10] This 'neutralization' of the past is intended to reduce the burden of a debt that might prevent any projection into the future. Its purpose is not to erase traces of the past, but the resentments that might be associated with them. Thus neutralized, the memory of battlefields, tombs and martyrs would no longer justify the shedding of one's own blood or that of others.[11] This is no easy undertaking. Indeed, how might we create a *single* narrative that everyone can relate to but whose central characteristic is its *plurality*?

According to Ricœur and many other authors working in the field of conflict resolution[12], only a change in the meaning given to the past can ultimately alleviate the emotional burden of painful past events. In the absence of such a change, some groups seem to be characterized by "unfinished grief"[13], reliving past events without end. The aim of Ricœur's work on remembrance is not to establish *the* truth with a capital "T", but rather to elaborate narratives that have the potential to bring different groups closer together. He wishes to generate "historical narratives that are themselves intersections between multiple histories".[14] In short, the objective is to tell the story in *another* way, that is to say, to tell it from the *other*'s point of view.[15] In this way, a plurality of memories is established.[16] The work of memory therefore remains work of

---

8   Ricœur 2000, 246.
9   Ricœur 1992.
10 Ricœur 1998.
11 See Irwin-Zarecka 1996.
12 See e.g. Krondorfer 1995; Tambia 1986.
13 Audoin-Rouzeau & Becker 2000.
14 Ricœur 1992, 110.
15 Ricœur 2000, 496.
16 Olick 1999.

memories – in the plural.[17] The aim is to reconfigure the past by "reshaping" the "stories we recount to each other about others".[18] This effort of "plural reading" or "cross narrative" appears as "the only way to open one's memory to that of the other"[19], as the only way to elaborate a narrative that may not be accepted by all but could potentially be shared by all.

2.2 The assumption of historical responsibility

Among the approaches mentioned to promote memory work, many scholars stress the importance of a form of recognition for past crimes, whether through requests for forgiveness, official apologies or truth and reconciliation commissions.[20] It is also from this perspective that Jean-Marc Ferry argues in favor of an *éthique reconstructive* (reconstructive ethics) between representatives of various national groups in order to bring former adversaries together.[21] This ethics is based on the critical assumption of historical responsibility for past crimes. From such a perspective, the official representatives of formerly war-torn states or communities are called upon to describe the wrongs suffered and committed so that generations to come can turn over the bloody pages of the past and work towards a shared future.

This reconstructive ethics approach has been mainly studied by scholars from two angles. The first is a normative angle from a political philosophy perspective. The aim of this perspective is to show that the processes involved are particularly promising in terms of conflict resolution. The second is a descriptive angle, carried out via case studies. Such studies have involved examining the normative principles showcased by the analysis of concrete situations, whether they are traditional post-conflict situations (following an international war or civil war) or transitions to democracy.[22] One angle, however, remains overlooked: that of the long-term effects of a critical assessment of the past. The negotiation processes that lead to the recognition or non-recognition of historical responsibility are the subject of many analyses. But little in-depth research has been devoted to the impact or, to put it another way, to the sociological depth of such gestures. However, it remains important to question the effectiveness of the official recounting narratives of the past to the public. Do the narratives emphasized by official representatives influence individual representations? If so, to what extent?

---

17 See Irwin-Zariecka 2017; Olick 2003; Rosoux 2001; Zerubavel 2003.
18 Ricœur 1992, 110.
19 Ricœur 1992, 115.
20 Barkan 2000; Brooks 1999; Lind 2008.
21 Ferry 1996.
22 Kritz 1995; Lefranc 2002.

As has been already mentioned, the two components of collective memory function according to their own logic, but they articulate and nourish each other. Political authorities can attempt to structure memory transmitted privately, whether through textbooks, monuments or commemorations. Nevertheless, the dissemination of a historical interpretation cannot simply be imposed from above. Citizens exposed to official discourses are not merely receptacles. Rather, they co-construct the messages conveyed to them. This allows researchers to observe discrepancies between official interpretations and individuals' perceptions of an event that prevail at the same time in a given society.[23] For this reason, it is worthwhile analyzing individual representations of the past in a comparative way.

3 Survey on the representations of the Great War

In order to achieve our objectives, an extensive online survey of university students in psychology, social sciences and history was conducted. The data collection took place between March 2014 and July 2015. 3081 participants from 21 countries[24] were invited to complete a questionnaire in their language of instruction. The survey took about 30 minutes to complete (only some of the questions asked in this survey are included in this study). Participants were informed that the survey was about sharing their personal opinions, not historical knowledge *per se*. In addition to a section concerning demographic information, the questionnaire consisted of the following items:

1. Perceived responsibility of the participant's country in the outbreak of the conflict: The recognition of the responsibility of a participant's country for the outbreak of war was measured by the following question: *According to you, how responsible was your country for the outbreak of war?* All items were measured using seven-point scales ranging from 1 = *Not at all* to 7 = *Extremely*.
2. Perceived violence of soldiers of participant's country and enemy soldiers: Perceived violence of soldiers during the First World War was measured separately for soldiers from the participant's country and enemy soldiers. This was evaluated by the following question: *According to you, what is the degree of violence that the soldiers from your country/enemy soldiers were capable of?*
3. Perceived collective victimhood and inflicted sufferings: Perceived collective victimization refers to "a mindset shared by group members that results from a perceived intentional harm with severe and lasting consequences inflicted on a collective by another group or groups, a harm that is viewed as undeserved, unjust and immoral and one that the group was not able to prevent".[25] Perceived collec-

---

23 Margry & Sanchez-Carretero 2011.
24 Argentina, Austria, Belgium, Croatia, Bosnia and Herzegovina, Estonia, Finland, France, Germany, Greece, Hungary, Italy, Norway, Poland, Portugal, Romania, Romania, Russia, Serbia, Spain, Turkey, Spain, Serbia, United Kingdom.
25 Bar-Tal, Chernyak-Hai, Schori & Gundar 2009, 238.

tive victimization was measured at historical and current levels by the following statements: *During the First World War, my country has suffered from the behavior of the enemy countries; my country is still suffering from the behavior of the enemy countries during the First World War.* Concerning historical suffering inflicted, this was measured by the following statement: *During the First World War, enemy countries have suffered from the behavior of my country.*

As the purpose of the survey was to highlight current representations of the First World War, the statistics used are descriptive in nature. The results included in this chapter can be found in the graphs below. Finally, it should be noted that the profile of respondents is not representative of the population of the same age in each country concerned. The samples on which the survey was based are made up of well-educated individuals. However, several studies show that historical representations obtained from student samples and national samples are relatively similar.[26] Moreover, differences in terms of representation are also likely to be minimal, given the influence of a certain (global) culture shared by university students; these students have grown up in a world that is more outward looking than the rest of the society.[27] Consequently, the differences in representation observed between the different countries are all the more noticeable.

4 Empirical evidences

The following results are based on data collected from participants in five countries: 281 Belgians (183 women and 98 men), 134 Germans (41 women and 93 men), 99 French (78 women and 21 men), 189 Bosnians belonging to the Serb community (139 women and 50 men), and 313 Serbs (179 women and 134 men). The average age of the students varied between samples, from 20.57 to 24.44 years of age. Few significant gender differences were found in the samples. These samples were therefore considered as a whole.

From a descriptive point of view, the results of the survey have allowed us to identify two groups of countries with special profiles: France and Germany and Bosnia-Herzegovina (Serbian Community) and Serbia. Based on all of the groups surveyed, the profiles of these two groups of countries sit at the extremes of a continuum. French and German participants expressed self-critical reflection on the Great War, whereas Serbian participants, whether citizens of Serbia or Bosnia and Herzegovina, emphasized the "victimized" character of their past.[28] The Belgian sample is characterized by specific representations that do not allow it to be classified in either group. It is therefore analyzed separately from the two main groups of countries.

---

26   See e.g. Liu *et al.* 2005.
27   See Paez *et al.* 2008.
28   See Chaumont 2017.

The results are presented here in four graphs.

Fig. 1: *Perceived responsibility of one's country in triggering the conflict*. Participants from Serbia, a country invaded at the beginning of the conflict, and Bosnia-Herzegovina, formally annexed in 1908 by the Austro-Hungarian Empire, had low perceived levels of responsibility (Figure 1). On the other hand, young Germans, whose country started hostilities on the western front, reported the highest perceived level of responsibility. They were followed by the French, whose perceived level of responsibility in the outbreak of hostilities was the second highest (Figure 1). The case of the French sample is particularly interesting because, although their country was partially invaded by Germany and was forced into a defensive position at the beginning of the war, French students acknowledged that their country had a high level of responsibility for the outbreak of the war. The fact of whether these countries belonged to the Triple Alliance (defeated countries) or the Entente (victorious countries) in the First World War does not appear to have been a determining factor in the representations of responsibility. These observations indicate a high level of recognition of responsibility on the part of the French and the Germans and a low level of recognition of responsibility on the part of young Serbs and Bosnians.

The level of perception of his/her own country's responsibility for the outbreak of war was relatively low in Belgium. Various hypotheses could be advanced to explain this result. One concerns the succession of historical events themselves. Belgium was

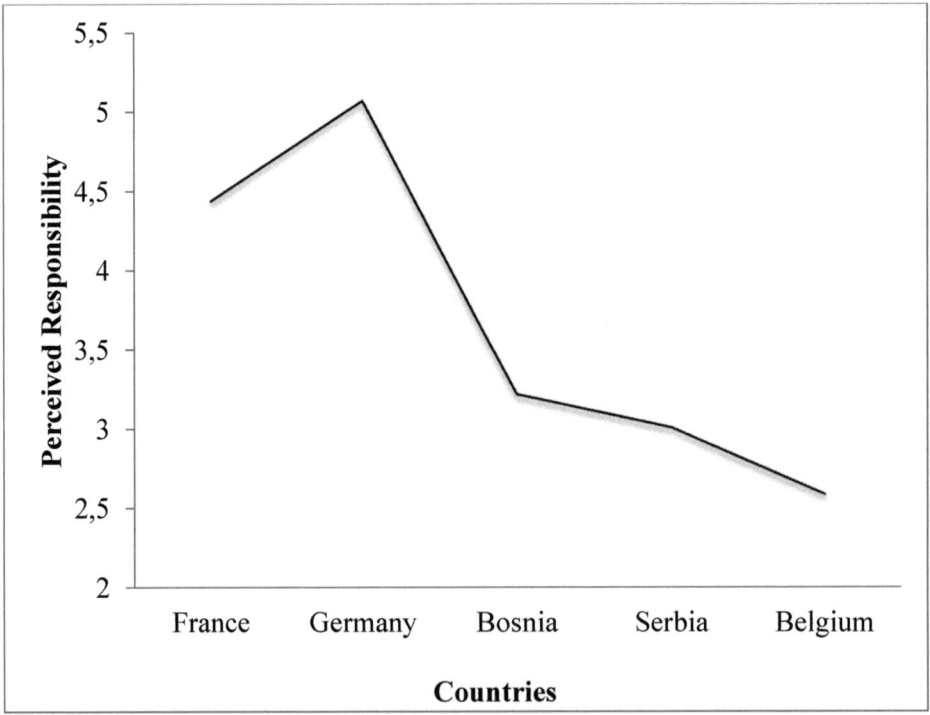

Figure 1: Perceived responsibility of participants' countries in triggering the conflict

invaded in spite of its neutral status, which was supposed to protect it from foreign attack. Another possible reason concerns the development, from the beginning of the war, of a widely shared representation among nations opposed to Germany, namely the need to save the Belgian civilian population. The expression *Poor Little Belgium* widely publicized during the volunteer campaigns in Great Britain and Ireland is particularly revealing from this perspective.

Fig. 2: *Perceived violence of soldiers of participant's country and enemy soldiers.* There is a strong consensus around the perceived level of violence of enemy soldiers during the Great War. This is relatively high in each sample (Figure 2). The most striking feature of Figure 2 is the similarity between French and German representations. Unlike the Serb and Bosnian samples, young French and Germans perceived a relatively similar level of violence of their own soldiers and those of the enemy. Conversely, the Serb and Bosnian-Serb samples are those where the perception gap between the violence of the country's soldiers and the enemy soldiers is greatest. The perception of the degree of violence committed by soldiers seems, as in the previous case, to be unaffected by the formal status of the countries during the war. The Belgian results are situated in between these two cases, although they are a little closer to those obtained in the Western European countries.

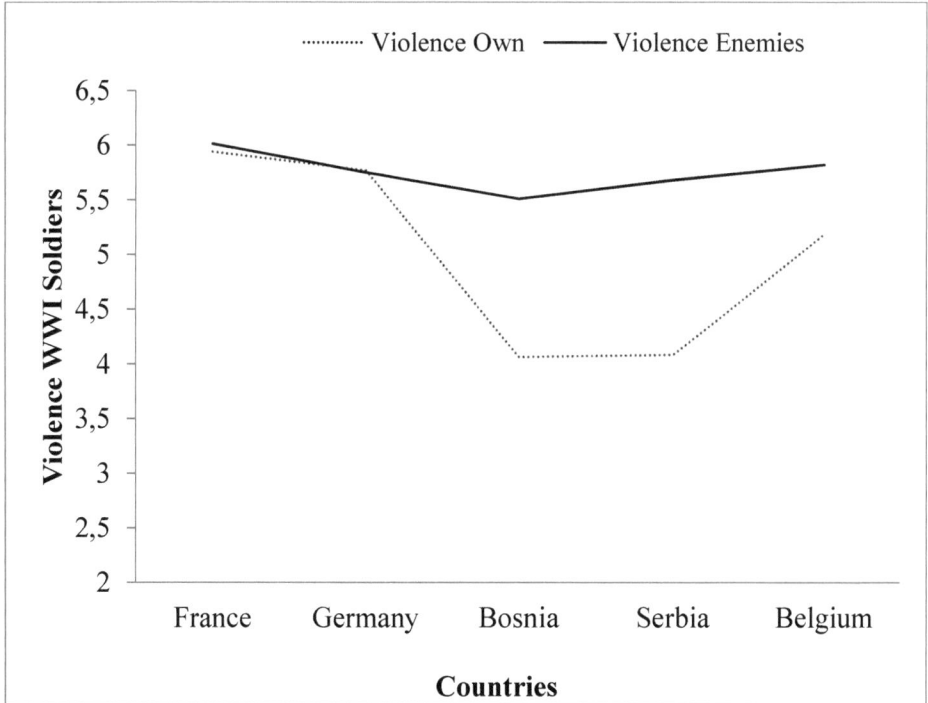

Figure 2: Perceived violence of soldiers of participant's country and enemy soldiers during the First World War

Fig. 3: *Historical collective victimhood and inflicted sufferings.* The level of perceived historical victimization is high in all four samples. What distinguishes them significantly is the recognition of suffering inflicted on enemy countries during the Great War. German and French students again share similar profiles (Figure 3). The former acknowledge that German soldiers inflicted more suffering upon their enemies than what they suffered while the latter acknowledge that French soldiers endured as much suffering as they inflicted. The Serb and Bosnian samples are characterized by a high perception of historical suffering and a relatively low perception of inflicted suffering (Figure 3). The Serbs are distinguished by the lowest level of recognition of suffering inflicted on enemies and the highest level of perceived historical suffering. They are then followed by the Serb speakers of Bosnia-Herzegovina.

Similar to the results obtained from the Balkan countries, although to a lesser extent, the data collected in Belgium shows that survey participants considered the level of suffering endured was higher than that related to the suffering inflicted. In the Belgian case, this representation is coherent with historical facts, as the role of the Belgian army was associated with a form of resistance rather than an aggressive attitude towards the enemies.

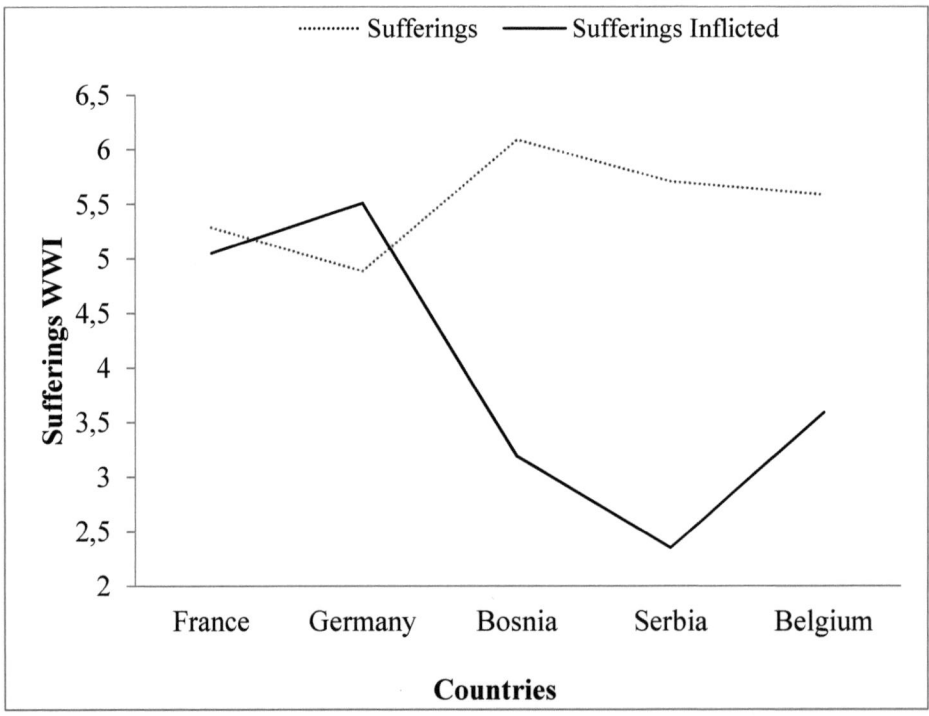

Figure 3: Perceived historical victimization and recognition of the suffering inflicted during the First World War

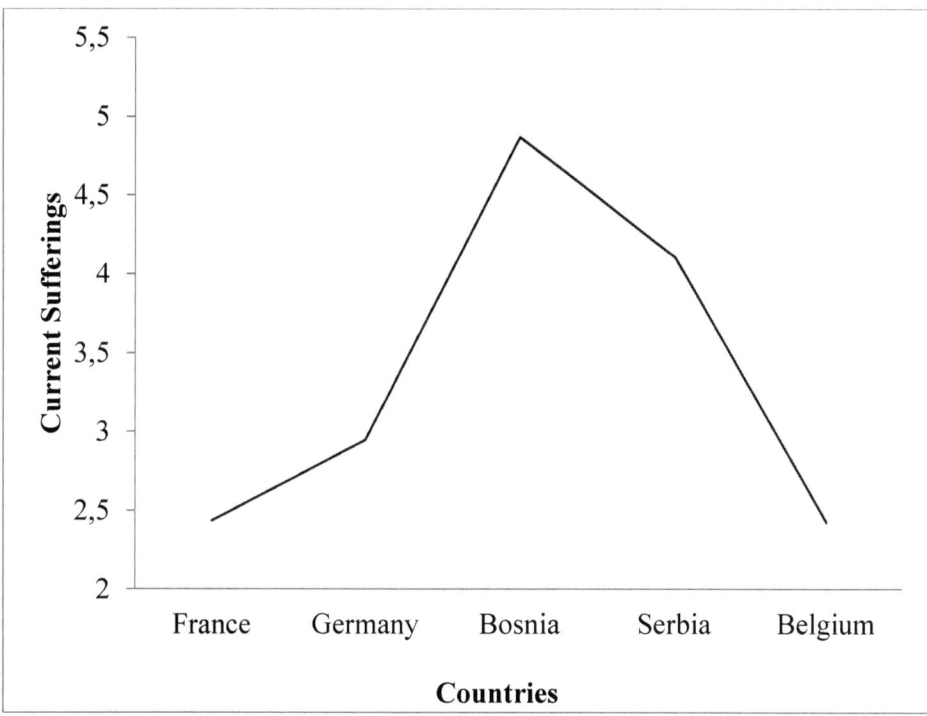

Figure 4: Perceived current victimization in the wake of the First World War

Fig. 4: *Perceived current victimization.* There seems to be significant cultural divergence in the perception of current suffering as a result of the Great War. Here again, young people in Western Europe appear to share a very low and relatively similar perception of suffering. In contrast, participants from Serbia and from Bosnia-Herzegovina are characterized by significantly higher perceptions of current suffering (Figure 4). As with the other variables, the perception of current suffering directly related to war seems to be independent of whether countries belonged to one side or the other during the conflict.

The results collected in Belgium indicate a very low current perception of suffering. There is therefore no reason to conclude that the Belgians interviewed harbor a sense of "victimhood" with regard to the First World War.[29] The events of 1914–1918 are too remote for them. While some testimonies illustrate the enduring, emotional nature of certain Great War memories, it would appear that these memories are linked to specific family events, rather than to a shared representation of a national past that is perceived as fundamentally unfair.[30]

---

29 See Chaumont 2017.
30 Concerning the highly emotional character of certain testimonies, see the documentaries directed by André Dartevelle, *Trois jours d'août 1914. Villages contre l'oubli* and *Les Murs de Dinant* (2013). In each of these documentaries, the director interviews descendants of civil-

At the end of the presentation of these results, it is striking to note the similarities between the representations shared by French and German participants. On both sides of the Rhine, the young people surveyed expressed a form of recognition for the harm their countries had suffered and committed. They recognised their countries as having considerable responsibility for the outbreak of war (1); their soldiers' violence as equivalent to that of enemy soldiers (2); their country's significant responsibility for the suffering inflicted on enemy countries during the war (3); and they felt a very low level of current suffering directly related to the conflict (4).

The contrast with the responses of young Serb speakers from Bosnia-Herzegovina and Serbia is clear. They perceived their country as having little responsibility for the outbreak of war (1); a lower degree of violence committed by their own soldiers than that of enemy soldiers (2); a low level of responsibility for the suffering inflicted on enemy countries during the war (3); and a high level of current suffering directly related to the conflict (4).

These results beg the question as to whether the extent and repetition of the divergences observed between these two sets of countries indicate the existence or absence of political and social memory work. This line of inquiry merits further attention (see below). Of course, the limitations of the survey do not allow us to establish a causal link between memory policies and individual representations.[31] Moreover, the responses provided by survey participants cannot be generalized.

However, they are revealing in at least two respects. First, they reflect the representations of a specific generation – that of students born at the end of the 20th century, more than 80 years after the First World War, and in the case of Serbian participants, in the midst of the Balkan War. Second, the answers gathered confirm how strongly individual memories are determined not only by the realities of the past but also – and above all – by the present context.[32] Worth to ask concerning this matter is how history is taught at school: such a question goes beyond the scope of political science and social psychology to embrace that of pedagogy.

In light of these results, the Belgian case deserves to be studied systematically. Ideally, future analyses should be based on larger samples of French, Dutch and German-speaking respondents. Particular attention could be paid to the specificities of the *bruxellois* in this area. No studies of this magnitude have been conducted to date. Political scientists, historians and social psychologists are only just beginning to examine the special case of German-speaking Belgians.

---

ian victims killed in August 1914. Beyond the documentary's interest in transmitting family memory, it is surprising to note the degree of sadness – and for some, anger – that persists four or five generations after the crimes in the martyrized city of Dinant and the villages in the South of Belgium where men were killed by German soldiers.
31 See Gensburger & Lefranc 2017.
32 Halbwachs 1925. For a comparison between the Franco-German case and that of the Balkans, see Moll 2008.

At this stage, the analysis of the French and German cases presented above sheds some light on the specificities of the Belgian situation. The representations of the Great War within the Belgian State are indeed both influenced by public debates on both sides of the Rhine and affected by the dynamics linked to the construction of Europe. However, the Belgian case seems to retain at least one particularity. Among the events related to the First World War, the major element that continues to raise questions in some villages is the massacre of civilians. It is striking, for example, that some localities, in which the population has changed relatively little, remain uncomfortable with any kind of German participation in First World War commemorations.[33] In the remainder of this chapter, we will focus on analyzing and discussing the main result of this study: the presence of two distinct groups of countries that have wildly differing representations of the world's first global conflict.

5 Analysis: Divergent or incompatible memories?

In his *Confessions*, the antique philosopher and theologian Saint Augustin defines memory as "the present of the past".[34] From this perspective, it is not surprising that survey participants perceived the First World War through the prism of their "present" situation. The Franco-German context of the last few decades is well known. Since the end of the Second World War, particularly from the late 1950s onwards, the relationship between these two countries has been a textbook example of post-conflict rapprochement. In these two nations, a succession of initiatives has been taken within civil society and at official levels to *jointly* re-appropriate the memory of the two world wars.

5.1 The reconciliation of hereditary enemies

For almost a century and a half, the incessant recollection of memories of confrontations had created national histories that were antithetical and ultimately incompatible on both sides of the Rhine. The hostility of the enemy was presented as ancestral and related to the nature of things. The European rapprochement after the Second World War radically challenged this perspective. The progressive construction of the European Community helped to do away with moralizing between the members of its own group and others. "We" no longer referred to a unanimously heroic people, and "others" were no longer stigmatized. And although dialogue between the French and Germans has not been without ambiguities and disagreements, the representatives of the two states have long based their cooperation on the recognition of a common past

---

33 It is the case of the villages of the South of Belgium (Rossignol, Tamines, Tintigny…), which are the topic of Dartevelle's documentary. See above.
34 Saint Augustin 1964, 269.

that "is filled with pride, but also painful regret" (to use the words pronounced by Heinrich Luebke, former President of the Federal Republic of Germany, on September 4 1962). Such an approach has required a new and more complex conception of otherness. The present groups are no longer seen as radically heterogeneous masses without internal conflicts and independent of each other, but as historically linked and reciprocally wounded peoples. In these countries, it is no longer a question of promoting a martyrological or sugar-coated version of the past, but of confronting it in all its complexity.

From the end of the Second World War, there were three successive waves of rapprochement. The first wave was supported by pioneers within the two states, including former prisoners, historians or members of religious associations. From 1950 onwards, there was a second wave based on the work of those who were later known as the founding fathers of Europe (such as Jean Monnet and Robert Schuman) and who launched the European Coal and Steel Community (ECSC) project in order to integrate the Federal Republic of Germany into the West. The third wave of rapprochement took place thanks to the initiative of Charles de Gaulle and Konrad Adenauer.[35] When General de Gaulle returned to power in 1958, the main points of contention between Paris and Bonn disappeared. Internationally, the division of the world between two politico-military blocs led by Washington and Moscow explains why France adopted a radically new European policy. Various factors, such as strategic developments in the nuclear and ballistic missile field, the shock of the Suez crisis and Hungarian crises and the Algerian war, also forced French and Germans to cooperate more closely. In these conditions, de Gaulle renewed his determination to maintain France's position as a significant power on the global stage. From a conception of power based on the maintenance of strong overseas influence, the General gradually shifted to a conception of power built on Franco-German understanding and cooperation. In order to achieve his aims, de Gaulle had to completely revise his stance towards Germany.

During a successful tour of Germany in the summer of 1962, the General ended all his speeches by raising his arms and shouting in the language of Goethe: "Es lebe Deutschland! Es lebe die Deutsch-Französische Freundschaft". Each time, this resounding exaltation of Franco-German friendship was met with wild cheers. One of the most important speeches of this trip was delivered on July 9th in front of young Germans gathered in Ludwigsburg. The General stirred the enthusiasm of his audience by denouncing all forms of collective condemnation and denying any Manichean and simplistic readings of the past. Like the President of the Federal Republic of Germany, Heinrich Luebke, he insisted on the need to distinguish between "bad" and "good" memories of the German people. For him, the great faults of the past could make the world forget that Germany had "spread fruitful waves of thought, science, art and philosophy throughout the world, enriched the universe with innume-

---

35 Grosser 1967.

rable products of its invention, technique and work, and displayed in the works of peace and in the trials of war treasures of courage, discipline and organization".[36]

Never since the Second World War had a foreign statesman eulogized the German nation in such a manner. This attitude of openness on the part of the French officer, who in 1940 had embodied resistance against the occupier, aroused a great deal of emotion in Germany. At the end of his speech, the Minister-President of Baden-Württemberg, Dr. Kiesinger, applauded the general saying: "You have won the hearts of German youth with a single gesture of your hand that erases all the past".[37] At the end of this journey, Charles de Gaulle and Konrad Adenauer could see what Briand and Stresemann had dared not to hope, namely that not only the statesmen, but also that the peoples were united on both sides of the Rhine.[38] Seventeen years after the Second World War, French discourse was no longer centered on revenge, but on "friendship".

Since then, all leaders of the Federal Republic of Germany have insisted on having to confront the darkest episodes of their past, while the French representatives have refused any Manichean reading of the past. In 1962, Charles de Gaulle reminded the French that they too had, "in certain circumstances", inflicted suffering upon the Germans and he stopped in Munich in front of the *Feldherrnhalle* built in memory of the victims of 1870 and 1914–1918.[39]

At the institutional level, the signing of the Elysée Treaty in January 1963 sealed the French and German commitment to one another. The two governments would now consult each other systematically in order to learn how to negotiate and make decisions together. From this point on, their cooperation resulted in biannual meetings held between the two Heads of State and Government, quarterly meetings be-

---

36 Grosser 1967.
37 Quoted in the French newspaper *La Croix* on September 11, 1962. Newspapers coming from all over Europe emphasised the significance of de Gaulle's gesture: "From a psychological point of view, General de Gaulle has had a success which undoubtedly exceeded his own expectations. He gave back to the Germans, many of whom still felt ashamed and humiliated, that priceless asset: self-confidence." (*Le Journal de Genève*, 11 September 1962); "This reconciliation has allowed Western Germany to regain its soul, its honour and confidence" (*Times*, 7 September 1962). Later, the President of the German Parliament, Eugen Gerstenmaier, confirmed the emotion felt by the population as a result of the General's trip: "This gesture was completely unexpected by the German people and its generosity touched deep layers of our history and affectivity that no other person had ever reached before. This was not just a matter of putting an end to the years 1940–1945. Additionally, a two centuries' old debt was all but erased." (Gerstenmaier 1964).
38 In 1926, the French Foreign Minister Aristide Briand and the German Foreign Minister Gustav Stresemann were awarded the Nobel Prize for reconciliation between Germany and France after World War I. Both were convinced that a peace treaty must not lay the foundations for a revanchist war. In 1925, accordingly, they signed an agreement of reconciliation between their two countries in Locarno.
39 Speech pronounced on December 21 1962.

tween foreign ministers and regular meetings between those responsible for defense, education and youth. The Treaty also created the Franco-German Youth Office (OFAJ), whose mission was to encourage stronger relations between young people from France and Germany to improve the image of the youths' home country in the other nation.[40] The same dynamic was adopted at all levels. In the field of historiography, historians on both sides of the Rhine began to write common history textbooks.[41] On the official stage, official representatives systematically recalled the past by softening its initial meaning (the confrontation of hereditary enemies) and by integrating a new meaning (the division of brotherly peoples).[42]

The commemoration of the First World War has been emblematic in this regard. For decades, French and German authorities have avoided describing the enemy soldiers' cruelty in order to consider the sufferings of combatants from both sides in commemorative ceremonies. When François Mitterrand and Helmut Kohl bowed together at the German and French graves of Verdun, their objective was clear: to mark the anniversary of "past battles [that had] definitely passed".[43] The 22nd September 1984 ceremony was a particularly important one for confirming the perpetuation of Franco-German reconciliation. It was, above all, aimed at younger generations. "Symbols are very important for stabilizing historical memory", noted François Mitterrand on the eve of this joint commemoration.[44] Unsurprisingly then, the following day was laden with symbolism. Among the most important symbols were: the image of the French president and the chancellor, shaking hands in front of a coffin covered with the two flags;[45] their act of silent contemplation in front of the imposing stone ossuary which shelters the bones of 130,000 unidentified French and German soldiers; the German military musicians slowly playing *Ich hatte einen Kamaraden* before their French counterparts played *La sonnerie aux morts*; the green and black berets of the French and German soldiers intermingling; the cries of joy of hundreds of children from both countries; and the two heads of state planting of a young maple tree near the ossuary.

---

40 Since then, more than seven million young French and Germans have participated in the exchange program.
41 The process was initiated in the 1920s by the French historian Jules Isaac. The first volume of a Franco-German history textbook was published in 2006 (Klett/Nathan).
42 See Rosoux 2007.
43 May 29, 1984.
44 September 21, 1984.
45 Afterwards, François Mitterrand explained that it (the gesture) was instinctive, without having previously spoken about it with the chancellor, he turned to him: "I extended my hand, his hand was extended at the same time, we sealed Franco-German reconciliation in this visible, sensitive and, believe me, deeply felt way" (30 September 1992). Jacques Attali also confirmed the unexpected and spontaneous nature of this handshake, stating that there was "no need for communication advisors when a real message is to be conveyed" (Attali 1993, 699).

The commemoration of one of the most emblematic battles of the First World War also had a personal dimension for Mitterrand and Kohl. Hans Kohl, the Chancellor's father, fought in the Verdun sector during the First World War. During the Second, Staff Sergeant Mitterrand was wounded in the shoulder. For the French president, this personal dimension was fundamental: "I spent my childhood in families torn apart by war, who cried over the dead and maintained grudges against and sometimes hatred for the former enemy". Hence the importance Mitterrand assigned to transmitting "not hatred, but – on the contrary – the hope of reconciliation".[46] This same impetus was apparent in the joint press release:

> "The war has left our peoples in ruins, in sorrow and in mourning. France and the Republic of Germany have learned from history. Europe is the home of a civilization shared by us all and we are the heirs of European tradition. It is for this reason that the French and German peoples chose to give up fratricidal infighting and work towards a shared future together almost forty years ago. We have reconciled our differences. We have come to understand one another. We have become friends."[47]

Twelve years later, Jacques Chirac struck the same tone when celebrating the 80th anniversary of the Battle of Verdun. The French president reminded some three thousand teenagers that Verdun was the symbol of solidarity and patriotism:

> "The soldier of Verdun, he explains, defended his country as he would defend his family. Engaged in a tragedy that surpassed him, he agreed to play, wherever he was stationed, the role assigned to him by fate."[48]

This message was not only aimed at French youth. It was also addressed to the 700 young Germans who had gathered at Douaumont, emphasizing that France remembers the "two armies" who attempted to destroy one another. It was "on both sides of the front line and regardless of the army in which they served" that troops were bled dry in this "reciprocal attempt at domination".

The messages shared at these diplomatic commemorations may have sought unanimity, but they could not drown out the plurality of Great War memories. For the vast majority of Germans, 11 November was (and still is) neither a holiday nor an occasion for commemoration, as the memory of Nazi crimes has somewhat overshadowed the memory of the 1914–1918 conflict. As historian Rudolf von Thadden argues:

---

46   Speech pronounced on January 17, 1995 at the European Parliament. Retrieved from http://discours.vie-publique.fr/notices/957000600.html
47   Quoted in Rosoux 2007.
48   *La politique étrangère de la France*, July – August 1996, 273–275.

"The French do not consider that their victory on 11 November as a defeat for Germany. November 11 also brought about the Treaty of Versailles, which led to Hitler. There is really nothing for Germany to commemorate [on this day]."[49]

Far from any notion of standardization or homogenization, it is about accepting that there are reasonable disagreements about the reality of the past. The elaboration of a common narrative of the past does not make it possible to erase the differences in approach between the two sides of the Rhine. As the former French Prime Minister Lionel Jospin pointed out, there are still gaps in and misunderstandings of memory that remain "as long as there are Germans and French, as long as our identities are different".[50] From this perspective, the challenge of a sustainable peace can be summed up in one sentence: the existence of tensions and conflicts concerning the interpretation of the past may not lead to contradictory and strictly incompatible visions.

5.2 The separation of brotherly peoples

In comparison to the current relationship between France and Germany, the Balkan framework is a sort of antithesis. Since the end of the wars that devastated the former Yugoslavian republics, the aim of many official speeches has been not to deconstruct or critique national narratives, but to strengthen them. Public references to history are often characterized by an exaltation of the past that identifies the nation as the victim and neighboring States as aggressors. Of course, the objective of these references cannot be reduced to the desire to stir up national and ethnic divisions. For example, in Republika Srpska (Serbia), nationalist radicalization seems above all to play a role in "partisan, intra-Serbian competition".[51] In all cases, the rejection of the other on the basis of past crimes allows elites to maintain their legitimacy and prevent political debate from turning towards socioeconomic issues that are likely to be more problematic for those in power. It is therefore not clear that the influence of such posturing on individual memories is most effective.[52]

Nevertheless, many testimonies confirm the persistence of conflicts, which most often mirror and draw on those of the past. As a Serbian veteran sent to the Sbrenica area in 1995 claimed,

"[…] we Serbs are a proud people who have fought for seven centuries for Europe and the defense of Christianity. We have always been, over the past century, on the side of those who

---

49 *Libération*, 11 November 1998, retrieved from http://www.liberation.fr/evenement/1998/-11/11/l-allemagne-ne-celebre-pas-sa-defaiteschroder-a-refuse-de-faire-commemoration-commune-avec-chirac_253182.
50 Genshagen, 25 September 1999.
51 Jouhanneau 2015.
52 On the limits of nationalist politicization, see Jouhanneau 2016.

fought against fascism."⁵³ This view was largely reinforced by NATO's raids. On 26 March 1999, Milan Panic, president of a democratic coalition of the Serbian opposition, claimed that, as "history has shown", the Serbian people "have a very long memory when they feel they are tims of aggression".⁵⁴

The political use of the past in the lead-up to the conflict has been the subject of much analysis. Here, we just wish to recall the logic underpinning and exacerbating tensions. As early as 1989, Slobodan Milosevic was accompanied by thousands of people to commemorate the 600th anniversary of the battle of Kosovo Polje. This battle symbolized the struggle against the Ottoman armies. It resulted in the defeat of the Serbs, the decapitation of their tsar Lazar and the occupation of their empire for five centuries. Until the restoration of the royal family in the 19th century, this defeat was remembered as a tragedy.⁵⁵

In addition to the bloodshed suffered under the Ottoman occupation, Serbs have clearly not forgotten the wars of liberation, nor the First and Second World Wars either. The detailed description by some Serb representatives of all the cruelties suffered in the past, the television screenings of current affairs films focused on massacres continue to have a profound effect on the population. Relayed in books, conferences and sermons, the discourse of victimhood attempts to reach out to all regions and social strata of the target community.⁵⁶ The objective of this discourse is to encourage Serbs to stand up and right historical wrongs so they might restore their nation. The antagonism which forms the basis of this discourse is expressed in absolute and immutable terms.

The rejection of any possible common understanding of the past has manifested itself throughout successive wars.⁵⁷ Some people talk about *urbicide* and *memorycide*. Urbicide refers to the desire to destroy cities such as Osijek, Vukovar, Zadar, Dubrovnik, Sarajevo and Mostar, whose architecture symbolized the coexistence of styles, civilizations and peoples. *Memorycide* evokes the desire to cut a people off from their past. The destruction of the Sarajevo Library, which houses all of Bosnia's archives, is a salient illustration of this.

However, more than two decades after the signing of the Dayton Accords, which put an end to the war in Bosnia, the representations of the *other* are not entirely stat-

---

53 *Le Monde*, 7 September 2000, retrieved from http://abonnes.lemonde.fr/archives/article/2000/09/07/un-sanctuaire-du-nationalisme-serbe_3709410_1819218.html?xtmc=fascisme&xtcr=1.
54 *Le Soir*, 26 March 1999, retrieved from http://www.lesoir.be/archive/d-19990326-W2WE8K.
55 It is interesting to note that the battle of Kosovo Polje was not a confrontation between Serbs and Turks alone, but a battle between various Balkan peoples – whether Bosnian, Albanian or Romanian – united against the invader. Thus, the battle of Kosovo Polje could have been mobilized to represent the symbol of friendship between the Balkan peoples (see Derens 2000).
56 Thual 1995.
57 In particular, the war in Croatia (1991–1995) and Bosnia and Herzegovina (1992–1995).

ic.⁵⁸ Certainly, some actions have been undertaken in favor of rapprochement. For example, Serbian President Boris Tadic visited Srebrenica in July 2010. A little less than three years later, his successor Tomislav Nikolic asked "on his knees" that "Serbia be forgiven for the crimes committed in Srebrenica".⁵⁹ On 11 July 2015, Serbian Prime Minister Aleksandar Vucic participated in a ceremony to commemorate the 20th anniversary of the massacre. The arguments put forward by the Serbian head of government on this anniversary showed a willingness to strike a reconciliatory tone:

> "It is time to show that we are ready for reconciliation, that we are ready to bow before the victims of others. […].It is the only way for them to begin to respect our victims."⁶⁰

Meanwhile, this process has provoked intense resistance. Tomislav Nikolic is suspected of complying with the instructions of Brussels, which considers reconciliation as a condition for Serbia's accession to the European Union. Aleksandar Vucic was physically targeted by stone throwing during the July 2015 ceremonies and rushed out of commemoration. These tensions recall that while the Serbian authorities may condemn a "heinous crime", they refuse to acknowledge the genocide committed in Srebrenica. According to a survey conducted in Serbia at the time, 54 per cent of respondents condemned what happened in Srebrenica, but 70 per cent of participants denied that it amounted to genocide.⁶¹ These results give an idea of the gap that continues to separate the former belligerents.

These divergent and divisive viewpoints are also found within Bosnia-Herzegovina. Although the Dayton Accords provided for the maintenance of a Bosnian state, the three major ethnic or religious communities in the country – Serb, Croatian and Muslim – now live more or less separately.⁶² In the schools of the three communities, history courses reject the very notion of common history. Schoolchildren learn that the other was the aggressor and that the other still is the enemy. As a consequence, Gavrilo Princip – the Bosnian Serb who killed Archduke Franz Ferdinand in 1914 – is a Serbian hero, whereas for Bosnians, who do not perceive the Austro-Hungarian

---

58 See Pingel 2009.
59 Interview on Bosnian television BHT (quoted in *Le Monde*, 25 April 2013, retrieved from http://abonnes.lemonde.fr/europe/article/2013/04/25/le-president-serbe-demande-par don-a-genoux-pour-le-massacre-de-srebrenica_3166633_3214.html?xtmc=srebrenica&xt cr=1). From 11 to 13 July 1995, 8,000 Bosnian Muslim men and teenagers were killed by Bosnian-Serbian soldiers commanded by General Mladic.
60 *Le Monde*, 8 July 2015, retrieved from http://abonnes.lemonde.fr/europe/article/ 2015/07/08/le-premier-ministre-serbe-ira-a-srebrenica-pour-le-20e-anniversaire-du-genocide_4674713_3214.html?xtmc=srebrenica&xtcr=3.
61 Quoted in *Le Monde*, 8 July 2015, retrieved from http://abonnes.lemonde.fr/europe/arti cle/2015/07/08/le-premier-ministre-serbe-ira-a-srebrenica-pour-le-20e-anniversaire-du-genocide_4674713_3214.html?xtmc=srebrenica&xtcr=3.
62 Bessone 2014.

Empire as an occupier, he is an assassin.[63] An author of history textbooks in Bosnia-Herzegovina has pointed out that there is a great deal of emphasis on the "genocide of Bosnians by the Chetniks during the Second World War" in new texts.[64] Conversely, in a Serbian elementary school in Sarajevo, the corridors are adorned with portraits of the great Serbian national and religious heroes. These courses are conceived as a "return to basics" for students throughout all three communities.

Serbian schoolchildren are taught that in the first Yugoslavia (1918), Croats and Slovenes did not get along with the Serbs and that after 1945, the Serbs' domination over these people increased. On the other hand, Croatian schoolchildren learn that their forebears could not hold leadership positions in Soviet Yugoslavia, the ruling regime of which implicitly accused them of being enemies of the people because of the crimes committed by the Ustaše.[65] Everywhere the same claims are repeated. Each group is stigmatized, if not persecuted. School teaching confirms the outcomes on the battlefields. Serbs seek to forget the events that Croats and Bosnian Muslims want to commemorate, and vice versa. And, if by chance, two parties remember the same event, it is glorious for one, and humiliating for the other. Beyond these disparities, there is a common goal: to erase all positive memories of Yugoslavia and coexistence between people of different nationalities.

Given this context, the results of the survey that we conducted in the Cost project *Social Psychological Dynamics of Historical Representations in the Enlarged European Union* are not all that surprising. They show how much the suffering associated with the First World War appears to resonate with that caused by subsequent wars. Without seeking to establish a strict causality, it is difficult not to link these results to the posture adopted by many Serbian officials (whether in Serbia or Bosnia-Herzegovina). The debates triggered by the commemoration of the First World War's centenary in Bosnia-Herzegovina demonstrate the emotionally charged and highly contested nature of memory in the Balkans.

6 Conclusion

The main objective of this chapter was to shed light on a problem which is located at the crossroads of several disciplines and rarely addressed in political science, namely the measurement of the possible impact of memory work carried out at social and political levels. The contrasting results of the survey showed that there were two very specific types of profiles among the participants. Each of them symbolically illustrates the range as well as the limits of reconciliatory ethics.

---

63   See Uzelac 1997, 37–38. The commemorations held in Andricgrad in June 2014 confirm this phenomenon.
64   Igric 1998.
65   Igric 1998.

On the one hand, French and German participants demonstrated a willingness to accept historical responsibility for crimes committed during the First World War. On the other, Serb-speaking participants (whether they resided in Serbia or Bosnia-Herzegovina) put more emphasis on crimes suffered during that same war. Faced with this contrast, the objective of this chapter was not to assess the more or less legitimate nature of the representations observed in a prescriptive manner; it was to reflect on the commemorative frameworks specific to the two identified cases.

The examination of these respective frameworks recalls the pragmatic nature of memory work. Such a process should not be seen as a normative model that can be applied in all circumstances. Like the accentuation of victimization or a glorious past, it constitutes one strategy among others. Its suitability depends on precise political and socio-economic conditions. The analyses carried out so far show that only the memory work which is perceived as beneficial by all protagonists is likely to be carried out successfully. It is only when cooperation guarantees the interests of each protagonist that it is advocated for on both sides of the former front line. Chancellor Adenauer neatly summed up the mechanism at stake in the Franco-German case:

> "Interest alone is the only thing that defines a country's foreign policy, not love or hatred, which can also play a role. It is the interest which is the decisive factor, and, thank God, (…) the interest of France coincides with that of Germany."[66]

Faced with a common enemy – the Union of Soviet Socialist Republics (USSR) –, French and Germans gradually chose to emphasise the plurality of Great War experiences. This development, however inspiring it may be, cannot be considered as a model for all post-conflict situations. Many authors and practitioners have highlighted the political, economic and sociological differences that distinguish the Franco-German context from that of the Balkans. The survey on which this reflection is based emphasizes those differences concerning representations of the past. Three points in particular deserve further emphasis.

Firstly, the two case studies are considerably different in terms of temporality. The Franco-German evolution allows us to reflect on the transformation of relations between former enemies in the long term. More than 70 years have passed since the end of hostilities between the two countries. In this time, initiatives at all levels, from schoolchildren and students' exchanges to joint ministerial meetings, have tended to replace confrontation with negotiation. They show that the work of memory after a war is not counted in years but in generations. Conversely, only twenty years separate the citizens of Serbia and Bosnia-Herzegovina from the fighting in the Balkans. In other words, only a single generation. From this point of view, the resistance to a historically and/or politically correct view of the past is hardly surprising.

Secondly, the uses of the past that characterize the official stage are radically different. French, German – and to a large extent Belgian representatives – refer to the

---

66 Quoted in Rosoux 2007.

past in order to underline what binds their people together, whereas Serbian spokespersons place their emphasis on sources of the past that demonstrate inevitable division.[67] Most of the representations of the past conveyed in the countries that once made up Yugoslavia take the form of a martyrological or glorious epic. This portrayal of the past, once common on both sides of the Rhine, is now inconceivable in Paris, Berlin or Brussels.

Thirdly, representations of the past reveal divergent identity processes. Beyond the Franco-German case, most western European leaders and populations take part in the slow – and never-ending – adjustment of their memories. This development is not a question of integration or homogenization, but a progressive and common "emplotment" of memories.[68] In this regard, Belgium is not an exception. The major trends are quite similar with those that characterize the French case. In the Balkans, the dynamics appear to have been reversed. Shattered by a violent fragmentation of memories, the shared past of a united Yugoslavia has been lost. A good example of the contraction or shrinking of identities in the region is the creation of the Federation of Bosnia-Herzegovina.

Behind each representation of the past is a representation of the *other* (designated as an ancient enemy or as a current threat). Behind each representation of the other is a representation of oneself (repentant or victim, victor or defeated). These roles form the base of a given group's identity. The transition from one to the other is, as a consequence, hardly self-evident. When former French Prime Minister Lionel Jospin declared that "a nation always wins by looking clearly at its past, including its darkest hours",[69] he not only invited French citizens but also neighboring states to confront "historical myths with real history".[70] The responses of French and Germans survey participants show that such a mentality does indeed have an impact on how people perceive the past. Faced with these results, our task remains immense: to get rid of a prescriptive – and often condescending – approach in order to refine the questions and keep thinking in a reflexive way.

The fruitful results of our research demonstrate the importance of promoting an approach that draws on a range of disciplines – in the present case, mainly social psychology and political science –, which are seldom associated with one another. Such an approach is crucial in revealing currently under-analyzed areas of research. At the same time, these research prospects require complementary methodological tools. We will mention just three here. Qualitative interviews have the potential to delineate as finely as possible the narratives chosen by each study group. It would also be useful

---

67 This study shows that further research is still needed. The Belgian case, in particular, is of interest. The attitude of Belgian representatives varies according to the period and the evolving institutional structures of the State.
68 Ricœur 1983.
69 Jospin 1998.
70 Jospin 1998.

to conduct surveys on other segments of the population. Representations of the past shared by individuals who are not confined to the student world would raise questions about the influence of factors such as generational affiliation, regional anchoring (which includes the question of the possible division between urban and rural areas), as well as the socio-economic characteristics of the groups observed. If previous research has shown that there are indeed discrepancies due to these factors, it is still necessary to identify and understand them. Finally, it would be interesting to cross-check these results with those from studies devoted to memory frameworks in order to understand the specific influence of each memory vector on individual representations (here we are not only thinking about official speeches or school textbooks, but also of stories relayed within families, on social networks or through the media). As daunting as it is, future research in this field will be an exciting and inspiring challenge.

References

Assmann, A. & Conrad, S. (2010). *Memory in a Global Age: Discourses, Practices and Trajectories*. Basingstoke: Palgrave Macmillan.
Attali, J. (1993). *Verbatim, I*. Paris: Fayard.
Audoin-Rouzeau, S. & Becker, A. (2000). *14–18, retrouver la guerre*. Paris: Gallimard.
Bar-Tal, D., Chernyak-Hai, L., Schori, N. & Gundar, A. (2009). A Sense of Self-perceived Collective Victimhood in Intractable Conflicts. *International Review of the Red Cross*, 91 (874), 229–258.
Barkan, E. (2000). *The Guilt of Nations: Restitution and Negotiating Historical Injustices*. New York: W.W. Norton.
Bell, D. (2010). *Memory, Trauma and World Politics: Reflections on the Relationship between Past and Present*. Basingstoke: Palgrave Macmillan.
Bessone, M. (2014). La réconciliation par l'histoire en Bosnie-Herzégovine. L'impossible réception d'un modèle multiculturel européen. *Revue d'études comparatives Est-Ouest*, 45(3-4), 149–175.
Brooks, R. (1999). *When Sorry isn't enough: The Controversy over Apologies and Reparations for Human Injustice*. New York: New York University Press.
Chaumont, J.-M. (2017). *La concurrence des victimes: génocide, identité, reconnaissance*. Paris: La Découverte.
Derens, J. A. (2000). *Balkans: la crise*. Paris: Gallimard.
Duroy, O. (2012). *L'hiver des hommes*. Paris: Julliard.
Ferry, J.-M. (1996). *L'éthique reconstructive*. Paris: Cerf.
Foong Khong, Y. (1992). *Analogies at War: Korea, Munich, Dien Bien Phu, and the Vietnam Decisions of 1965*. Princeton: Princeton University Press.
Grosser, A. (1967). *Die Bundesrepublik Deutschland: Bilanz einer Entwicklung (Vortrag)*. Tübingen: Rainer Wunderlich Verlag.
Gensburger, S. & Lefranc, S. (2017). *À quoi servent les politiques de mémoire*. Paris: Presses de Sciences Po.

Gerstenmaier, E. (1964). L'influence de la France sur le sentiment national en Allemagne. *Articles et documents.* 1606, 2.

Halbwachs, M. (1950/1980). *The collective memory.* New York: Harper Colophon Books.

Halbwachs, M. (1925/2013). *Les cadres sociaux de la mémoire.* Paris: Albin Michel.

Igric, G. (1998). "Relectures de l'histoire yougoslave". *Manière de voir,* 40, 30–32.

Irwin-Zarecka, I. (1996). "Neutralising the Past", *Peace Review,* 8 (2), 273–274.

Irwin-Zarecka, I. (2017). *Frames of Remembrance: The Dynamics of Collective Memory.* London: Routledge.

Jospin, L. (1998). Discours du 28 novembre 1998 devant le CRIF – Conseil représentatif des institutions juives de France.

Jouhanneau, C. (2015). La 'société civile' entre protestation et prestations. Organisations de victimes, compétition partisane et néo-corporatisme en Bosnie-Herzégovine. *Politix,* 110 (2), 85–110.

Jouhanneau, C. (2016). *Sortir de la guerre en Bosnie-Herzégovine. Une sociologie politique du témoignage et de la civilité.* Paris: Khartala.

Kritz, N. (1995). *Transitional Justice: How Emerging Democracies Reckon with Former Regimes.* Washington DC: United States Institute of Peace.

Krondorfer, B. (1995). *Remembrance and Reconciliation: Encounters between Young Jews and Germans.* New Haven, CN: Yale University Press.

Langenbacher, E. & Shain, Y. (2010). *Power of the Past. Collective Memory and International Relations.* Washington DC: Georgetown University Press.

Lavabre, M.-C. (1994). *Le fil rouge, sociologie de la mémoire communiste.* Paris: Presses de la Fondation nationale des sciences politiques.

Lavabre, M.-C. (2001). Peut-on agir sur la mémoire? *Les cahiers français,* 303, 1–13.

Lefranc, S. (2002). *Les politiques du pardon.* Paris: Presses de Sciences Po.

Lind, J. (2008). *Sorry States: Apologies in International Politics.* Ithaca: Cornell University Press.

Liu, J. H., Goldstein-Hawes, R., Hilton, D. J., Huang, L. L., Gastardo-Conaco, C., Dresler-Hawke, E., Pittolo, F., Hong, Y. Y., Ward, C., Abraham, S., Kashima, Y., Kashima, E., Ohashi, M., Yuki, M. & Hidaka, Y. (2005). Social Representations of Events and People in World History across 12 Cultures. *Journal of Cross-Cultural Psychology,* 36 (2), 171–191.

Margry, P. J. & Sánchez-Carretero, C. (2011). *Grassroots Memorials: The Politics of Memorializing Traumatic Death.* New York: Berghahn Books.

May, E. (1975). *'Lessons' of the Past: the Use and Misuse of History in American Foreign Policy.* Oxford: Oxford University Press.

Moll, N. (2008). La réconciliation franco-allemande et les Balkans: une motivation, pas un modèle. *L'Europe en formation,* 3, 3–54.

Olick, J. K. (1999). Genre Memories and Memory Genres: A Dialogical Analysis of May 8, 1945 Commemorations in the Federal Republic of Germany. *American Sociological Review,* 64 (3), 381–402.

Olick, J. K. (2003). *States of Memory: Continuities, Conflict and Transformations in National Retrospection.* Durham: Duke University Press.

Paez, D., Liu, J. H., Techio, E., Slawuta, P., Zlobina, A. & Cabecinhas, R. (2008). "Remembering" World War II and Willingness to Fight Sociocultural Factors in the Social Representation of Historical Warfare across 22 Societies. *Journal of Cross-Cultural Psychology,* 39 (4), 373–380.

Pingel, F. (2009). From Ownership to Intervention – or Vice Versa? Textbook Revision in Bosnia and Herzegovina. In Dimoun A. (Ed.), *Transition and the Politics of History Education in Southeastern Europe.* Göttingen: Vandenhoek & Ruprecht.

Ricœur, P. (1983). *Temps et récit, I*. Paris: Seuil.
Ricœur, P. (1992). "Quel ethos nouveau pour l'Europe?". In Koslowski, P. (Ed.), *Imaginer l'Europe. Le marché intérieur européen, tâche culturelle et économique*. Paris: Cerf.
Ricœur, P. (1998). "La crise de la conscience historique et l'Europe". In Lopes Alvez, J. (dir.), *Etica e o Futuro da Democraticia*. Lisboa: Edicoes Colibri.
Ricœur, P. (2000). *La mémoire, l'histoire, l'oubli*. Paris: Seuil.
Rosoux, V. (2001). *Les usages de la mémoire dans les relations internationales*. Bruxelles: Bruylant.
Rosoux, V. (2007). La réconciliation franco-allemande: crédibilité et exemplarité d'un "couple à toute épreuve"? *Cahiers d'histoire. Revue d'histoire critique*, 100, 23–36.
Saint Augustin (1964). *Les confessions*. Paris: Garnier-Flammarion.
Tambiah, S. J. (1986). *Sri Lanka: Ethnic Fratricide and the Dismantling of Democracy*. New York: IB Tauris.
Thual, F. (1995). *Les conflits identitaires*. Paris: Ellipses.
Uzelac, A. (1997). Apprendre aux petits Bosniaques que leur voisin est un ennemi. *Gazeta Wyborcza – Courrier International*, 325, 23–29 January.
Zerubavel, E. (2003). *Time Maps: Collective Memory and the Social Shape of the Past*. Chicago: University of Chigaco Press.

Part III
**The Centenary of the First World War in Belgium:
Commemorations and Memory Dynamics**

Chantal Kesteloot and Laurence van Ypersele

The Commemorations of the First World War as Seen through Postage Stamps[1]

1 Introduction

The First World War left deep impressions on the histories of many societies. From the beginning, it has also been the subject of an unprecedented number of commemorations, which have changed dramatically over the decades. Seen as a whole, they allow us to understand and analyse the memories which societies have kept of this conflict. These memories are the result of lived experience and the transmission thereof, on the one hand, and of the policies of commemoration that States put in place, on the other.

Among the methods of commemoration undertaken by public authorities, there is one which has, until very recently, barely garnered the attention of researchers: postage stamps. In 2016, two French researchers attempted to fill in that gap. *Timbres en guerre. Les mémoires des deux conflits mondiaux* ('Stamps at War: The Memories of the Two World Wars') aims to consider how the postage stamp has been able to contribute 'to sustaining and forming memory' worldwide from 1914 to the present, while adding that the postage stamp itself 'also feeds on the state of memory at the moment when it was conceived'.[2] More so than other methods of commemoration, the widespread distribution of the postage stamp as well as its status as a form of 'official' language, submitted to regulations, makes it worthwhile to spend time looking at it.[3] Postage stamps, like banknotes and coins, are essentially objects used on a daily basis: 'nothing else comes between everyone's hands so often'[4]. It emerges thus as a reflection of the policies of memory undertaken by public authorities, in this case, the post office. It too is susceptible to being used by everyone.

The development of the stamp happens alongside that of mass communication and society based around the written word. It therefore becomes a banal object. It is precisely in this banality where the interest lies.[5] The post became an essential form

---

1 Translation: David Hensley.
2 Croix and Guyvarc'h 2016, 16.
3 Besides the aforementioned book, see Schwarzenbach 1999 and Parker 2015. Similar studies have been undertaken in other countries. See especially Wallach 2010, Raento & Brunn 2005 or Aupiais 2014.
4 Banque nationale de Belgique 1991, 7.
5 On this question of 'banal nationalism', see Billig 1995.

of communication which would go hand-in-hand with the whole 20th century, before facing competition from the telephone at first, followed by the internet. We need to admit that in 2018, the stamp has lost much of its lustre and its ubiquity, while, perhaps paradoxically, the number of stamps produced has never been higher. We will get back to this.

In the wake of this large-scale international research, it seemed to be a good opportunity to return to the Belgian case. If Belgium is certainly not absent from the book *Timbres en guerre*, it nevertheless seems legitimate to consider this national approach in its uniqueness, and in more detail than possible in a general survey. We will look back at some of the observations made on the international level and we will see to what extent Belgian stamp production reflects these observations or, to the contrary, differs from them, which will lead us to concentrate on what makes the Belgian case unique.

The goal of this chapter is to analyse the iconography of the First World War as seen through postage stamps, beginning with stamp production during the war itself. What kind of representation is conveyed via the postage stamp? Is this representation part of a general pattern, or can we find traces of more specific developments? What place does King Albert I occupy in this representation, given how much stamps have contributed to popularising the image of the royal family since their first appearance? Were certain stamps the subject of debate, even polemics? We have in mind especially the question of Eupen-Malmedy and the stamps that followed the annexation of this region by Belgium after the First World War. We will also try to understand the decision-making process in regard to putting stamps into circulation, and to get at the always difficult question of these stamps' reception. Let us say upfront that these two dimensions remain very difficult to talk about in detail, as the archival record is so poor.[6] How can we measure them? Using which parameters? To which criteria does the production of stamps respond? Who makes decisions about this production? Is the production strictly determined by political forces, or can we also consider the stamp as a commercial product, the visual appeal of which is supposed to contribute to its success? And to what extent is there an educational aspect? In the context of the commemoration of the 100th anniversary of the Great War, in Belgium and elsewhere, the production of stamps has exploded at the same time that the sending of letters has become rarer. We can therefore also ask why this has happened.

---

6   The closure of the Postal Museum in 2003 was followed by the dispersal of its collection and archives. Some documents may be consulted on the premises of the printing press of the B-Post in Mechelen. Others (including some of the documents to which Alexis Schwarzenbach was able to get access) have not been found. Recently, a new inventory (Jacquemin 2018) of what has been able to be collected by the State Archives has been published. Unfortunately, it seems more and more likely that we will have to come to accept the irreversible loss of some documents.

2 The first stamps

Introduced in Belgium in 1849, the image on the front of the stamp served first of all as a way to represent the Belgian monarchy. From 1849 to 1866, only one portrait of Leopold I in three-quarter view was in circulation. From the latter date on, different versions of a small Belgian lion also appeared. The first stamps were monolingually French. It took until 1891 for the issuance of the first stamps with bilingual inscriptions. In 1894 a series commemorating Belgium appeared for the occasion of the International Exposition of Antwerp. Afterwards, this kind of event provided the material for numerous printings. For the first time, a pressure group, the *Anvers en Avant* ('Antwerp First') league, asked the Post Office for and received the issuance of specific stamps acting as promotional material for a future event.[7]

Until the First World War, no stamp made reference to traumatic events. In this regard, as in others, the conflict was a point of rupture. The phenomenon spilled over national borders. The stamp became 'a document' and, as such, it was the reflection of 'the extraordinary period which the entire world [was] going through'.[8] The stamp was used 'in and for the war'.[9]

3 Who decides?

Decisions regarding the choice of images were the responsibility of the minister in charge of the administration of the Post Office. Since 1879, there had been a *Commission des timbres postaux et télégraphiques* ('Commission of postal and telegraphic stamps'). Its role remains poorly known, but its aim was above all to improve the artistic quality of stamps and to fight against counterfeiting.[10] It was not, therefore, a body whose remit included interfering in the choice of the themes of imagery.

Quite obviously, from the beginning the monarchy paid particular attention to its image as conveyed via stamps; its intervention is difficult to trace, though. It is clear that the approval of the royal family was necessary when they were represented.[11] But did they go further, as far as to suggest certain images? The question remains open. According to Alexis Schwarzenbach, from 1936 onwards, not only was the approval

---

7   Schwarzenbach 1999, 74.
8   'Timbres de guerre' (*Le Temps*, 18 Februar1916, 3).
9   Croix and Guyvarc'h 2016, 35.
10 Schwarzenbach 1999, 49 ff.
11 'It is these considerations which cause me to submit for Your Majesty's assent the attach draft project for a stamp, the drawing of which is inspired by the first Belgian stamp, printed with the effigy of Leopold I', letter of the Minister of Railways to the King, 9 May 1919 (concerning the 'Liberation' postage stamp project), Archives of the Post Office.

of the royal family required, but they had to be informed ahead of time of each plan for an issue of stamps including a theme that was connected to them.[12]

Until 1928, the minister and his administration were the only persons responsible for the design of stamps. In this year, the Philatelic Commission was formed. It was presided over by the director-general of the Post Office, in addition to four members with qualifications regarding stamps. But originally, it had the mission to classify and conserve the collection of Belgian and foreign postage stamps that the Belgian Post Office possesses. It does not seem, then, that the commission weighed in on the content of particular issues of stamps.[13] Each issue was the subject of a royal or ministerial decree. These decrees contained the date of the issue, the print run, the face value and a brief description of the stamp in question. On the other hand, there was no information as to the decision-making process or the least reference to the Philatelic Commission. It was only from 1951 that the function of the Commission would evolve and it would be called on to give its opinion about the proposals for stamps given by the minister.[14] Originally made up of employees of the postal administration, the Commission opened to exterior members in 1956. Their number kept growing: 10 in 1954 and 14 in 1956.

Today, the Philatelic Commission is composed of representatives of B-Post, of scholars, and of stamp specialists. Besides the president, it has 12 members. Its mission consists of drawing up an annual calendar of stamp issues. The proposed program is then approved by the appropriate minister and published in the *Moniteur belge*, the official government publication of laws and decrees.

4 Stamps in wartime

A little under 3000 different designs of stamps were printed worldwide between 1914 and 1918: 400 of them, that is around 15 %, had the war as their subject.[15] It was the first time that an event of international dimensions had such an impact on the production of stamps. The reasons are obvious, given the importance of the conflict. It was also the first time that stamps themselves participated in the war effort, both through the surcharge system which allowed for the collection of funds and through messages which supported wartime propaganda.[16]

The position of the stamp during wartime is all the more important because this extraordinary event provoked an unprecedented amount of letter-writing.[17] While in

---

12 Schwarzenbach 1999, 125.
13 See the Royal Decree of 1 October 1928.
14 See the Royal Decree of 21 November 1951.
15 Croix and Guyvarc'h 2016, 39.
16 Schwarzenbach 1999, 104.
17 See Trévisan 2003, Pignot 2006, Vidal-Naquet 2006, Hanna 2006, Prochasson 2008. Vidal-Naquet 2009.

the 19th century maintaining correspondence was the prerogative of an aristocratic and bourgeois elite, suddenly tens of millions of men and women took up their pens to keep family ties strong, to wipe out the distance between those at the front and those behind the lines, to stay present when one could not be there in person and to affirm one's existence in this universe of death. So, over the course of four years, for the first time, millions of letters and postcards were exchanged on a daily basis, written by individuals from every stratum of society.[18] The stamp therefore appeared on private, intimate messages as the extension of a discourse which the belligerents wanted to promote, at the same time that the daily lives of all citizens – under arms or not – were dominated by the ongoing conflict.

It was not a surprise, then, when the German occupiers imposed their own stamps in occupied Belgium from 1 October 1914.[19] The whole postal sector was subjected to sustained attention on the part of the Germans, with specific guidelines for both the General Government, the area of occupied Belgium with a full-fledged bureaucracy, and the *Etappengebiet* ('staging area' or 'rear area'), the area of occupied Belgium subject to tighter military oversight.[20] At the same time, the occupying power confiscated the Belgian stamps in circulation. The German stamps that were imposed were overprinted with *Belgien*. Their value was given in German marks and Belgian francs. They showed different allegories of German unity. They seemed to be one of the signs of the Germans' total occupation of the territory, where every aspect of everyday life was dominated by the realities of wartime. After the introduction of administrative separation, the occupying power tried to push things even further, wanting to overprint a certain number of stamps with *Flandern (i.e. Flanders)* and *Wallonien (i.e. Wallonia)*. However, were these really used, or did this stall at the planning stage? The question remains open.[21]

On the other hand, in the small part of Belgium that remained free, it was most certainly those Belgian stamps that were in circulation in 1914 which continued to be used. On 3 October 1914, two stamps were even issued before the almost complete occupation of Belgium. The first was dedicated to the Mérode Monument, an allusion to Count Frédéric de Mérode, a hero of the Belgian Revolution of 1830. Given the complex process of manufacturing and the launch date, the decision to print it was taken before the conflict.[22] It seems to have been connected to the reactions towards the first stamp issued with a portrait of King Albert in 1912. This latter stamp was

---

18 "One of the most powerful vectors for the maintenance of family ties was letter-writing. One estimates that in the order of two billion letters were exchanged between families at home and men in uniform during the conflict. That figure is probably an underestimate. The epistolary history of the war has yet to be written, but it includes parcels, objects, letters and postcards of all shapes and kinds" (Winter 2014, 52).
19 See Van der Mullen 2008.
20 See Van der Mullen 2011.
21 See Stes 2001, 782–83.
22 Retrieved from http://www.postzegelsdemerode.be/FR/inhoudsopgave.html

typically judged to be of mediocre quality, with a rather disappointing representation of the sovereign. A new series of twelve stamps had been under consideration. Among these, nine were supposed to represent the king – the most common denominations, from 1 to 40 centimes; one of the nine was supposed to represent the monarchy as a whole, with King Albert in a medallion surrounded by Leopold I and Leopold II. The three other stamps were supposed to be dedicated to the colonisation of the Congo, the opening of the Scheldt, and finally national independence, with the evocation of the death of Frédéric de Mérode. These stamps were almost ready when the declaration of war intervened. The printing of October 1914 therefore took place in a very distinct context. The message seems to have been directed at the German invader. Belgium does not intend to capitulate: it will prove itself worthy of the patriots of 1830 and defend its independence. This message could be immediately deployed in the context of the war, though as it happened it predated the war.

The other stamp issued from Antwerp had the king as its subject and seemed to complement the message: the sovereign continues the struggle. Here again, the project preceded the outbreak of the war. But the two stamps complement one another. The one representing the Mérode Monument roots Belgium in the past and in tradition while that of the king, represented in three-quarter view, facing right, is turned toward the future. This new stamp had been created by John MacDonald, with whom the postal administration signed an agreement in February 1914. The goal of the agreement was two-fold: MacDonald was to introduce a new machine that used intaglio procedures; as a graphic designer, he was charged with developing a new series of stamps with the royal portrait.

The fall of Antwerp had the consequence of shutting down printing. The original print runs, anticipated at 75,000 copies for the denominations of 20 and 40 centimes and 600,000 copies for those of 5 and 10 centimes, were never reached.[23] Nevertheless, sheets were sent out to the part of the country that had not yet been invaded, the provinces of East and West Flanders, and some of the stock was sent to the government *en route* to Le Havre. The royal portrait stamp of 1914 was very popular. It came in denominations of 5 to 20 centimes and was in circulation until 1920, in different forms: sometimes monocolour, sometimes bicolour.[24] These stamps of King Albert were also the first to be sold with a surcharge to benefit the Red Cross.[25]

Actually, the first stamps of the Belgian Post Office with any kind of surcharge date from 1910 and were issued to benefit the *Œuvre Nationale Belge de Défense contre*

---

23 The Mérode stamp was to have had 24,000 copies printed at the face value of 5 centimes, 30,000 at 10 centimes, and 12,000 at 20 centimes. See Toulieff, *Série Monument de Mérode*. Retrieved from http://postzegelsdemerode.be/NL/toulieff.html.

24 Created in October 1914, it was printed in Antwerp (Mechelen being occupied by the Germans). This issue only lasted for a few days, but it was taken back up by the government in Le Havre in 1915 and printed in Paris and London. See Bouckaert 1934.

25 Likewise, in France, the first stamps with a surcharge to benefit the Red Cross date from 18 August 1914. See Aupiais 2014, 2.

la Tuberculose ('Belgian National Charity for Fighting Tuberculosis').[26] The war would popularise this practice of adding a surcharge. Throughout the conflict, most belligerents, on either side, had recourse to such surcharges.[27] This approach was part of the cultures of war which presented the conflict as the incarnation of the struggle of Right and Justice against Barbarism.[28] The printing of these two stamps by the Verscheuren firm in Antwerp – the print shops in Mechelen were already out of service – could only take place for a few days, being suspended because of the advance of the German army. In theory, all the plates were supposed to have been destroyed, which was not the case. The Verscheuren print shop printed new sheets between March 1915 and October 1916. The two stamps were the subject of large-scale counterfeiting – more than 100,000 series of stamps were seized in 1920. This offence was brought before the courts. The case was closed in April 1926: only a fine was imposed, as the State had not been adversely affected.[29]

Starting in January 1915, the government-in-exile in Le Havre (in France) issued a new series of stamps which circulated in the small part of Belgian territory that remained free and that was confronted with a lack of stamps. A Belgian post office was opened at Sainte-Adresse (also in France) on 18 October 1914.[30] During the invasion, the German seized the available stock of stamps. Did they sell them to neutral countries, did they simply hold on to them? The question remains open. In reaction, the Belgian government in Le Havre decided to suspend their validity by way of a Royal Decree of 15 September 1915 – including the two series printed in Antwerp in October 1914 – 'considering that large quantities of postage stamps of the currently circulating series have been stolen from Belgian post offices'.[31] It was in this context that new stamps were issued. Their usage remained rather limited during the war. However, they acted as a way both to exult about their country's national identity as well as to evoke key episodes of the First World War. Unsurprisingly, the king occupied an essential place in them. In January 1915, the Belgian government-in-exile had a series of stamps printed in London with the royal portrait. The king strikes the same pose on each of seven stamps having different face values and colours. These stamps were sold with surcharges for the benefit of the Red Cross; this was the third series where this was the case. Like the stamp of October 1914, the king is represented in three-quarter view facing right; its size was larger than the one printed in a hurry in Antwerp. The 5- and 10- centime stamps had 3 million copies printed, which was

---

26 Royal Decree of 30 September 1914. 'Émission des timbres spéciaux avec surtaxe au profit de la Croix-Rouge', Archives of the Post Office.
27 See Legrand 1914.
28 See Audoin-Rouzeau and Becker 2000.
29 De Vos, *De Belgische Rode Kruis zegel nummer 130.* http://postzegelsdemerode.be/showpic turezm.html?ImgNr=187
30 It was in service until 22 November 1918.
31 Royal Decree of 16 September 1915.

plainly a much larger quantity than the number of potential buyers given the circumstances, which explains why, in the space of two years, fewer than 10 % were sold.[32]

In the autumn of 1915, another series was printed in London, by Waterlow and Sons. It was clearly placed in the context of the war. Three emblematic sites were chosen: Ypres (Figure 1), Dinant (Figure 2) and Leuven (Figure 3). The iconography remained sober, however. For Leuven, the stamp represented the pre-war library; for Ypres, the famous Cloth Hall and Dinant was symbolised by the profile of the Collegiate Church of Notre Dame. In other words, these three stamps provided a view of the prestigious buildings that characterised each of these martyred cities before their destruction by the Germans. There is no direct evocation of the violence to which these three cities had fallen victim, not even through the representation of ruins, as if to remind one of the original beauty of this heritage which one now knew had been destroyed. The message was more implicit than explicit. It was the context of war and the intense Allied propaganda denouncing German atrocities which gave these stamps their full meaning.[33]

On the other hand, the war was directly evoked, while still avoiding a representation of violence, by a stamp dedicated to the presentation of the flag to the 7th Regiment of the Line at Veurne by the king himself. This regiment shone brilliantly during two deadly sorties during the siege of Antwerp, as well as during the First Battle of Ypres. It is clear that these were two important moments during the 'war of movement' for the Belgian army. This was the only reference to the strictly military dimension of the conflict. We do not know why the 7th Regiment of the Line was preferred to the 12th of the Line, which was actually better known. Can we see a communitarian dimension? The 7th of the Line was essentially an Antwerp regiment, while the 12th of the Line was from Liège… That being said, it is interesting to note that only the infantry was given such an honour, which corresponds to a change in the perception of its role. Infantrymen, whose sacrifices on the battlefield were highest, took precedence over the cavalry, and even the artillery, which were traditionally more prestigious. Another series of seven stamps (from 1 to 25 centimes) represented the king alone. He appears again in three-quarter view facing left; the image is similar to that of 1912.

The other stamps issued by the Le Havre government, from 1915 onwards, found their origin in decisions taken before the war. They had themes that were symbolic of a Belgium which had struggled for freedom since the 19th century: Antwerp and the abolition of the toll on the Scheldt in 1863, the Congo and the antislavery campaign as part of an emancipatory approach to colonialism, and the first three kings of the

---

32   The stamp with a face value of 5 centimes had 220,154 copies sold, that of 10 centimes, 195, 154 out of a print run of 3 million between January 1915 and April 1917. See Van San.

33   So, for example, the message was immediately understood in France, while in Japan the Belgian ambassador had to explain their meaning during a postage stamp exhibition in Tokyo in 1919. See Schwarzenbach 1999, 104.

realm. This joint presence of the first three kings around the national motto was a first. These stamps would circulate across all of Belgium's territory from November 1918 – they were on sale at Brussels post offices starting on 27 November – and would remain in circulation until 1931. Their impact thus extended long after the end of the conflict. They would later be available in different colours and would be sold for the benefit of the Red Cross through a surcharge.[34]

5 The post-war period: an immediate turn to a commemorative perspective

Once the war ended, the top priority was to combat the lack of stamps. The German post office's last day of operation in Belgium was 12 November. Four days later, Belgian employees took up their jobs, still using German stamps overprinted with *Belgien* until 20 November. On this date, those stamps ceased to be used, while a number of post offices were simply out of stock and the print shops in Mechelen were not yet operational. At first, the cost of sending a letter was paid directly at the post office and the delivery was accompanied with the words *port payé* ('postage paid') while waiting for the situation to return to normal.

New stamps would thus be printed quickly. From the beginning, they were envisioned from a commemorative point of view. For the minister in charge of the Post Office, the Catholic Jules Renkin, they had to perpetuate 'the memory of the war through the postage stamp'[35], an approach which was also rapidly adopted regarding postcards, as in that case the Post Office published pre-stamped postcards which served to spread the image of the king.[36] In that vein, in a note from the management of the Belgian postage stamp to its director-general, dated 13 December 1918, we can read:

> "Through the postage stamp, Belgium already commemorates the painful events that she has just gone through. We put out a series of different denominations representing views of cities destroyed by the Germans, and the faces of our sovereigns since Leopold I. But, to really connect with the people, the commemoration of this period should also be done by means of stamps of lower denominations used by everybody. A stamp linking the memory of our battles with that of our liberation would be timely and, in a note of this past 24 November, I put forward the idea of a postage stamp representing H. M. the King in field dress, with a helmet on his head."[37]

---

34 We have little information regarding the size of the print run. Only that dedicated to Dinant, with a face value of 40 centimes, is known: 54,000 copies. See Philippe 2013.
35 Quoted in Schwarzenbach 1999, 113.
36 'Émission de cartes postales avec timbre "Roi casqué"', Ministerial Decree of 10 May 1920, Archives of the Post Office.
37 Note taken from the Archives of the Postal Museum and reproduced in Deneumoustier (1988).

Figure 1: Ypres. The famous Cloth Hall before its destruction by the Germans, 1915–1919, expirity 1920, © BPost.

Figure 2: Dinant. The Collegiale Church of the city before its destruction by the Germans, 1915–1919, expirity 1920, © BPost.

Figure 4: King Albert with a helmet, 1919, expirity 1931, © BPost.

Figure 5: The heroic defense of Liège symbolized by the perron, symbol of the liberties of the city, 1919, expirity 1931, © BPost.

Figure 3: Leuven. The University library before its destruction by the Germans, 1915–1919, expirity 1920, © BPost.

Figure 6: The martyrdom of the city of Dendermonde symbolized by the City Hall, 1920, expirity 1931, © BPost.

Figure 7: The postage stamps for the fiftieth anniversary of the end of the First World War. The "Joyous Entry of Bruges", 1968, © BPost.

Figure 8: The postage stamps for the fiftieth anniversary of the end of the First World War. The "Joyous Entry of Brussels", 1968, © BPost.

Figure 9: The postage stamps for the fiftieth anniversary of the end of the First World War. The "Joyous Entry of Liège", 1968, © BPost.

Figure 10: The postage stamps of 2008 dedicated to the First World War. The front is the major topic, 2008, © BPost.

Figure 11: The postage stamps of 2014 dedicated to the First World War. The topic "invasion" is at the forefront, 2014, © BPost.

Figure 12: The postage stamps of 2018 dedicated to the First World War. The major aspects of the Liberation are at the forefront, 2018, © BPost.

Unsurprisingly, the major personality was that of King Albert. For the director-general of the Post Office, it was about offering 'the satisfaction of glorifying [Belgium's] heroic Soldier-King and his valiant army before the whole world'.[38] This approach was unsurprising in that it was in the tradition of the Belgian Post Office. But in this case, it was definitely the Soldier-King who was being highlighted, and who personally embodied the valour of the Belgian army. In 1919, he appeared in a helmet with the dates 1914–1918 on stamps with common denominations (Figure 4). At first, the artist Anto Carte was approached for the work. His proposal was refused though, because the appearance of the king, inspired by a photograph taken in 1917 by the famous British photographer Richard Speaight, did not glorify the king enough.[39] With time running short, the bureau in charge of the stamp production called on one of its foremen, Jan De Bast (1883–1975), who was paid extra for his creation: he 'put soul, talent and pride into it, wanting to achieve a good result'.[40]

Initially three denominations had been planned (5, 10 and 25 centimes). But when the time of for the order came around, it was in fact a series of 14 stamps – that is, 14 different face values – printed intaglio, which was ordered. Production was entrusted to the Dutch firm Enschedé en Zonen, rather than the firm Waterlow with which the Post Office was nevertheless contractually bound, because during the war the former had supported the Belgian charity based in The Hague, *Le sou du Mutilé* ('The Invalid's Mite').[41] This stamp circulated until 1931, but from 1920 onwards it became rather rare. The print run, limited at first, was nevertheless considerable: 10 million copies for the denominations of 2, 10 and 15 centimes, 5 million copies for the denominations of 1 and 5 centimes and one million copies for the denominations of 20 and 25 centimes. It was clearly the most popular Belgian postage stamp, with a total print run of over 40 million copies.

In 1920, the Post refused to cede to public demand to issue a new print run of the almost sold-out denominations of 1 and 2 francs – the print run of which, it is true, had only been 100,000 copies for the one-franc stamp and 30,000 for the two-franc stamp. It justified its decision by reminding people that that the print run was limited from the beginning, and that disrespecting this limit would displease collectors, as well as the fact that a new stamp (King Albert, 'Montenez' type, see below) was in preparation. Commercial and speculative reasons were at the heart of the matter. On account of the limited print run of these two denominations, all of the stock had been

---

38 Letter from the General Director to the Minister in Charge of the Post Office, 13 October 1918 (quoted in Schwarzenbach 1999, 149).
39 Note of the director of the postage stamp service to the director-general, 5 February 1919 (Deneumoustier 1988).
40 Note of the Service Director (Stamp Print Shop 117) to the attention of the General Director, 6 June 1919 (Deneumoustier 1988).
41 Note of Neven, Director-General of the Post Office, 3 May 1919 (Deneumoustier 1988). Agreement signed with Enschedé en Zonen, June 1919 and Royal Decree signed 30 June 1919 as well as Ministerial Decree, 1 July 1919.

quickly bought up by resellers. The success of this stamp was confirmed by a parliamentary question of 5 August 1920, which waxed indignant about the fact that, at that moment, the two-franc stamp was selling for 12 francs in unofficial circles! For Minister Poullet, there was however no room for attacking the freedom of trade which permitted the selling of stamps at a price higher than their face value ('we cannot stop businesspeople from taking a fair profit for the work from which they are sparing their buyers'). The only measure that he foresaw was stopping the entire print run from being hoarded by speculators.[42] As it turned out, the print run was nevertheless revised upwards, though we do not know exactly when. In the official catalogue of the Belgian Post Office, we learn that the stamp with a face value of one franc had 330,000 copies printed and that of two francs, 109,000 copies. In total, more than 45,000,000 copies, all denominations combined, were printed.[43]

The two other stamps of the Liberation celebrated, on the one hand, the heroic defence of Liège (Figure 5) and, on the other, the martyrdom of the city of Dendermonde (Figure 6). Since August 1914, the resistance of the forts of Liège benefitted from an international renown, and the city received the French Legion of Honour on 7 August 1914. In September 1914, the town of Dendermonde was bombed; the majority of its buildings were destroyed and hostages were taken to Germany.[44] These two stamps reflect a use of the national memory of 'heroic and martyred' Belgium to reinforce local identities. From December 1918 onwards, the *Ligue Wallonne de Liège* ('Walloon League of Liège'), a regionalist association, asked the Minister of the Post to denounce the absence of the city on war stamps and to demand that its internationally recognized heroism be honoured.[45] The demand was accepted, and the stamp showed a drawing of the *perron*, a stone column which symbolises the liberties of Liège. The first printing of the stamp – 19 July 1919 – also coincided with the visit of French president Poincaré from 21 to 24 July.[46] During this visit, he went to Liège to officially award the Legion of Honour to the city, and the French delegation received *perron* stamps. The first print run was only distributed in the city of Liège. The following print runs were sold in all Belgian post offices. This stamp, printed intaglio by the Dutch firm Enschedé en Zonen on sheets of ten copies each, was intended to replace the stamp with the portrait of Albert printed since October 1915 and used all over Belgian territory since liberation. Afterwards, its use diminished, almost completely disappearing in 1925. It was still in circulation until 1931, however.[47]

---

42 *Annales parlementaires Chambre*, 5 August 1920, 848–850.
43 *Catalogue officiel* 2005, 33.
44 Tixhon & Derez 2013.
45 Schwarzenbach 1999, 161.
46 Balace & Lanneau 2017, 203–205.
47 Royal Decree of 30 June 1919: 'remplacement du timbre de 25 c à l'effigie royale par un nouveau type "Perron liégeois"', Archives of the Post Office.

The Dendermonde stamp was clearly part of a policy of balance. The initiative for it was put forth by a Member of Parliament from Dendermonde, Oscar Vermeersch, less than a week after the publication of the stamps featuring Liège. He referred to the *perron* stamp to justify his demand to the Minister of the Post.[48] It was not until a year later, though, that the stamp was made available to the public. Between the printing of the Liège and the Dendermonde stamps, several changes were made. They concerned not only the quality of the stamp which represented Dendermonde in ruins, but also its denomination and print run. Initially, the face value was supposed to be 20 centimes. Given the change in postal rates, it was raised to 65 centimes (in the meantime, the price to send a regular letter went from 20 to 50 centimes; 65 centimes for express delivery). More interestingly, the initial print run of 15 million copies was ultimately reduced to 10; the remaining 5 million were reserved for a new print run of the *perron* stamp, whose face value was 25 centimes. If the *perron* stamp was an incontestable success, the same cannot be said for that portraying Dendermonde. In November 1921, the minister took the decision to lower its face value from 65 to 55 centimes for the remaining supply; a lower face value was supposed to ease sales.[49] Apparently, its initial face value did not solicit enough demand for a stamp with an unusually long manufacturing time; besides, Dendermonde did not seem to be the most emblematic martyred city.

As we can see, both these stamps revealed a memory-oriented stamp-making policy and a desire to promote local identities within a shared national narrative.

5.1 Asserting Belgian sovereignty in the Eastern Cantons

At the same time, there was another memory-related issue, focussed on the territories annexed by Belgium. The postal administration in the municipalities annexed from Germany was handed over to Belgium from 15 January 1920. During the annexation of the Eupen-Malmedy region (the 'Eastern Cantons'), Belgian stamps were immediately imposed, and German stamps banned starting 27 January 1920. This approach clearly corresponds to a political will to assert Belgian sovereignty over these populations. It also seems to be a response to the policy of the German occupiers who had imposed their own stamps in occupied Belgium on 1 October 1914.

Belgian stamps carried an overprint of *Eupen, Malmédy*, or both. Note that the name *Malmedy*, even when written fully in upper case, where French orthography traditionally does not use diacritical marks, had an 'e' with an acute accent, another sign of the desire to promote the francophone – and therefore, Belgian – nature of the town. These stamps were denominated in marks, the Belgian franc not being introduced in the region until 1925, during the total and complete annexation. The stamp

---

48 Vermeersch to the Minister of the Post, 26 July 1919, Dendermonde stamp.
49 Royal Decree of 3 November 1921, Archives of the Post Office.

therefore served to help promote Belgian identity at a time when the inhabitants of the Eastern Cantons were still considered second-class citizens (not having the right to vote, for example).[50]

The Belgian stamps that were introduced were none other than the series issued by the government in exile in Le Havre in 1915: in other words, stamps about the martyred towns (Ypres, Dinant and Leuven), about the presentation of the flag to the 7th Regiment of the Line as well as those which exulted national identity (the three kings, the 'antislavery' stamp and the navigation of the Scheldt). Added to these were the stamps dedicated to the Liberation, that is, all of those representing the king wearing a helmet as well as those representing Liège and Dendermonde. These would also be used during the Belgian occupation of the Rhineland.[51]

5.2 Surcharges benefitting charitable works

Besides the series dedicated to the liberation, surcharges for the benefit of charitable institutions were the most important way that the memory of the war was expressed and these multiplied in the beginning of the 1920s. This practice was not unique to Belgium. During the war, it spread among nearly all the belligerent countries to raise funds for the war effort. It continued after 1918, even in neutral countries such as Switzerland.[52]

For the benefit of wounded veterans

In 1920, for the occasion of the Olympic Games in Antwerp, a choice which was itself linked to the war, three stamps, of 5, 10 and 15 centimes were issued.[53] They were dedicated to three sporting events: the discus throw, the chariot race and the marathon. The minister was convinced that this initiative would be a success. The initial print run of 5 million copies for each of the stamps was thus doubled.[54] Each stamp also carried a surcharge for the benefit of wounded veterans. But as it happened, these stamps stayed in post offices for the most part. At first, they were planned to be valid

---

50   Fickers 2005, 620–21.
51   Ministerial Decree of 10 September 1919. 'Pour l'utilisation dans la zone belge d'occupation en Allemagne', Archives of the Post Office.
52   Croix and Guyvarc'h 2016, 53; Schwarzenbach 1999, 133–34.
53   5 centimes was the rate for sending a card with a maximum of 5 words, 10 centimes was the rate for sending a postcard, starting 15 December 1919 and 15 centimes was the rate for sending a letter of less than 20 grams by domestic mail; rates were adjusted upwards by 5 centimes for letters and postcards without any restriction on content on 1 November 1920.
54   A telegram dated 15 March 1920 planned for doubling the initial order. See Van Rompay (n. d), 3.

until 15 January 1921, but they ultimately remained in circulation until 1931. It is estimated that 70 % of the production was unsold by the end of 1920.[55]

Was it the association of a sporting theme with the image of wounded veterans that was the issue? Or was it simply the overly large print runs? One of the difficulties in selling off the stamps could have been the provision that forbade the use of stamps with a surcharge for foreign correspondence. But this explanation is insufficient. In October 1920, a Royal Decree authorised their use – even with a surcharge – for a certain number of foreign countries. But by then, the Olympic Games had been over for three weeks. The situation remained problematic: millions of stamps sat in post offices, even after the decision to eliminate the surcharge. The size of the print run seems to be the major reason for the lack of sales. That said, beyond the stamps, the Olympic Games themselves were not very successful for reasons connected to the lack of time and money, the shortage of lodging and the resentment by a majority Dutch-speaking population towards an extremely francophone event. To this was added the very unpredictable weather.[56]

Subsequently, the image of the Soldier-King and Nurse-Queen was put to use for war veterans. In 1922, a stamp designed by Anto Carte was printed in New York for the benefit of the *Œuvre Nationale des Invalides de Guerre* ('National charity for Wounded Veterans'). It only included a 20-centime denomination but was printed in one million copies, that is, a much more limited print run than that for the Antwerp Olympics.[57] On the stamp, we see a wounded veteran offering a palm frond to King Albert whose very small portrait appears in a medallion. The representation of the veteran was clearly sanitised. He is shown from the back, nude; his body muscular and intact. Only the bandage on his head indicates his wound.

In 1923, another stamp came out for the benefit of the war wounded. Printed in one million copies, it was the work of the famous Dutch artist Louis Raemaekers and was intended to be more realistic.[58] It featured a one-legged man on crutches, wearing a long coat and a kepi. He walks with difficulty but also with dignity, in a scene which evokes a devastated landscape, the trees themselves missing limbs.

In 1926–1927, a series of 'antituberculosis' stamps in five different denominations went on sale. The print runs ranged from 200,000 copies (for the highest face value, 5 francs) to 1,700,000 for the face values of 5 and 20 centimes. They carried surcharges of between 5 centimes and one franc.[59] This series was intended for wounded veterans with tuberculosis. Even this considerable print run was much lower than that

---

55 At the initial date when they were to lose validity (15 Januar 1921), the 5-centime stamp had only sold 774,524 copies, that of 10 centimes, 1,462,393 and that of 15 centimes, 1,076,655. See Van Rompay (n.d.), 7.
56 See Renson 1996.
57 Ministerial Decree of 28 April 1922, Archives of the Post Office.
58 Royal Decree of 6 June 1923, Archives of the Post Office.
59 Royal Decree of 26 November 1926, Archives of the Post Office.

for the Antwerp Olympic Games. It seems that the lesson had been learned, because we can read in a letter of 1926 addressed to the Minister of the Post that it 'is essential that [charitable stamps] have an aspect that appeals to the public in some way'.[60] This stamp presented just the royal couple, each in their own medallion, presented in three-quarter view and turned towards each other. The king was in a khaki uniform and the queen in that of a nurse. Note that this was the first time that a Queen of the Belgians was represented in stamps.

In 1934, the first stamp with a portrait of Leopold III, who had just succeeded his father, was also dedicated to wounded veterans. Initially destined for a limited number of buyers and sold only during a philatelic exposition on postal cancellations of the war of 1914–1918; it was later sold in all post offices.[61] These two stamps did not represent the wounded veterans for whose benefit they were sold but rather the monarchy.

For the benefit of commemorative charities

In 1932, a series of stamps carrying a surcharge was issued with the portrait of Cardinal Mercier, the national hero who symbolised the moral resistance in the occupied country during the war. These stamps, the work of Anto Carte, had a commemorative significance, because the surcharge was intended 'first of all' to 'collect the funds necessary for raising the monument to the memory of Cardinal Mercier'[62]; part of the surcharge of this printing was supposed to be set aside for finishing work on the Collège Cardinal Mercier, a school in Braine-l'Alleud.[63] This series was available in four types and nine denominations. The complete series was sold for 95 francs. On the 1.75-franc stamp, the 'patriotic' Cardinal appeared as 'the insurmountable barrier of right… protecting a tearful mother with her children and three men holding on to each other as if to escape the deportations'.[64] On the 10-franc stamp, the portrait of the Cardinal-Archbishop of Mechelen is framed by the words *Civitatis Defensor*. Here, then, it was the war hero, the embodiment of the moral resistance of the occupied country, which was represented. In other words, this series was the first to be directly dedicated to the experience of the population in the occupied country. It was also accompanied by the printing of illustrated postcards on the same theme. If it was

---

60   Quoted in Schwarzenbach 1999, 124.
61   These stamps were only sold at the special post office of the exposition on postal cancellations of the war of 1914–1918, organised by the *Club Royal Philatélique des Invalides à Bruxelles* (Royal Philatelic Club of Wounded Veterans in Brussels', from 15 to 17 September 1934, as well as the Brussels first post office from 18 to 22 September 1934 (*Catalogue officiel de Timbres-Poste. Belgique* 2009, 51).
62   Royal Decree of 14 May 1932, Archives of the Post Office.
63   Bosse 2017, 30 ff.
64   *Revue de la Poste*, June 1932, MP, Timbres-poste 'Cardinal Mercier Monument'.

heavily criticised in the press[65], it was not on account of the theme, but rather the surcharges, judged to be exorbitantly high (from 10 centimes to 40 francs) and the cause for which these surcharges were being collected. At any rate, this series encountered some success, because it raised more than 2 million francs.[66]

Also in 1932, the Belgian Post issued a stamp intended 'first of all to complete the necessary funding for raising the *Monument national à la gloire de l'infanterie* (National Monument to the Glory of the Infantry), which would be inaugurated in 1934 in Place Poelaert in Brussels.[67] This stamp was available in two denominations and two colours, each printed in 40,000 copies, that is, a very limited print run. It was only made available to the public by subscription, from 4 August to 30 November 1932. The imagery was not intended to be that of glorification. Rather, it was the image of a solitary soldier, suffering under the load of his gear, making progress with difficulty, in a ruined landscape. Only the light that surrounds him speaks to the nobility of his efforts. Remember that since 1915, 'the' Belgian soldier of the First World War was, in the imaginations of the belligerent populations, above all the infantryman. No surprise then that the monument to the infantry was the only one dedicated to specific branch of the army to benefit from the support of the Post Office, even though there were a number of other similar monuments, like those dedicated to aviators or to the dead of the Corps of Engineers, both in Brussels.[68]

6 The permanence of the Soldier-King

We know that King Albert paid more attention to his image than his predecessors. The postage stamp was used in this image-making. Generally speaking, throughout his whole reign, it was the royal function which was highlighted, that is, the intuition more than the man. Nevertheless, a few exceptions, some details, added details, frames etc. reveal, even if in a small way, the way in which the monarch was seen to embody his function. Since 1912, on stamps, the king was often represented in three-quarter view, his gaze turned to somewhere beyond the viewer: the county's destiny! In 1919, it was the image of the conquering king which was given pride of place. From then on, reference to the war went along with his image.

In 1921, a new portrait was created by Montenez. Also printed in the Netherlands, then later in England, it was initially printed in 200,000 copies just for the International Exposition of Postage Stamps.[69] It was used on several stamps until 1948.

---

65 See notably *Pourquoi pas?*, 1 July 1932. The surcharges amounted to 75 centimes for the 1.75-franc stamp and to 40 francs for that of 10 francs!
66 Summary of special postage stamp issues with surcharges that appeared since 1932, Archives of the Post Office.
67 Royal Decree of 15 June 1932, Archives of the Post Office.
68 See van Ypersele, Debruyne and Kesteloot 2014, 147–151.
69 Ministerial Decree of 10 May 1924, Archives of the Post Office.

In it, the king was presented in left profile, bareheaded and wearing a khaki uniform. However, from 1922 to 1948, the most widespread stamps were of the Hoyoux (1856–1940) type. There are five different series of it, encompassing 19 different denominations from 1 centime to 10 francs. They were printed in the print shops of Mechelen, which had finally been rebuilt. In these the king was represented in a khaki uniform and bareheaded, in three-quarter view right. Finally, in 1931, a stamp designed by Jean Malvaux presented a very realistic portrait of the king: older, more human, wearing a military kepi. Here was the image of the Soldier-King, close to his men, at their side throughout the whole war and protecting their lives.[70] This stamp, called *Albert en casquette* ('Albert in a helmet')[71], also circulated until 1948. In 1934, the year of the king's death, this stamp would have a special edition with a black border, printed in 32 million copies. This shows the aura that Albert I had in his country, and even abroad.

In addition to these ordinary stamps, we need to mention two stamps created for special occasions. The first, in 1925, is a stamp commemorating 'the 75th anniversary of the "epaulette" postage stamp' with portraits of Leopold I (1849 type) and Albert (1924 type) in three-quarter view and both in a general's field uniform. It was printed in 100,000 copies for each of 13 denominations. It was in circulation until 1938 and represented a widespread discourse in which Leopold I gave Belgium its body and Albert gave Belgium its soul. The second, in 1930, the year of the centenary of Belgian independence, was part of a series dedicated to the dynasty, the work of the engraver De Bast for the print shop in Mechelen: Albert was presented for the first time down to his knees in a khaki uniform and coat, hand at his belt, solemn and majestic. This stamp, with an indeterminate print run, remained in circulation until 1938.

The aura of King Albert did not end with his death in 1934. After his passing, to celebrate anniversaries and commemorations, several stamps still appeared with his portrait. In 1938, a stamp appeared for the King Albert monument in Nieuwpoort, which had been inaugurated the same year.[72] Sold by subscription from 5 to 15 February, its surcharge value (7.55 francs for a stamp with a face value of 2.45 francs) went to the building of the monument. The stamp portrayed the model of the monument, which would be inaugurated three months later. Considering its print run (205,000) and the high surcharge, it was most likely intended for collectors and veterans who had worked for the building of the monument. On the sheet surrounding the stamp, there was an extract of the speech given by the king on 4 August 1914: 'a country that defends itself demands everyone's respect'. We can speculate if this little phrase was just a simple quotation, or if it had a particular meaning in the context of

---

70 See van Ypersele 2006.
71 The one-franc stamp was printed in Mechelen in rotogravure, the first in Belgium printed via this new procedure. The other denominations were printed intaglio.
72 This monument, inaugurated in 1938 in the presence of King Leopold III, was the work of sculptor Karl Aubroeck.

1938, when the Belgian authorities were looking to remobilize public opinion facing the risk of a new war. In any case, this stamp had an undeniable financial success: while the organisers hoped to gain 700,000 francs from the surcharge, they collected more than double that amount.[73] In other words, all the stamps were sold.

In 1939, the Post Office issued a stamp of Orval Abbey surrounded by busts of Albert in a khaki uniform and of Leopold III. It circulated until 1950. In 1954, three stamps were issued to commemorate the twentieth anniversary of his death. One evoked Marche-les-Dames, his place of death, with the portrait of the king in a helmet in a small medallion. The other two represent the equestrian monument to the king in Namur[74] in profile, which was inaugurated the same year. In 1968, for the fiftieth anniversary of the victory in the First World War, stamps were issued representing the 'Joyous Entry' ceremonies of 1918 in Bruges, Brussels, and Liège. Three years later, a stamp commemorating the fiftieth anniversary of the *Académie Royale de Langue et de Littérature Françaises de Belgique* (the Belgian Royal Academy for French Language and Literature) represented the buildings of the Academy with, in one medallion, King Albert wearing glasses, and in another, Jules Destrée, a Walloon Socialist politician, author, and art critic who had been a member.

In 1972, the 1919 style stamp of the king in a helmet as well as the Montenez type in profile were reprinted for the philatelic exposition Belgica 72. In 1974, on the occasion of the fortieth anniversary of King Albert's death, Luc De Decker (1907–1982) created a stamp that reproduced the famous portrait by Isidore Opsomer (1878–1982), showing him at a mature age, bareheaded, in a khaki uniform, giving off a kindness lightly tinged with melancholy, with his birth and death dates. For the centenary of his birth, a stamp showed him in civilian clothing wearing a bowtie, an homage to the democratic king associated with the granting of universal suffrage after the Great War and to the king who was a patron of the arts and sciences. This image of King Albert had been distributed during the interwar years, mostly by the Socialists, but it remained marginal for the majority of Belgians. This stamp was an exception to the mostly military representation of the king in postage stamps. In 1980, for the 150th anniversary of Belgian independence, a series of stamps showed each of the royal couples, surrounded by greenery and the dates 1830–1980. King Albert is there, yet again in a khaki uniform, rather young, looking at Queen Elisabeth, who is wearing a nurse's uniform. With this work from Henri Decuyper, we are looking at the return of the Soldier-King and Nurse-Queen of 1914–1918. In 2005, for the 175th anniversary of independence, a 'dynastic' stamp brought together all of the royal couples from Belgian history, as well as Prince Regent Charles: Albert and Elisabeth were there again, in the image inherited from the Great War.

---

73 Schwarzenbach 1999, 206.
74 This monument, the work of sculptor Victor Demanet, was inaugurated for the 20th anniversary of the king's death, in 1954.

Thus, until quite a while after his death, stamps linked King Albert only with the Great War. Be it by his khaki uniform, his helmet or the equestrian monuments to his glory, in stamps, Albert was at first the glorious Knight-King (1938 and 1954), then conqueror (1968) and finally human (1974). Starting in the 1970s, the king as a civilian, democratic, patron of the arts and sciences, competed with the warrior king, but never replaced him.

7 Forgetting the Great War

However, except for the figure of the king, the Great War progressively disappeared from memory. At the same time, in France and Germany, the situation was completely different.[75] In the Hexagon, it was the pacifist theme which was given pride of place on many stamps. In Germany, except for a surcharge for the benefit of war victims in 1919, no stamp was created to evoke the First World War. The situation changed radically when the Nazis came to power. Unsurprisingly, stamps were used to promote militaristic propaganda: stamps which carried the memory of the First World War embodied force, violence, domination.

However, it was obviously the Second World War which would largely displace the memory of the First pretty much everywhere in Europe. As in the Great War, there was a policy of instituting surcharges for the benefit of specific categories of people affected by the war. This time, it was prisoners of war. Two issues of stamps with a surcharge were dedicated to them, in 1942 and 1943. From December 1944, a 'Liberation' series was printed. Just as after the end of the First World War, commemorative stamps were issued starting in 1945.

These had a series of emblematic representations: the resistance fighter, the deportee, the prisoner and even the victim of the firing squad. Other stamps, whose imagery had nothing to do with the recent conflict, were sold for the benefit of prisoners of war and deportees or other (unidentified) charitable works.

The various anniversaries of the end of the Second World War would serve as occasions to evoke that conflict to the detriment of the Great War, which disappeared bit by bit from the field of stamp production, a situation that was not unique to Belgium. In numerous European countries, popular memory, publishing trends and academic research focussed heavily on the period from 1939 to 1945.

It was not until the fiftieth anniversary of the Great War that it reappeared in the field of postage stamps. It remained within the limits of a very traditional representation with two foci: the first dedicated to the soldiers (1964) and the second dedicated to the end of the war (1968). The three stamps dedicated to soldiers gave homage to infantrymen, to the Guides as well as to the grenadiers and drum majors. These three stamps were each printed in 700,000 copies, a print run similar to that of the two

---

75 See Croix and Guyvarc'h 2016, 54–55.

stamps dedicated to the resistance and issued the same year, but significantly less than other thematic stamps with similar denominations issued around the same time for the 20th anniversary of Benelux (7,500,000) or the series 'Europa' (two denominations, sold respectively at 3 million and 8 million copies).

In 1968, four stamps were issued for the fiftieth anniversary of the end of the First World War. The illustrations were classic: King Albert and Queen Elisabeth were portrayed in three stamps that depicted the ceremonies of the 'Joyous Entries' in Bruges (Figure 7), Brussels (Figure 8), and Liège (Figure 9): that is, victory. The fourth represented the Tomb of the Unknown Soldier. Their print runs ranged from 830,000 to 960,000 copies. Here again, these were rather small print runs if we compare them, for example, with that of the Christmas stamp for 1968, of which 9,000,000 copies were printed.

On the occasion of the 175th anniversary of Belgium (2005), ten themes were chosen to summarise the major issues of its history. War was one of them. If the image evokes primarily the suffering of civilians – a universal theme – the image chosen was that of May 1940, and therefore the Second World War.

8   The ever-present Great War (2008–2018)

From 2008 onwards, we can talk of a real sea change. The First World War was again at the heart of popular concerns about memory. From this moment, it was already clear that the centenary would be the subject of a massive (over)investment by Belgian society. This situation is a product of the evolution of Belgium into a federal state. Since this evolution, commemorative policies have been put in place not only at the federal level but also, and more importantly, at the level of the federal entities. We can now see a veritable competition of memory. In this context, stamp production reflects the general tendency. But even beyond Belgium, there has been a more general inflation in the production of stamps.

Three stamps were issued on the occasion of the 90th anniversary of the end of the war (Figure 10). Yet again, it was the front which was given pride of place, with the monument to King Albert in Nieuwport, the Menin Gate at Ypres and the emblematic British poppy. These three stamps were part of a sheet whose background represented, in black and white, a desolated landscape of the front.

But it was the commemorations of the Centenary that really rang in the return of the Great War to the stamp world. This time, the engagement is centred on the period from 2014 to 2018. It is no longer a case of just representing the beginning or the end of the war. From now on, it is not just the military aspects of the conflict which are highlighted. Five themes were chosen for each of the anniversary years. Each time, the Post Office printed a sheet of 5 stamps. Each time, the principle is the same: a short text from the time period is displayed as a way to put things in context. The particular themes are extended by the images in the background. The goal is that at the end of the five years, by way of the five sheets, the essential aspects of the conflict will have been treated.

It is an exercise in striking a balance between the expected themes, which have already been largely represented and new concepts which demonstrate the evolution of representations and of research on Belgium during the Great War. This evolution reveals the place of 'experts' in the decision-making process. Unsurprisingly, in 2014, it was the invasion which was at the forefront (Figure 11). Besides the German attack itself, two stamps were dedicated to martyred towns. Linguistic equilibrium being necessary, one was from Wallonia (Dinant) and the other from Flanders (Leuven). Other towns were mentioned on the sheet, but the smaller villages were forgotten, which garnered some reactions from the province of Luxembourg.

Refugees were also the subject of a stamp, as well as the withdrawal of the Belgian army behind the Yser. The background of the sheet extends – via a watermarked cardstock – the depiction of the front and the flight of civilians in a war-torn landscape. An extract from the socialist newspaper *Le Peuple*, dated 7 August 1914, evoked the resistance of Liège, under the title 'Courage, patience and tenacity'. The sheets printed in 2015 and 2016 both dedicated a lot of space to occupied Belgium. In 2015, the theme chosen was life behind the lines, and the following year, the resistance. The depiction of life behind the lines allowed for a consideration of not only material difficulty and hunger but also the large philanthropic movement that developed. It was also an occasion to depict the role of women in occupied society. In a more classic turn, the sheet also depicted the government-in-exile in Le Havre. For the theme of the resistance, the stamps depicted the clandestine press, the efforts of Gabrielle Petit (who was executed in 1916) and the historian Henri Pirenne, deported to Germany for his opposition to the *Flamenpolitik* (German policy of co-opting Flemish nationalism). The sheet also portrayed the forced labour imposed by the occupier as well as the Battle of Tabora in German East Africa in which Belgian and Congolese troops participated.

For 2017, the theme chosen was communication. An extract from a soldier's letter to his '*marraine de guerre*' (a war godmother) was used as an epitaph. The stamps were dedicated to wireless transmission, messenger pigeons, the military postal service and the border post of Baarle-Hertog, a small Belgian exclave within the neutral Netherlands. But the war itself continued through the last stamp of the sheet, which concerned the terrible Battle of Passchendaele during which British troops confronted German troops.

The series ended in 2018 with a sheet evoking several major aspects of the Liberation, including not only the monumental memory, but also the question of lodging and redeployment of injured and disabled soldiers (Figure 12). The figure of the king, who had been absent throughout this series despite usually being ubiquitous in postal stamp imagery, will be there. The commemoration will end with the printing of a final sheet, which will present a kind of summary.

Through this series, the Belgian Post Office reflects the evolution of historiography over the past twenty years, which has turned towards the history of civilians, the problems and material difficulties of daily life and the concept of a 'culture of war'. These themes were chosen by the Philatelic Commission, which decides on the stamps to be printed each year. Open to exterior members since 1956, it today has some twenty members, including two historians, one from each linguistic community.[76] The commemorative sheets of 2014–2018 give evidence of their participation.

The number of stamps dedicated to the Great War is higher than ever. It is worth stopping and thinking about this inflation of commemoration. It is not a specifically Belgian phenomenon in any way. Never before have so many stamps been printed worldwide; and among these, the Great War has never played as big of a role. But today, the stamp has lost most of its lustre. Personal letter-writing has become rarer and commemorative stamps have become collector's items.

Their status has changed. They are no longer objects that embody a banal nationalism, to which everyone is exposed almost despite themselves. Today, there are two kinds of stamps: those that pass through all the normal points of sale and those that are only known to collectors. Stamps that portray the Great War belong to the second category. Absent from the traditional retail outlets, they are totally unknown to the public at large, only known and appreciated by philatelists. All the evidence indicates that the philatelic milieu remains interested in historical themes.

Current print runs would make the buyers of the twenties smile, as they would not have hesitated to accuse the Post Office of artificially maintaining the rarity of stamps, including those with print runs of several millions. Each of the commemorative sheets dedicated to the Great War – made up of five stamps – is today printed in 65,000 copies, that is, a total of 325,000 individual stamps. These stamps are only sold to collectors, both Belgian and foreign; modern-day philately is more and more thematic in its approach.

9   Conclusion

In wartime, the stamp, something so banal and so common, can be a powerful tool of mobilisation. At the very moment when the Belgian army was fighting for control of Antwerp, two stamps were hastily issued. It is true that they had been planned since 1912, but the imagery of each of them set the tone of a Belgium that fights for itself: an homage to the soldiers of 1830 and the representation of King Albert turned towards the future. It was the first stamp issued with the king on it since the heavily-criticised stamps of 1912. The importance of the postage stamp was not lost on the German occupiers either; from October 1914, they imposed their own stamps in occupied Belgium. Likewise, soon after its arrival at Le Havre, the Belgian govern-

---

76   One of these historians co-authored this text.

ment-in-exile issued new stamps. This goes to show the importance of the stamp at the time.

The impact of the Great War on Belgian society was immense. It is not shocking then that its production of stamps reflected that impact, even if that was only one aspect of that impact, one which was less permanent than the naming of streets and buildings or construction of monuments. Starting with the Liberation in November 1918, a policy of memorialisation was put in place, of which King Albert was unquestionably the figurehead. As in other aspects of life, the representation of the monarch became part of the daily life of Belgians, much more so than in the case of the Soldier-King's predecessors.[77] If the war itself was evoked, it was never done so with reference to violence. Even when destruction was alluded to, there was a preference for showing buildings in all their pre-destruction glory; no devastated countryside, no soldiers who fell in combat. It was instead anonymous, stylised figures of victims who were represented, or sometimes even just alluded to by a surcharge which raised funds for them. French policy in this matter was not different.[78]

Beyond the figure of the king, no other soldier is represented in an identifiable way before 1974 and the stamp dedicated to Corporal Trésignies. But undoubtedly the most striking absence was that of occupied society. While the civilian memory of the war was to be found in the names of streets and buildings and in monuments,[79] it was not until 1932 and a stamp dedicated to Cardinal Mercier that we see Belgium behind the lines finding a place in the philatelic landscape. Nevertheless, the memory of Belgium in combat was not a triumphant one, as it was usually embodied in an image of a fighter who had suffered and paid a high price.

As in other countries, the Second World War displaced the First in terms of public memory, even if Belgium did not, in this case, have an emblematic hero to honour. Leopold III was not Albert, and his image was almost completely absent from stamps after the war, given his controversial actions during the invasion and occupation, and his abdication in the face of opposition from some sections of Belgian society in 1951. But if we make an exception for the Soldier-King, whose representation was a given, the Great War disappeared from stamps until the commemorations of its fiftieth anniversary. The figure of the king thus appears to be the most important visual aspect of the stamps.[80]

The representation of the Great War during the 1960s remained very conventional, and in the vein of that which immediately followed the war. The stamps for the fiftieth anniversary of the Armistice of 1918 also demonstrate a desire for balance in a Belgium undergoing a transformation into a federal country: three cities were rep-

---

77 See Kesteloot 2015.
78 Croix and Guyvarc'h 2016, 188.
79 See van Ypersele, Debruyne & Kesteloot 2014.
80 As Alexis Schwarzenbach has already observed, 'the most important Belgian symbol was the representation of the monarchy' (Schwarzenbach 1999, 258).

resented, one in Flanders, one in Wallonia, and of course the capital. But their print runs were fairly modest if compared to that of the 1919 style with the king in his helmet, the champion of all categories. Despite this brief burst – necessary, given the fiftieth anniversary – it was the Second World War which was the focus of nearly all representations of memory. Like the wounded veteran or invalid of the First World War, the resistance fighter and the deportee of 1940–1944 were anonymous, intentionally stylised figures. Violence was never represented directly.

That production was centred on the Second World War reflected not just institutional policies, but also societal representations. In this sense, and indeed more generally, stamp production was the reflection of not only government decisions, including those of the monarchy, but also public opinions. Stamps accompany, comfort and consolidate phenomena of memory, but do not create them. Their convergence with feelings rooted among the population assures them a measure of legitimacy. In turn, they help reinforce pre-existing sentiments.

Since the 1980s, a time when the production of stamps increased dramatically[81], societies have progressively rediscovered the Great War, and the production of stamps reflects this trend in public memory. This time around, the representation goes beyond strict national boundaries, with, for example, the representation of the Menin Gate or the poppy, emblematic of British memory. The commemoration of the centenary is linked with an historic attempt to more closely follow the development of a flourishing historiography. However, the role of the stamp is no longer what it once was. It has now become a collector's item.

Not only has letter-writing become much less common, but now only certain stamps are available at all points of sale. The productions put in place by the Philatelic Commission thus only have a very limited impact among the public, if they even have one at all. What then is the impact of the Commission's choices? What does it matter if, from now on, occupied society gets pride of place, that the anonymity of yesteryear has disappeared with emblematic personalities like Gabrielle Petit or Henri Pirenne, if the reality of the Great War is finally shown in all of its complexity?

---

81 Alain Croix and Didier Guyvarc'h have calculated that between 1914 and 2000, Belgium issued 1900 stamps and France a bit under 2000. From 1981 to 2015, Belgium issued around 2500 stamps and France 2800. See Croix and Guyvarc'h 2016, 187.

References

Audoin-Rouzeau, S. and Becker, A. (2000). *14–18, retrouver la guerre*. Paris: Gallimard.

Aupiais, G. (2014). Le patrimoine postal de la Grande Guerre. *In Situ*, 25, http://insitu.revues.org/11591. Consultation april 2018.

Balace, F. & Lanneau, C. (2017). De la Première Guerre mondiale à aujourd'hui. In Demoulin, B. (Ed.). *Histoire de Liège. Une cité, une capitale, une métropole*, Liège-Brussels: Les Grandes Conférences liégeoises & les éditions Marot.

Banque nationale de Belgique (1991). *La monnaie et le portrait royal (1830–1991)*. Brussels: musée de la Banque nationale de Belgique.

Billig, M. (1995). *Banal nationalism*. London: Sage Publications.

Bosse, R. (2017). L'émission du Cardinal Mercier de 1932. *Delcampe Philatélie*, 11, April.

Bouckaert, A. (1934). L'iconographie du Roi Albert en philatélie. *Le Soir Illustré*, 24 March, 31, 7.

Catalogue officiel de Timbres-Poste. Belgique (2009). Brussels: CPBNTP.

Croix, A., Guyvarc'h, D. (2016). *Timbres en guerre. Les mémoires des deux conflits mondiaux*. Rennes: Presses Universitaires de Rennes.

Deneumoustier, E and M. (1988). Émission de la Libération dite "roi casqué", 13.12.1918, Mechelen: Belgian Post Office Archives.

Fickers A. (2005). De la 'Sibérie de la Prusse' aux 'Cantons rédimés': l'ombre diffuse de la Grande Guerre dans la mémoire collective des Belges germanophones. In Jaumain, S. et al. (Eds) *Une guerre totale? La Belgique dans la Première Guerre mondiale. Nouvelles tendances de la recherche historique*, Brussels: Archives générales du Royaume, 615–633.

Hanna, M. (2006). *Your death would be mine*. Cambridge: Harvard University Press.

Jacquemin, M. (2018). *Inventaire des archives de La Poste (1830–2009)*, Brussels: Archives générales du Royaume.

Kesteloot, Ch. (Ed.) (2015). *Albert & Elisabeth. Le film de la vie d'un couple royal*. Brussels: Mardaga.

Legrand (1914). Les Sociétés de la Croix-Rouge dans les différentes Nations. *La Vie Internationale*. 5(20), 59–75.

Parker, D. (2015). *European Stamp Issues of the Second World War: Images of Triumph, Deceit and Despair*. Stroud: History Press Limited.

Philippe, E. (2013). La quiétude de Dinant, avant l'atrocité et le drame, figée à jamais sur un timbre. *Traces mosanes*, 12, 2–4.

Pignot, M. (2006). Les petites filles dans la Grande Guerre. *Vingtième Siècle. Revue d'histoire*, 89, 9–16.

Prochasson, C. (2008). *14–18 retours d'expériences*. Paris: Texto.

Raento, P. & Brunn, S.D. (2005). Visualizing Finland: postage stamps as political messengers. *Geografiska Annaler*, 87(2), 145–164.

Renson R. (1996). *The Games reborn. The VIIth Olympias Antwerp 1920*. Antwerpen: Snoeck Ducaju.

Schwarzenbach, A. (1999). *Portraits of the Nation. Stamps, Coins and Banknotes in Belgium and Switzerland, 1880–1945*. Bern: Peter Lang.

Stes, J. (2001). *Essais de Belgique. Catalogue raisonné des essais des timbres en Belgique/Belgium Proofs. Descriptive catalogue of the proofs of Belgian stamps, 1849–1949*. Brussels: Ed. Williame.

Tixhon, A. and Derez, M. (Eds) (2013). *Villes martyres: Visé, Aarschot, Andenne, Tamines, Dinant, Louvain, Termonde. Belgique, août-septembre 1914*, Namur: Presses universitaires de Namur.

Trévisan, C. (2003). Lettres de guerre. *Revue d'Histoire littéraire de la France*, 2, 331–341.

Van der Mullen, M. (2008). Les "timbres de l'occupation" (OC) dans le COB: une lecture différente. *Belgaphil*, 12, 4–8.

Van der Mullen, M. (with Stes, B.) (2011). *De Duitse Post in België en in Noord-Frankrijk tijdens Weeldoorlog I, 1914–1918.* http://www.academiebelgium.be/pdf/WO1-boek%20MVDM.pdf

Van Rompay, R. (n.d.). *De olympische spelen van 1920 te Antwerpen*. Belgian Olympic Philatelic Club.

Van San, P. (n.d.). *Hoe kon de 3de Rode Kruis uitgifte zo snel verschijnen in W.O II (sic)?*, http://postzegelsdemerode.be/showpicturezm2.html?ImgNr=3.

van Ypersele, L. (2006). *Le roi Albert, histoire d'un mythe*. Brussels: Labor.

van Ypersele, L., Debruyne, E. and Kesteloot, C. (2014). *Bruxelles, la mémoire et la guerre. 1914–2014*. Brussels: La Renaissance du Livre.

Vidal-Naquet, C. (2006). S'épouser à distance. Le mariage à l'épreuve de la Grande Guerre. *Revue d'Histoire moderne et contemporaine*, 53 (3), 143–158.

Vidal-Naquet, C. (2009). Imaginer le retour. L'anticipation des retrouvailles chez les couples pendant la Grande Guerre. In Cabanes, B. & Piketty, G. (Eds). *Retour à l'intime au sortir de la guerre*, Paris: Tallandier, 215–228.

Wallach, Y. (2010). Creating a Country through Currency and Stamps: State, Symbols and Nation-building in British-ruled Palestine. *Nations and Nationalism*, 17 (1), 2011, 129–147.

Winter, J. (2014). Families. In *Cambridge History of The First World War*, vol. III: Civil Societies. Cambridge: Cambridge University, 46–68.

Pierre Bouchat, Olivier Klein, Valérie Rosoux

The Paradoxical Impacts of the Commemorations of the Great War in Belgium

1 Introduction

In Western Europe[1], the centenary of WWI is marked by what observers called "a commemorative fever".[2] Since 2014, from Portugal to France, hundreds of commemorative activities have attracted thousands of citizens.[3] Belgium is at the epicentre of this dynamic. In this country – that was occupied during the four years of war and endured huge destructions and massacres – the commemorations of the centenary are qualified as the largest commemorative event ever organized.[4] They are anchored at the local, the regional and the national levels and take different forms such as ceremonies, exhibitions, lectures, book presentations, TV shows and series. An important amount of resources (e.g., public and private funding; time spent by academic experts) has been invested in these initiatives. However, to date, little is known about the potential effects of the commemorations on the individuals who participated in them. Do commemorations influence psychological variables? If so, to what extent, and how does it happen? To address these questions, the present chapter investigates the influence of commemorations from a social psychological perspective. More specifically, it focuses on the impact of two forms of commemorations – namely: exhibitions and documentaries – on a specific kind of psychological variable especially emphasized by the designers of WWI commemorations: pacifist attitudes.

Attitudes are a key concept in social psychology. They correspond to "evaluations individuals hold towards elements in their environment".[5] We will analyze pacifist attitudes, conceived in this case as a mix of negative attitudes towards war and positive attitudes towards peace.

The starting point of our approach lies in the belief, widely shared in the political and academic spheres, that commemorations are likely to change the knowledge and attitudes of the public.[6] Commemorations are based on certain values and mobilize

---

1 A shorter version of this article has been published in *Matériaux pour l'histoire de notre temps* (2016). See references.
2 See e.g. Fillière 2016; Verreycken 2015.
3 See e.g. Wellings 2016; Winter 2014.
4 Wouters 2016.
5 Aronson, Wilson & Akert 2005, cited by Sammut 2015, 97.
6 See Lavabre 2001.

a set of representations. In terms of values, the notion of peace constitutes the central axis of most memorial activities in Belgium.[7] Given this focus, we could expect that participation in commemorative activities will influence the level of pacifist attitudes of the participants. But what are the mechanisms that could explain the influence of the commemorations on attitudes?

2 Commemorations and persuasion

In Belgium, the individualization/personalization of the relation to the past constitutes one of the fundamental aspects of some of the most successful commemorative activities and especially of documentaries and exhibitions. This individualization is made possible, among other things, by portraying everyday life during the war and the reference to characters with which individuals can more or less easily identify. This effect is typically palpable in museums and exhibitions.[8] Interactive visits are organized around stories of the war experience of specific characters. This immersion in the narrative of an individual experience is reinforced by the use of a specific scenography and music, arousing visitors' empathy and emotions.[9] According to Wouters, "this approach of identification is mostly a continuation and reinforcement of the most essential, traditional core-narrative of WWI commemorations, namely the pacifist one".[10] This focus on pacifism constitutes the core of the commemorations in Flanders and is an important value of the commemorations in the other Belgian communities. Given these specificities, we will address the question of the effects of the commemorations by considering a mechanism where emotions and identification hold a key role.

"All forms of human communication need to be seen fundamentally as stories".[11]

This strong assertion underlies what was then a new concept in communication theory, the narrative paradigm. This approach to human communication has influenced a wealth of literature far beyond its original realm. In psychology and communication research, Fisher's insights have been imported into the field of narrative persuasion. Narrative persuasion occurs when "stories" or narratives, influence individuals' beliefs, attitudes, behaviors.[12] This research particularly focuses on attitudes. That stories can be used to convey messages or foster attitudes is familiar to anyone who has been exposed to a parabola from the Bible such as *the Good Samaritan*, a fable by Jean

---

7   See Bost & Kesteloot 2014; Wouters 2016.
8   Bedford 2001.
9   This is especially the case in the two exhibitions we studied: *J'avais 20 ans en 14* and *14–18: c'est notre histoire* (for a description, see below).
10 Wouters 2016, 83.
11 Fisher 1987, xi.
12 See e.g. Green, Strange & Brock 2003.

de La Fontaine, such as *the Hare and the Tortoise,* or watched a film by Charlie Chaplin, such as *Modern Times* (to borrow examples from Western culture only). Basically, information presented in the form of narratives has much more chance of impacting the audience than information presented in another way (see next paragraph). The contribution of narrative persuasion research has resided in the empirical observation of this phenomenon through methods inspired by experimental psychology.[13] So far, narrative persuasion has been studied via written extracts, books, short video clips and full-length movies. Moreover, the impact of the narratives on attitudes has been mainly studied in relatively controlled environments.[14] However, if one returns to Fisher's original formulation of the narrative paradigm, storytelling is not limited to such messages and environments. Humans are continually exposed to communications (e.g., radio spots, artistic representations, exhibitions). These narratives form the bulk of everyday communication and exert a great variety of effects on people's attitudes. We could then expect narrative persuasion to occur also through specific forms of commemorative activities. But how does narrative persuasion work?

Basically, narration immerses the receiver in the narrative, reduces his/her capacity to process information in depth, leading to potential attitude change. Identification with a character plays a key role in the effects of a narrative on attitudes.[15] Most stories involve characters audiences can identify with. Identification is a process in which individuals' self-awareness decreases and is replaced by a heightened emotional and cognitive connection with a character in the story.[16] Through this process, individuals come to feel what the character feels (emotional empathy), endorse the character's perspective (cognitive empathy) and even have the sensation of being the character (merging).[17] As an immersive process, identification reduces the ability to counter-argue, leading the individual to more easily adopt beliefs and attitudes related to those contained in the message.[18] For instance, if the message of a story is related to peace, we could then expect that identification with a character of this story will lead to an adoption of pacifist attitudes.

While evidence supports the link between identification with characters and attitudes, the question of its underlying mechanisms is still open. In a recent study, Hoeken and Sinkeldam put forward the role of emotions in the narrative persuasion process.[19] Emotions have traditionally been considered as an effect of exposure to

---

13 See e.g. Cho, Shen & Wilson 2014; Dal Cin, Zanna & Fong 2002; Diekman, Gardner & McDonald 2000; Hoeken & Sinkeldam 2014; Igartua 2010; Morgan, Movius & Cody 2009; Moyer-Gusé & Nabi 2010; Slater, Rouner & Long 2006.
14 See e.g. Hoeken & Sinkeldam 2014; Mazzocco, Green, Sasota, Jones 2010.
15 See e.g. De Graaf, Hoeken, Sanders & Beentjes 2011; Slater & Rouner 2002.
16 Cohen 2001.
17 Cohen 2001; Green & Dill 2013; Hoeken & Fikkers 2014.
18 Igartua 2010; Igartua & Barrios 2012; Slater & Rouner 2002.
19 Hoeken & Sinkeldam 2014.

narratives[20], but their impact on attitudes has also been acknowledged.[21] According to a recent model,[22] specific (sadness-related) emotions are believed to mediate the relation between identification with characters and attitudes while other emotions do not. Building on Frijda's work,[23] Hoeken and Sinkeldam consider emotions as signals to the individual that his or her interests are at stake. In this sense, negative emotions would alert individuals that are identified with characters that what is happening in the narration is not in their interest. This would in turn, influence individuals' attitudes.

Could this mechanism of narrative persuasion account for the potential change of attitudes following participation in a commemoration? This is what we will see as the result of five studies conducted at two kinds of commemorative activities: exhibitions and documentaries. In its modern sense, commemoration is a more or less ritualized and more or less official cultural practice, which consists in the recall in the present of a past event. It is a manifestation of memory that can take the form of monuments,[24] images[25] and more often celebrations.[26] What is usually commemorated are events perceived as important by a society or group of individuals (often victories and founding events). Commemoration is defined as a political act and fulfils a key function in the shaping of social identity. It is an opportunity to develop a common narrative of the past and the reaffirmation of shared values. In this regard, it allows the creation of a link between the members of the society and the affirmation of their collective identity.[27] But beyond this identity-shaping function, commemoration can also serve as a tribute. The latter is particularly important in the case of commemorations of wars and other conflicts. In this case, expressing some form of mourning for the victims of war would make sense of the sacrifices made during the conflict.[28]

Over the last few decades, commemorations have taken an increasingly important place at the societal level. This phenomenon, noticeable since the 1980s, has been described as *frénésie/fièvre/course/obsession/boulimie commémorative*.[29] Their forms have also evolved. They now exceed traditional collective gatherings and ceremonies. Thus, according to Nora,

> "l'esprit de la commémoration s'exprime dorénavant bien plus à travers la télévision, les musées, les théâtres, l'exposition "obligatoire" et le "fatidique colloque"" [The spirit of com-

---

20 See e.g. Oatley 2002.
21 See e.g. Dillard & Anderson 2004; Earl & Albarracin 2007.
22 See Hoeken & Sinkeldam 2014.
23 Frijda 1986.
24 Prost 1984; Savage 2007.
25 Schwartz 1982.
26 Cottret & Henneton 2010.
27 See Ashplant, Dawson & Roper 2000; Spillman 1997.
28 Loyd 2014; Mosse 1991; Simpson 2006.
29 See e.g. François 1994; Gillis 1996; Nora 1992.

memoration is now expressed more and more through television, museums, theatres, the "compulsory" exhibition and the "fateful colloquium"].[30]

This process unfolds globally and its inflation seems supported by public media.[31] Although these new forms of commemorations are characterized by the lesser role they give to social gatherings, they involve a fairly similar set of cognitive and emotional processes as prototypical commemorations.[32] It is these new kinds of commemorations that we will investigate in the following studies. The first activity we will focus on is the visit of exhibitions.

3 Exhibitions

The goals of historical exhibitions are multiple. One of them is generally to draw lessons from history, where historical events are a vehicle for generating such lessons. And they rely more and more on narratives in order to transport the visitor in the historical events they portray.[33] As such, exhibitions and museums can be interpreted as conveyors of stories.[34] The biggest exhibitions organized in Belgium on the occasion of the centenary of WWI – *J'avais 20 ans en 14 [I was 20 in 14]* and *14–18: c'est notre histoire! [14–18: It's our History!]* – rely heavily on narratives. The first exhibition took place at the Liège-Guillemins railway station and was opened to the public between August 2014 and May 2015. It extended over 4,000 m² and presented some aspects of the day-to-day life in Belgium during WWI. It has been designed to put an emphasis on emotions and character identification:

> "Walk through an ultra-realistic 30-meter long trench with striking sound and light effects"; "Enter a peaceful chapel that overlooks the poignant scene of an execution of civilians".[35]

Reconstitutions of trenches with noises of explosions, a destroyed house with cries of a young child, made the exhibition extremely realistic and emotional. Six months after its official opening, the exhibition had attracted more than 150,000 visitors.[36] It explicitly focused on pacifism, as its development is one of the major effects of WWI:

> "The exhibition underlines the importance of the fundamental value of peace, a guarantee of democracy, freedom, justice and solidarity".[37]

---

30 Nora 1992, 985.
31 Cottret & Henneton 2010.
32 See Bouchat & Rimé 2017.
33 Lambert 2009.
34 Bedford 2001; Rounds 2002.
35 Press File 2014, 11.
36 Newsletter 2015.
37 Press File 2014, 10.

The second exhibition, *14–18: c'est notre histoire!*, which constitutes the frame of the second and third studies, took place between February 2014 and November 2015 at the Royal Museum of the Army and of Military History in Brussels. It attracted over 175,000 visitors. The main theme of the exhibition was the war and everyday life in Belgium during WWI. A deep emphasis was placed on emotions with the aim of making the visitor concerned by the story of the exhibition:

> "The exhibition appeals to the minds and hearts of visitors, making them both understand and feel that this history concerns them and involves them – it is *their* history".[38]

Building on Fisher's formulation of the narrative paradigm, we believe that narrative persuasion constitutes a privileged medium for the study of the influence of exhibitions about WWI on pacifist attitudes. Indeed, exhibitions that rely on the value of peace may in principle influence pacifist attitudes (e.g. fostering greater pacifism) by allowing the individual to identify with characters and feel specific emotions. This leads us to formulate the following hypotheses:

1. the level of pacifist attitudes of the participants will be higher after visiting the exhibition than before;
2. stronger identification with characters will produce stronger pacifist attitudes.
3. stronger identification with characters will evoke stronger emotions.
4. emotions will mediate (explain part of) the relation between identification with characters and pacifist attitudes (see Figure 1).

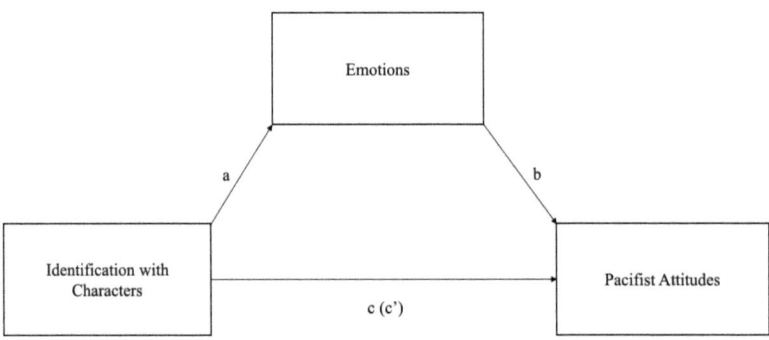

Figure 1: Hypothesized Mediation

---

38 Press Release 2014.

3.1 J'avais 20 ans en 14

We test these hypotheses using a step-by-step approach. Study 1 is conducted in the context of a historical exhibition of WWI: *J'avais 20 ans en 14*, at the Liège-Guillemins railway station. As already mentioned, it aims at investigating the effects of narrative persuasion on pacifist attitudes (Hypotheses 2 to 4).

276 Belgian participants, (124 males) were asked to fill in a paper-pencil questionnaire at the end of the exhibition. The average age is 48.62 (SD = 32.22). Data collection lasted for three weeks and was conducted by two experimenters at random times of the day. The questionnaire was composed of three kinds of measures: Identification with characters, emotions and pacifist attitudes.

Identification with characters: During their visit, participants were exposed to several characters (i.e., a soldier, a nurse, a child) with which they identified. The level of identification with characters during the exhibition was appraised by the identification with characters scale (EDI) adapted from Igartua and Páez.[39] All variables were measured on 7-point scales, ranging from 1 = not at all to 7 = very much. Given that individuals were able to identify with several characters at varying levels of intensity, identification with characters has been considered generically[40] following the procedure used by Igartua.[41] Identification with characters used in the following analyses is this generic vision.

Emotions elicited by the exhibition: Three emotions experienced during the commemorative activity were measured by asking "To what extent did you feel the following emotions during your visit of the exhibition". The emotions were sadness, anger and pride.

Pacifist attitudes: The level of pacifist attitudes of the participants was measured using a French version of the Attitudes toward Peace and War Scale (APWS).[42]

For the sake of readability, we do not present the results of statistical tests in text but rather in two tables. Descriptive statistics are reported in Table 1. The dominant emotion was in this case sadness. But the levels of anger and pride were also above the mid-point of the scale. With regard to Hypothesis 2, it was tested whether stronger identification with characters would produce stronger pacifist attitudes. In order to do so, a simple linear regression was run (results of the regressions are presented in Table 2). Consistent with our Hypothesis, results show that identification with characters is positively linked with pacifist attitudes. Next, we tested whether identification with characters would evoke stronger emotions during the commemorative ex-

---

[39] Igartua & Páez 1998.
[40] Generically means that a global level of identification has been measured, that corresponds to the aggregation of the identification with all characters the individuals have identified with.
[41] Igartua 2010.
[42] Van der Linden, Leys, Klein & Bouchat 2017.

perience. Results of a linear regression show that this is the case. The more individuals identify with characters, the more they feel sadness and anger and the less they feel pride. This brings empirical support to Hypothesis 3.

Finally, we tested whether emotions would mediate (i.e. explain) the relation between identification with characters and pacifist attitudes. In order to test this Hypothesis, we ran mediation analyses.[43] Results of the mediations are displayed in Table 2. They suggest that only one type of emotion, pride, partially mediates (explains) the relation between identification with characters and pacifist attitudes. Hypothesis 4 is thus only partially supported. So, what did we learn from this first study?

Study 1 was designed in order to investigate the presence of narrative persuasion mechanisms during the commemorative experience. First, it shows that the exhibition actually elicits strong emotions. It also shows that individuals do identify with characters. Next, the main contribution of Study 1 is that it replicates the basic mechanism of narrative persuasion in a brand-new field: Historical exhibition. Identification with characters is indeed significantly linked with pacifist attitudes. However, only one specific emotion (pride) successfully mediates the relation between identification with characters and pacifist attitudes. The present results also suggest that narrative persuasion would constitute an appropriate mechanism in order to explain the impact of an exhibition on pacifist attitudes. However, Study 1 is characterized by a number of limitations. The first resides in the possible selection bias of the participants. Despite the presence of experimenters at various times of the day during three weeks, it is possible that a specific category of participants refused to complete the questionnaire. We try to overcome this limitation in the next studies by following classes of secondary school students. A second limitation resides in the absence of a baseline measure of pacifist attitudes. The absence of such a measure prevented us from appraising the effect of the visit on pacifist attitudes (Hypothesis 1). Moreover, as all variables were measured simultaneously, causality is difficult to establish with certainty. Such design is widespread in the study of narrative persuasion.[44] However, we try to establish causality in a more controlled design.

---

[43] See Hayes 2013. In this case, mediation analyses are used to explore potential explanatory mechanisms of the relation between identification and attitudes. They are classical statistical analyses basically composed of three linear regressions.
[44] See e.g. Hoeken & Sinkeldam 2014.

3.2 14–18: c'est notre histoire

The next two studies were conducted in the context of the temporary exhibition *14–18: c'est notre histoire!*. Their design has been enhanced with measures taken at two times. The repeated measures design was created to appraise the evolution of pacifist attitudes after the visit (Hypothesis 1). It also allows studying the effects of narrative persuasion while controlling for the baseline level of pacifist attitudes (Hypotheses 2 to 4). Participants visited the exhibition as part of their history lessons.

In Studies 2 and 3, participants were secondary school students: French speakers in Study 2 ($N = 83$; 35 males, $M_{age} = 16.43$, $SD = .74$) and Dutch speakers in Study 3 ($N = 45$; 40 males, $M_{age} = 16.58$, $SD = .76$). Participants were asked to fill in questionnaires in their language of instruction at two measure times. A baseline measure was taken 15 days before the exhibition (at school with a paper-pencil questionnaire). They were asked to fill in a second questionnaire after their visit (in a room at the end of the exhibition). Questionnaires were matched with an individual code. Baseline measures were taken for pacifist attitudes (APWS). Then, just after the visit, participants were asked to complete again the APWS, the EDI (Identification with characters scale) and to rate to what extent they felt sadness, anger and pride during the visit.

Descriptive results are presented in Table 1. They show that participants in Studies 2 and 3 feel a different pattern of emotions than in Study 1. In this case, pride is the emotion that is felt the most intensely. Moreover, Dutch speakers report a lower mean level of emotions and of identification with characters than the French-speaking students. Such results suggest that the experience of the exhibition may have been different for the two linguistic groups. However, the impact of the visit on their level of pacifist attitudes is similar for both samples. The design of Studies 2 and 3 allows for testing the evolution of pacifist attitudes after the visit. We ran paired t-tests in order to test Hypothesis 1. Contrary to what was expected, results show that pacifist attitudes of the participants drop after visiting the exhibition (see Table 1).

Next, we used simple linear regressions in order to test Hypotheses 2 to 4. As the repeated measures design allows controlling for the baseline level of pacifist attitudes, we introduced it in the analyses. When controlling for pacifist attitudes at T1 (15 days before the visit), identification with characters is not significantly linked to pacifist attitudes at T2 (just after the visit), neither in Study 2 nor in 3. Hypothesis 2 is thus not confirmed. Next, still controlling for pacifist attitudes at T1, results of linear regressions show identification with characters is linked with the three emotions (see Table 2). Hypothesis 3 is thus confirmed in both studies. Finally, we did not run mediation analyses, given the absence of a significant link between identification and attitudes when controlling for the baseline level of pacifist attitudes. What are the additional lessons learned from these two studies?

Studies 2 and 3 were designed in order to appraise the impact of an exhibition on pacifist attitudes and to investigate the narrative persuasion processes during the commemorative activity. However, instead of confirming our insights, the present results are quite unexpected. First, descriptive statistics suggest that the experience of the exhibition may have been quite different for French and Dutch speakers. Indeed, the latter report lower levels of identification with characters and of emotions. The exhibition was presented in both languages. Still, we could suppose that the students did not experience it the same way. It is actually possible that given their cultural differences, they have been attracted by different aspects of the exhibition. They can also have identified with different characters. However, the design of the studies did not allow investigating the content of the exhibition. The role of the experience of the visit is thus an issue left open.

Another finding of Studies 2 and 3 is the result of the improvement of their design. The inclusion of a baseline measure of pacifist attitudes led us to reconsider the prior findings of Study 1. When a baseline measure of attitudes is taken, the effect of identification on attitudes is not significant anymore and we do not find mediation by the emotions. This absence of significant effect can be explained in at least four different ways. First, the sample size of Study 3 is small. Such a small number of observations can lead to an absence of effect per se. However, this is not the case in Study 2. Second, the inclusion of a baseline measure of attitudes is not a constant in narrative persuasion research. For instance, Hoeken and Sinkeldam[45] did not control for the baseline level of attitudes when they observed a mediating effect of specific emotions. It is thus possible that, in some situations, when not controlling for a baseline level of attitudes, narrative persuasion processes are less robust than expected. Third, the absence of a significant effect suggests that it can be quite arduous to show clear narrative persuasion processes in situations that differ from laboratory settings. Indeed, in the case of an exhibition, the participants are exposed to many different – and maybe even contradictory – messages. Moreover, as a less controlled environment, the exhibition could be characterized by an increased presence of distractors, reducing the capacity of the individuals to follow one clear message. Finally, while most studies on narrative persuasion used explicit messages, it is not especially the case for exhibitions. It is then possible that more implicit arguments would lead to an absence of clear persuasive effects.

But the most interesting results of the present studies concern the evolution of the pacifist attitudes. While the experience of the visit seems to have been different for the two groups, their participation in the exhibition is linked to a similar evolution of their level of pacifist attitudes: The mean level of pacifist attitudes is lower after the visit than 15 days before. This result is quite paradoxical given the fact that the value of peace is central in the program of the exhibition. How is such an effect possible? The Elaboration Likelihood Model (i.e. a model of persuasion from which the E-ELM is a direct extension)[46] can provide a tentative answer to this question. In this model,

---

45   Hoeken & Sinkeldam 2014.
46   Petty & Cacioppo 1986; Petty & Wegener 1999.

an attitude change in the opposite direction to that held in the message is called "boomerang effect".[47] It is the result of the generation of more negative thoughts than positive ones about the message topic.[48] The boomerang effect may occur especially when the arguments in the message are considered weak, irrelevant, but also aversive.[49] In the case of the exhibition, it is conceivable that secondary school students did not consider the arguments presented in favour of peace/pacifism as relevant or persuasive enough to increase or even maintain their level of pacifist attitudes. They could also have perceived the message as an aversive one, leading to a decrease in their level of pacifist attitudes.

Still, recent findings could also explain this paradoxical effect. Indeed, Bouchat and colleagues[50] have shown that WWI-related indicators of victimization were linked to the current level of pacifist attitudes of young Europeans. More specifically, the death toll by country during the war is positively linked to the level of pacifist attitudes. By contrast, the presence of an ancestor who was victimized during WWI in the family of the participant was negatively linked to his level of pacifist attitudes. These results suggest that a national *ethos* of reconciliation may coexist with a vindictive logic at the individual level.

The commemorations in Belgium can also be appraised from this point of view. Indeed, most of the observed commemorations focus on the figure of the victim, whether civilian or military. Knowing that the results of the previous survey suggest that the presence of a conflict victim in their families is negatively associated with the level of pacifist attitudes of individuals, it seems useful to question the impact of commemorations that promote empathy for the victims. In the eyes of many of the protagonists involved in the commemorative field, it goes without saying that participation in commemorative activities increases – or at least does not affect – the level of pacifist attitudes of individuals. However, in line with the above results, we could assume that the commemorations that focus on the victims of the Great War and their concrete suffering will influence pacifist attitudes in a negative way. This constitutes our new Hypothesis (H1b): Commemorative activities that focus on the figure of the victim will lead to a decrease in the level of pacifist attitudes of the participants while activities that do not put a high focus on victims would not affect it. We test this Hypothesis using larger samples and via a medium allowing for more control: Historical documentaries.

---

47 See Petty, Briñol & Priester 2009.
48 Byrne & Hart 2009; Petty, Wegener Fabrigar, Priester & Cacioppo 1993.
49 Haugtvedt, Petty, Cacioppo & Steidley 1988.
50 Bouchat *et al.* 2017.

4 Documentaries

Historical documentaries generally report the unfolding of important historical events. In order to do so, they often rely on the narrative form to describe the experience of ordinary individuals immersed in these events. An example is the recent TV show "Apocalypse",[51] which was aired during prime time on French television. In its first instalment, broadcast in 2014, this show described the history of World War I using colorized archives. It heavily relied on the use of personal narratives. The avowed goal of the documentary was to "preserve the memory of WWI."

The use of the documentary format is not common in narrative persuasion studies. However, it is quite usual to use films as a medium for inducing narrative persuasion.[52] Unlike studies in the exhibitions, the use of video material allows more control of the content of the message and of eventual distractors. We thus use WWI-related documentaries in order to test our Hypotheses.

Documentaries and focus on victims

The commemorations of the centenary have been characterized by the large-scale distribution of documentaries produced for the occasion. The following studies are based on the screening of documentaries with low-focus (Study 4) vs. high-focus on victims (Study 5). Both are Belgian documentaries about WWI in Belgium. They last for 20 minutes and are of two types. The first, *Les trois serments*[53] focuses on the experience of a Belgian soldier at the beginning of the war. The story is built around a letter that a grandfather wrote to his granddaughter, and alternates between past and present. It begins with a presentation of the situation in Belgium and Europe before the war. It then focuses on the invasion of Belgium by the German troops and ends with the fall of the Belgian fortress of Loncin in August 1914. Central facts are punctuated by the intervention of historians. The second extract *Les Murs de Dinant*,[54] focuses on the experience of the massacres of civilians in the town of Dinant in August 1914. It also alternates between past and present, due to the use of testimonies of descendants of victims. This second extract places a particular emphasis on the figure of the victim and the long-term consequences of the massacres. Both documentaries are privileged means of expanding individuals' knowledge of WWI. Unlike books and history classes, they offer low cost and less sober access to knowledge in terms of cognitive efforts (because of the level of illustration).

---

51 Costelle & Clarke 2014.
52 See e.g. Costabile & Terman 2013; Igartua 2010; Igartua & Barrios 2012.
53 Pireaux & Donjean 2014.
54 Freres, Dardenne & Dartevelle 2014.

Participants in Studies 4 and 5 were university students in psychology (first year): $N = 98$; 12 males, $M_{age} = 21.25$, $SD = 6.82$ & $N = 60$; 12 males, $M_{age} = 19.42$, $SD = 1.99$. The design of the data collection is similar to the one used in Studies 2 and 3. Participants were asked to complete questionnaires 15 days before their viewing the movie and then immediately after it. The main difference was that participants were asked to fill in questionnaires in a psychology laboratory rather than in a classroom. The same measures were taken in Studies 4 and 5 as in Studies 2 and 3. Baseline measures of pacifist attitudes: (APWS); pacifist attitudes after the viewing; identification with characters in the documentary: (EDI); emotions.

First, descriptive results show that the level of sadness is quite high in both studies, but the level of pride is quite different between the samples (see Table 1). In the study with a high focus on victims, the level of pride is very low (1.56 on a 1–7 scale) while it is higher than the mid-point of the scale in the study with a low focus on victims. Results also show that participants in Study 5 (high focus) do identify less strongly with characters than participants in Study 4 (low focus). Next, we tested our new Hypothesis using paired t-tests. Consistent with it, results show that in the case of the movie with a low focus on victims (Study 4), the level of pacifist attitudes does not significantly evolve. On the contrary – and still in line with our Hypothesis – we notice a decrease in the level of pacifist attitudes after the viewing of the movie with a high focus on victims (Study 5; see Table 2). Hypothesis 1b is thus confirmed.

Next, we tested Hypotheses 2 to 4. Results are similar as in Studies 2 and 3. More specifically, when controlled for the baseline level of pacifist attitudes, identification with characters is not significantly linked with the level of pacifist attitudes after the visit. Hypothesis 2 is thus not confirmed. Then, as in the previous studies, Hypothesis 3 is mainly supported: with the exception of pride in Study 5, identification with characters is positively linked with emotions. Finally, given the absence of a significant relation between identification and pacifist attitudes, the Hypothesis concerning the mediation has not been tested (see Table 2).

Table 1: Mean levels of the main variables & paired t-test score of pacifist attitudes between T1 and T2

Study	Identification Characters M & (SD)	Sadness M & (SD)	Anger M & (SD)	Pride M & (SD)	Pacifist Attitudes T1 M & (SD)	Pacifist Attitudes T2 M & (SD)	Score t-test Pacifist Attitudes & (Effect Size)
1. Expo Liège	4.67 (1.25)	5.57 (1.56)	4.61 (2.11)	4.62 (1.96)	–	5.42 (.80)	–
2. Expo Brussels French	4.21 (1.13)	4.26 (1.90)	3.38 (1.96)	5.05 (1.71)	5.34 (.77)	5.12 (.87)	3.66*** (.423)
3. Expo Brussels Dutch	2.86 (1.25)	3.21 (1.76)	3.05 (1.65)	3.71 (1.58)	4.76 (1.10)	4.40 (.60)	2.26* (.343)
4. Movie low victim	4.53 (1.29)	4.88 (1.50)	3.84 (1.73)	4.59 (2.05)	5.23 (.80)	5.23 (.80)	.03 (0)
5. Movie high victim	3.80 (1.23)	5.07 (1.76)	3.19 (1.86)	1.56 (1.25)	5.50 (.76)	5.31 (.78)	2.89** (.370)

Notes

Numbers in the first three columns are mean scores and standard deviations. Fourth column is the paired t-test value between pacifist attitudes at T1 and T2. *: $p < .05$. **: $p < .01$. ***: $p < .001$.

Table 2: Results of the mediations

	a	b	c'	c	Sobel's Z
Study 1 (No control for baseline PA)					
Sadness	.43**	.07*	.13**	.09*	1.87
Anger	.31**	.06*	.13**	.09*	1.68
Pride	.32**	−.12**	.13**	.09*	−2.61
Study 2					
Sadness	1.34**	.11	–	−.01	–
Anger	1.29**	.00	–	−.01	–
Pride	1.01**	.03	–	−.01	–
Study 3					
Sadness	.61**	−.10	–	−.03	–
Anger	.68**	−.04	–	−.03	–
Pride	.55**	.17	–	−.03	–
Study 4					
Sadness	.30*	.07	–	.05	–
Anger	.32*	-.03	–	.05	–
Pride	.56**	-.02	–	.05	–
Study 5					
Sadness	.77**	−.04	–	−.07	–
Anger	.74**	.04	–	−.07	–
Pride	.24	.03	–	−.07	–

Notes

b: path from mediator (emotions) to dependent variable (attitude); c: direct path (from identification to attitude) without mediator, c': direct path with mediator (see Figure 1). Coefficients are unstandardized regression coefficients. *: p < .05. **: p < .01.

The main goal of Studies 4 and 5 was to investigate whether portraying figures of victims during commemorative activities would influence the pacifist attitudes of the participants. Results show that in the instance of a documentary, it is the case. The vision of a documentary with a high focus on victims led to a decrease of the level of pacifist attitudes of the participants. By contrast, with respect to the documentary that was not specifically focused on the victims' experience, we did not witness a significant evolution of the pacifist attitudes. Starting from the findings by Bouchat and colleagues,[55] we could suppose that this effect is the result of identification with victimized characters, identification associated with a vindictive logic. The simultaneous presence of a message of peace whether implicit or explicit and of figures of victims to which it is possible to identify with, would therefore not be appropriate in the case of commemorations aiming at increasing the level of pacifist attitudes. This tentative explanation should be studied more systematically in future studies.

Next, Studies 4 and 5 showed that when controlling for the baseline level of pacifist attitudes, no significant effect of narrative persuasion was found. This result was not expected because the media we used is similar to the one applied in several studies on narrative persuasion.

5 General discussion

The starting point of our approach lies in the premise that commemorations are likely to modify the knowledge and attitudes of the individuals who take part in them. After five studies on the topic, it is clear that, under certain circumstances, commemorations do not produce the desired effects. Indeed, the studies conducted lead to a set of observations that may seem surprising: Those who focus on the figure of the victim generate a decrease of the level of pacifist attitudes of the participants. This result is all the more striking as the values underlying the commemorations are often explicitly linked to peace. The paradoxical nature of this phenomenon highlights the contrast between the objectives displayed by the designers of the commemorations and the effects observed here. It also indicates the existence of a tension between, on the one hand, the valorisation of peace as an almost absolute value and, on the other hand, the accentuation of the emotional devices put in place to favour empathy of participants called to identify with the victims of war.

This point seems particularly interesting for further reflection. The expected effects of the commemorations on pacifist attitudes appear a priori to be obvious. Yet they are challenged. This finding helps reflect the expectations pursued by all the protagonists involved in this type of commemorations. Public authorities, historians who assume most of the time the status of experts, donors, artists or filmmakers certainly do not pursue the same objectives. But one of the most consensual aims is probably to

---

55 Bouchat *et al.* 2017.

promote a culture of peace, which, it is hoped, will constitute a bulwark against the repetition of past violence. This is especially the case of Flanders where the main objective of the commemorations is to promote Flanders as an international centre in terms of peace and reconciliation.[56] Hence the need to think about the measures to adopt: if they are able to influence individual attitudes, is it in the direction of an increase or a decrease in pacifist attitudes?

The comparative analysis of commemorative activities in Belgium shows that in terms of importance and cost, none of them has ever reached the commemorations organized in 2014. The choice to play with the emotions of the visitors reflects to some extent the expectations of the public. In any case, it reminds us that beyond the "civic" objective pursued by the public authorities, the touristic aspect of the commemorations is often at the forefront.[57] This phenomenon, which has been present in most European countries for several decades, is particularly massive.[58] Commemorations are thus considered to be sources of income by the different Belgian communities but also by a set of private actors.[59] This phenomenon is particularly marked in Flanders, where the commemorations are first of all regarded as a "total marketing product" accompanied by an "added ethical value".[60] The Flemish authorities, and in particular the Minister of Tourism in charge of commemorations, emphasized the absurd and cruel aspects of the conflict and the absolute necessity of avoiding the repetition of the war. Such a vision is relatively consensual in the eyes of the general public. However, historians of the Great War do not fail to point out that by presenting fallen soldiers as "passive victims" crushed by the war machine, commemorations erase the dimensions of commitment and consent to the war.[61] As for the impact of such a vision on pacifist attitudes, this reflection calls for great caution.

In a next step, our study aimed at exploring the mechanisms responsible for the paradoxical effect of the commemorations of WWI on pacifist attitudes. Building on the narrative paradigm,[62] we considered the commemorative activities (i.e., exhibitions and documentaries) as conveyors of persuasive messages. Given the wide use of emotions and characters by the designers of the commemorations in order to reinforce the implication of the participants, we considered that the narrative persuasion model would be well suited for explaining the attitude change of the participants. Indeed, the narrative persuasion model gives a central role to the identification with characters in the persuasion process. More specifically, identifying with characters would lead to attitude change by decreasing the ability of the participants to counter-

---

56 Wouters 2016.
57 See Bost & Kesteloot 2014; Wouters 2016.
58 Iles 2008; Loyd 2014; Winter 2014.
59 See e.g. Wouters 2016.
60 Bost & Kesteloot 2014.
61 Audoin-Rouzeau & Becker 2000.
62 Fisher 1987.

argue. And the emotions experienced during the commemorative activity would play the role of mediator of this relation. However, the results of the different studies do not support our hypotheses. When controlling for the baseline level of pacifist attitudes, identification with characters does not significantly predict the level of pacifist attitudes after the commemoration. Several explanations have been advanced in order to explain these unexpected results: presence of a control measure of the baseline level of pacifist attitudes, "noises" inherent to ecological situations, and the inability of the narrative persuasion model for appraising the attitude change during the commemorative process. None of these explanations being completely satisfying, one could suppose that the narrative persuasion mechanism is not appropriate to account for the commemorative experience.

6 Conclusion

The present chapter revealed that the effects of commemorations are sometimes quite paradoxical. However, it is not without limitations. The first resides in the restricted number of commemorative activities studied: two documentaries and two exhibitions. Even if the exhibitions were two of the most visited in Belgium and the documentaries were seen by a large number of people, commemorations are not limited to these media. The study of ceremonies, for instance, could reveal precious information on the collective dynamics at stake in the commemorations (here, we think especially about the role of collective emotions). A second limitation lies in the limited diversity of the samples. Indeed, the Dutch-speaking group of participants seemed less involved in the exhibition than their French-speaking counterparts (they identified less with characters and experienced a lower level of emotions). The inclusion of groups of participants from diverse generations and cultures (especially participants from immigrant origins) could help nuance our results. Finally, the content of the exhibitions and documentaries and the singular experience of the visit/viewing for each participant were not addressed. However, recent works suggest that these factors are of the utmost importance in the study of the impacts of the exhibitions.[63] Here, this is paradoxically the fact of not having sufficiently contextualized the commemorative experience, which reminds us of how contextualization is critical in the study of attitudes.

The commemorations of the centenary of WWI constituted an unprecedented event by the number and type of activities organized. These were a popular success and attracted a wide and diverse audience. The results we obtained through these five studies therefore reflect only a minimal part of the reality of the commemorative experience. Nevertheless, by highlighting the sometimes paradoxical effects of the commemorative activities, they confirm the relevance of a social psychological approach in the study of commemorations.

---

63 See Gensburger, Antichan, Teboul & Torterat 2016.

References

Aronson, E., Wilson, T. & Akert, R. (2005). *Social Psychology*, 5th ed. Upper Sadd, NJ: Prentice Hall.

Ashplant, T. G., Dawson, G. & Roper, M. (2000). *The Politics of War Memory and Commemoration*. London: Psychology Press.

Audoin-Rouzeau, S. & Becker, A. (2000). *14–18, retrouver la guerre*. Paris: Gallimard.

Bedford, L. (2001). Storytelling: The Real Work of Museums. *Curator: the Museum Journal, 44* (1), 27–34.

Bost, M. & Kesteloot, C. (2014). Les commémorations du centenaire de la Première Guerre mondiale. *Courrier hebdomadaire du CRISP, 30,* 5–63.

Bouchat, P., Licata, L., Rosoux, V., Allesch, C., Ammerer, H., Bovina, A., … Klein, O. (2017). A Century of Victimhood: Antecedents and Current Impacts of Perceived Suffering in World War I across Europe. *European Journal of Social Psychology, 47,* 195–208.

Bouchat, P., Klein, O. & Rosoux, V. (2016). L'impact paradoxal des commémorations de la Grande Guerre. *Matériaux pour l'Histoire de Notre Temps, 121–122,* 26–31.

Bouchat, P. & Rimé, B. (in press). National Identity and Collective Memory: A Social Psychological Perspective. In D. Ingenhoff, C. White, A. Buhmann & S. Kiousis (Eds), *Bridging disciplinary perspectives on the formation and effects of country image, reputation, brand, and identity*.

Byrne, S. & Hart, P. S. (2009). The Boomerang Effect. A Synthesis of Findings and a Preliminary Theoretical Framework. *Annals of the International Communication Association, 33*(1), 3–37.

Cho, H., Shen, L. & Wilson, K. (2014). Perceived Realism: Dimensions and Roles in Narrative Persuasion. *Communication Research, 41*(6), 828–851.

Cohen, J. (2001). Defining Identification: A Theoretical Look at the Identification of Audiences with Media Characters. *Mass Communication & Society, 4*(3), 245–264.

Costabile, K. A. & Terman, A. W. (2013). Effects of Film Music on Psychological Transportation and Narrative Persuasion. *Basic and Applied Social Psychology, 35*(3), 316–324.

Costelle, D. & Clarke, I. (Producer) & Clarke, I. (Director). (2014). *Apocalypse, la Première Guerre Mondiale*. France-Canada: CC&C, Idéacom international & ECPAD.

Cottret, B. & Henneton, L. (Eds) (2010). La commémoration, entre mémoire prescrite et mémoire proscrite. *Du bon usage des commémorations. Histoire, mémoire et identité*. Rennes: Presses universitaires de Rennes.

Dal Cin, S., Zanna, M. P. & Fong, G. T. (2004). Narrative Persuasion and Overcoming Resistance. In Knowles, E. S. & Linn, J. A. (Eds), *Resistance and Persuasion*. Mahwah, NJ, US: Lawrence Erlbaum Associates Publishers, 175–191.

De Graaf, A., Hoeken, H., Sanders, J. & Beentjes, J. W. (2012). Identification as a Mechanism of Narrative Persuasion. *Communication Research, 39*(6), 802–823.

Diekman, A. B., Gardner, W. L. & McDonald, M. (2000). Love Means Never Having to be Careful: The Relationship Between Reading Romance Novels and Safe Sex Behavior. *Psychology of Women Quarterly, 24*(2), 179–188.

Dillard, J. P. & Anderson, J. W. (2004). The Role of Fear in Persuasion. *Psychology & Marketing, 21*(11), 909–926.

Earl, A. & Albarracín, D. (2007). Nature, Decay, and Spiraling of the Effects of Fear-inducing Arguments and HIV Counseling and Testing: A Meta-analysis of the Short-and Long-term Outcomes of HIV-prevention Interventions. *Health Psychology, 26*(4), 496–596.

Fillière, M. (2016). L'émotion de la fièvre commémorative. Retrieved from http://www.lamontagne.fr/clermont-ferrand/social/2016/01/14/la-rubrique-du-mediateur-lemotion-de-la-fievre-commemorative_11737977.html

Fisher, W. R. (1987). *Human Communication as Narration: Toward a Philosophy of Reason, Value, and Action*. Columbia: University of South Carolina Press.

François, E. (1994). Nation retrouvée, "Nation à contrecœur": l'Allemagne des commémorations, *Le Débat, 78* (1), 58–65.

Freres, J. & Dardenne, J.-P. (Producer) & Dartevelle, A. (Director). (2014). *Les murs de Dinant*. Belgium: Dérives.

Frijda, N. (1986). *The Emotions*. Cambridge: Cambridge University Press.

Gensburger, S., Antichan, S., Teboul, J. & Torterat, G. (2016). *Visites scolaires, histoire et citoyenneté. Les expositions du centenaire de la Première Guerre mondiale*. Paris: La Documentation Française.

Gillis, J. R. (1996). *Commemorations: The politics of National Identity*. Princeton: Princeton University Press.

Green, M. C. & Dill, K. E. (2013). Engaging with Stories and Characters: Learning, Persuasion, and Transportation into Narrative Worlds. *The Oxford Handbook of Media Psychology*. Oxford: Oxford University Press, 449–461.

Green, M. C., Strange, J. J. & Brock, T. C. (Eds). (2003). *Narrative Impact: Social and Cognitive Foundations*. London: Taylor & Francis.

Haugtvedt, C., Petty, R. E., Cacioppo, J. T. & Steidley, T. (1988). Personality and Effectiveness: Exploring the Utility of Need for Cognition. *NA-Advances in Consumer Research, 15*(1), 209–212.

Hayes, A. F. (2013). *Introduction to Mediation, Moderation, and Conditional Process Analysis: A Regression-Based Approach*. New York: Guilford Press.

Hoeken, H. & Fikkers, K. M. (2014). Issue-relevant Thinking and Identification as Mechanisms of Narrative Persuasion. *Poetics, 44*, 84–99.

Hoeken, H. & Sinkeldam, J. (2014). The Role of Identification and Perception of Just Outcome in Evoking Emotions in Narrative Persuasion. *Journal of Communication, 64*(5), 935–955.

Igartua, J. J. (2010). Identification with Characters and Narrative Persuasion through Fictional Feature Films. *Communications*, 35 (4), 347–373.

Igartua, J. J. & Barrios, I. (2012). Changing Real-World Beliefs with Controversial Movies: Processes and Mechanisms of Narrative Persuasion. *Journal of Communication*, 62 (3), 514–531.

Igartua, J. & Paez, D. (1998). Validez y fiabilidad de una escala de empatía e identificación con los personajes. *Psicothema*, 10 (2), 423–436.

Iles, J. (2008). Encounters in the Fields–Tourism to the Battlefields of the Western Front. *Journal of Tourism and Cultural Change,* 6 (2), 138–154.

Kesteloot, C., Bost, M. (2014). Les commémorations de la Première Guerre mondiale. *Courrier hebdomadaire du CRISP,* 2235–2236.

Lambert, S. J. M. (2009). Engaging Practices: Re-thinking Narrative Exhibition Development in Light of Narrative Scholarship. Unpublished Thesis. Massey University, Palmerston North, New Zealand.

Lavabre, M.-C. (2001). Peut-on agir sur la mémoire? *Cahiers français,* 303, 8–13.

Loyd, D. W. (2014). *Battlefield tourism: Pilgrimage and the Commemoration of the Great War in Britain, Australia and Canada, 1919–1939*. London: A&C Black.

Mazzocco, P. J., Green, M. C., Sasota, J. A. & Jones, N. W. (2010). This Story is Not for Everyone: Transportability and Narrative Persuasion. *Social Psychological and Personality Science,* 1(4), 361–368.

Morgan, S. E., Movius, L. & Cody, M. J. (2009). The Power of Narratives: The Effect of Entertainment Television Organ Donation Storylines on the Attitudes, Knowledge, and Behaviors of Donors and Nondonors. *Journal of Communication,* 59 (1), 135–151.

Mosse, G. L. (1991). *Fallen Soldiers: Reshaping the Memory of the World Wars.* Oxford: Oxford University Press.

Moyer-Gusé, E. & Nabi, R. L. (2010). Explaining the Effects of Narrative in an Entertainment Television Program: Overcoming Resistance to Persuasion. *Human Communication Research,* 36 (1), 26–52.

Newsletter (2015). Retrieved April 1, 2015, from http://www.liegeexpo14-18.be/expo14-18/in dex.php/fr/infos-2/newsletter

Nora, P. (1992). L'ère de la commémoration [The Commemoration Era]. In Nora, P. (Ed.), *Les lieux de mémoire,* 3, Paris: Gallimard, 975–1012.

Oatley, K. (2002). Emotions and the Story Worlds of Fiction. In Green, M. C., Strange, J. J. & Brock, T. C. (Eds), *Narrative Impact: Social and Cognitive Foundations.* Mahwah, NJ, US: Lawrence Erlbaum Associates Publishers, 39–69.

Petty, R. E., Brinol, P. & Priester, J. R. (2009). Mass Media Attitude Change: Implications of the Elaboration Likelihood Model of Persuasion. *Media effects: Advances in Theory and Research,* 3, 125–164.

Petty, R. E. & Cacioppo, J. T. (1986). The Elaboration Likelihood Model of Persuasion. In *Communication and Persuasion.* New York: Springer, 1–24.

Petty, R. E. & Wegener, D. T. (1999). The Elaboration Likelihood Model: Current Status and Controversies. In Chaiken, S. & Trope, Y. (Eds), *Dual-Process Theories in Social Psychology.* New York, NY, US: Guilford Press, 37–72.

Petty, R. E., Wegener, D. T., Fabrigar, L. R., Priester, J. R. & Cacioppo, J. T. (1993). Conceptual and Methodological Issues in the Elaboration Likelihood Model of Persuasion: A Reply to the Michigan State Critics. *Communication Theory,* 3 (4), 336–342.

Pireaux, C. (Producer) & Donjean, J. (Director). (2014). *Les trois serments.* Belgium: Les Films de la Passerelle & RTC Télé-Liège.

Press File (2014). Retrieved April 1, 2015, from www.liegeexpo14-18.be/docs/Liege-Expo-14-18-EN.pdf

Press Release (2014). Retrieved April 1, 2015, from http://www.klm-mra.be/klm-new/14-18-press/14-18-pr-100000.pdf

Prost, A. (1984). Les monuments aux morts. In Nora, P. (Ed.), *Les lieux de mémoire 1.* Paris: Gallimard, 195–225.

Rounds, J. (2002). Storytelling in Science Exhibits. *Exhibitionist,* 21 (2), 40–43.

Sammut, G. (2015). Attitudes, Social Representations and Points of View. In Sammut, G., Andreouli, E., Gaskell, G. & Valisner, J. (Eds), *The Cambridge Handbook of Social Representations.* Cambridge, UK: Cambridge University Press, 96–112.

Savage, K. (2007). *History, Memory, and Monuments: An Overview of the Scholarly Literature on Commemoration.* Pittsburgh: University of Pittsburgh.

Schwartz, B. (1982). The Social Context of Commemoration: A Study in Collective Memory. *Social forces,* 61 (2), 374–402.

Simpson, D. (2006). *9/11: The Culture of Commemoration.* Chicago: University of Chicago Press.

Slater, M. D. & Rouner, D. (2002). Entertainment – Education and Elaboration Likelihood: Understanding the Processing of Narrative Persuasion. *Communication Theory*, 12 (2), 173–191.

Slater, M. D., Rouner, D. & Long, M. (2006). Television Dramas and Support for Controversial Public Policies: Effects and Mechanisms. *Journal of Communication*, 56 (2), 235–252.

Spillman, L. (1997). *Nation and commemoration: Creating National Identities in the United States and Australia*. Cambridge: Cambridge University Press.

Van der Linden, N., Leys, C., Klein, O. & Bouchat, P. (2017). Are Attitudes Toward Peace and War the Two Sides of the Same Coin? Evidence to the Contrary from a French Validation of the Attitudes Toward Peace and War Scale. *PloS one, 12*(9):e0184001.

Verreycken, S. (2015). *Le pédalo mémoriel. Les commémorations de 14–18 et les arts de la mémoire: une approche institutionnelle*. Retrieved from https://parenthese.hypotheses.org/656

Wellings, B. (2016). First World War Commemorations in Belgium and the Netherlands: Comparative Perspectives. *BMGN-Low Countries Historical Review*, 131 (3), 99–109.

Winter, J. (2014). Commemorating Catastrophe: Remembering the Great War 100 Years On. *Matériaux pour l'histoire de notre temps*, 113–114, 166–174.

Wouters, N. (2012). Poor Little Belgium? Flemish- and French-language Politics of Memory (2014–2018). *Journal of Belgian History*, 2–3, 192–199.

Wouters, N. (2016). The Centenary Commemorations of the Great War in Belgium. *BMGN-Low Countries Historical Review*, 131 (3), 76–86.

Bernard Rimé

Conclusions
Traces of Wartime Emotions in our Collective Memory

1   Interdisciplinary research with a panoramic view

This book provides the reader with an overview of the main results of a vast research program that focused on a detailed examination of the traces left today by a proximal historical past. With the First World War, indeed, we are facing a past to which we are still bound by experience, and not by knowledge alone. Each of us can still find in the family echoes of war experiences that were lived and reported by an identifiable great-grandfather or -grandmother, great-uncle or great-aunt. The experience of these elders is still currently circulating in conversations and family evocations. As a result, this past retains emotional power over us, sometimes at a very high level. Those who have seen André Dartevelle's documentary film "The walls of Dinant" will not forget this person who undertakes to tell the fate of his ancestors in Dinant in 1914 and who suddenly finds himself overcome by an emotion that he did not expect, to the point that he must stop and that the viewers themselves cannot escape experiencing an empathic emotion. Or, we only need to travel to the Menin Gate in Ypres and attend there the daily *Last Post* ceremony to experience a sense of deep emotional resonance with events that took place a hundred years ago. This is therefore a past still largely likely to affect us personally. No evocation of a distal past – let us think, for example, of the Battle of Waterloo – can bring about a comparable emotion and communion. However, we are probably close to reaching the limits of the experiential impact of this war. Those who suffered from the First World War are still "ours", that is, an extension of ourselves. But for our own descendants, these personal bonds we still hold will be very thin – if it still exists at all. The research reported in this book thus comes at a critical time. This is the moment when collective memory is shifting from living memory, memory still composed of lived episodes, to a memory entirely made up of abstract knowledge.

The research reported in this book is distinctive because of the disciplinary diversity of its authors. Each of the projects pursued was led by an interdisciplinary team. This is a very unusual situation in scientific work. Usually, scientific work is mono-disciplinary. Everyone works and interacts with colleagues in their own field. Such a practice presents considerable drawbacks. If it favors controversies, it also promotes implicit social consensus. A scientific discipline is not only the theatre of competition between different theories and contradictory results. It is also a cocoon in which we lock ourselves in to share preconceived ideas and blinding stereotypes that we do not question. In this book, researchers from four disciplines of the social sciences and humanities, namely political science, history, literature and social psychology, have linked their concepts and methods. Each chapter provides another set of results from this integration. Each of them went off the beaten track and proposed a line of questioning and analysis that enriches the reader. At the end of this reading, we feel amazed at the sum of what we have learned.

Basically, with this investigation, researchers, and their readers after them, are wondering how the human mind – perhaps we should say the human soul – manages to cope with the gigantic set of inconsistencies that emerge from our contemplation of these war events. Everyone is aware that the sequence of events that humans produce has the capacity to generate this type of fatality. Afterwards, however, the emotions that motivated these sequences are no longer there. Only the traces of the disaster remain – and the pain that these traces are still capable of arousing. We are irremediably confronted with these traces because we live in a country that bears them and we share links that remind us of them. How do we manage? The human mind is fundamentally a generator of meaning. It awakens to this endeavor with the countless "why?" that children ask as soon as they achieve their mastery of language. Each of us is looking for answers. Everyone participates in the fundamental mission of better understanding – and therefore better mastering – of this world in which we exist. And this search is never more active than when emotions prevail. Emotions signal critically when things do not go as planned. They thus inform us that there is a gap in our knowledge. To illustrate, when an air disaster occurs, we put our experts to work. They collect all the remaining pieces. They subject them to questioning and careful analysis, with all the rigor that science and technology are capable of. And in a majority of cases, after long processes, their efforts are successful. They are able to trace the sequence of facts and events that caused the disaster. Their work then makes it possible to develop the necessary corrections on aircraft in service. This is done so that the same disaster will not happen a second time. It may be a similar motivation that guides our study of the First World War today. Admittedly however, the historical, political, sociological, psychological – and other – variables involved in triggering the disaster are far more complex than the technical failure that causes an aircraft accident. We can only try to gather the available pieces and to weave enough links between them so that our minds can shed the best possible light on these facts that overtake us. That, in my opinion, is what this book offers us. I will therefore devote the rest of this conclusion to charting my own path, and to noting what struck me particularly in the reading, and which will continue to feed my personal meditations on this theme. Being convinced of the merits of shared knowledge and shared emotions, I dare to hope that my path will resonate with that of the reader.

2 Written traces from diaries or poems

Within the written records left by the participants and direct witnesses of the Great War, soldiers' diaries seem to have been in large numbers. Their study in the first chapter of the book reminds us of the situation of these soldiers. They experienced day after day events that were completely beyond their control and that stirred up extreme emotions. They were deprived of connection with relatives with whom they had formerly found refuge in distress. And they had serious reasons to doubt that they would ever see these relatives again. For them, writing was then an attempt to maintain a certain order through this chaos. The study notes quite judiciously that for these soldiers writing a diary was a strategy to take care of themselves and to maintain a psychological balance. Writing is a powerful tool. Much more than speech, it makes it possible to recreate the experience while ordering and filtering it. The study evidences the extent to which writing makes it possible to manipulate experience. The texts of the diaries regularly oscillate between the detached, distanced narrative and the confrontation-oriented one. This latter movement denotes the soldiers suddenly overwhelmed again by what they have just experienced. They then meticulously recount particularly dramatic events. Such events will be more difficult for them to bear in the future. Yet, the soldier who writes is no longer alone. Through his writing, he is connected. He addresses his own people, those who speak his language and share with him the same worldviews. He is returning to his country.

The historians Fredericq and Pirenne whose journals were studied in the second chapter also responded to the need to re-examine their experience during the peregrinations to which they were forced by the war events. The study reminds us of the edifying history of these two professors in their role as leaders of opposition to the manoeuvres of the German occupier. Worthy of inclusion in a *De Viris Illustribus*, their posture earned them deportation to Germany. The study shows how, at the time of the conflict, the social identity of these professors brought about the collapse of the friendly relations they had maintained until then with their German counterparts. But the study also shows how strongly the social context – and in particular social contact – could influence the evolution of Fredericq's and Pirenne's attitudes. Indeed, during their forced stay in Germany, the two professors were able to observe that not all Germans were in favor of the war and that the German population was also exposed to suffering. But their differentiated attitude towards the Germans vanished upon their return to Belgium, particularly in the wake of the shock they felt at the sight of the devastation their country had suffered. The study of the testimonies of these two actors thus intersects with concepts such as "social belonging", "social context", "contact", to which social psychology attaches central importance with regard to intergroup attitudes and attitude change.

With the study of First World War poetry, a very different form of written testimony was examined in the research program. Poetic expression is the antithesis of the diary narrative produced by direct witnesses. The narrative account mobilizes the power of articulation of the logico-rational approach. It thus enables you to put your experience in order. Poetic expression mobilizes a more archaic form of expression. The low articulation and high activation power of images and symbols are ways through which poetry powerfully conveys emotions and thus fosters emotional bridges between individuals. This is what the study shows: for over a century Lanoye's verses have aroused intense emotions in the students who discovered them. In particular, these verses have generated a high degree of empathy, pity and respect. Furthermore, the data revealed that these emotions stirred by poetry were accompanied as well by a mobilization of attitudes towards peace and war. The more the students were touched by the poems, the more they expressed a pacifist attitude.

3 Traces in streets, on walls and on envelopes

The exploration of traces has extended to the study of public space, in the streets and squares of cities that have played a pivotal role in the history of this war. Surprisingly, the study shows the extent to which these traces speak and thus represent what the authors refer to as "city-text". The comparative study of the former fortified cities of Liège and Antwerp reveals that the way in which the events were experienced there is reflected in the traces that the public spaces bear today. Thus, the distant echo of emotions, whether of glory or of shame, still resonates in our public space. A new issue then arises: Who among the inhabitants is still able to read and decode these traces? And what are the conditions of historical knowledge that support such a capacity? What use would it be for our cities to be richly endowed with historical traces of an important past if their inhabitants stand before them as before hieroglyphics prior to the Rosetta stone?

The research was taken one step further with the study of the iconographic traces left in the postage stamps of the war period and the years that followed. One must realize the place of the postage stamp at a time when the letter was the only way to maintain written communication with correspondents. All moments of written communication, in love or business, were linked to these small indented images that were carefully bought, cut, wet and pressed on an envelope, or that were found on letters coming sometimes from distant countries. Stamps decorated the envelopes. They were harvested and collected with religious care. The study of their production in relation to the evocation of the Great War reveals the very particular position of this small medium amidst the other traces. Only images are displayed on stamps, and the study suggests that the option taken in their design was one of great restraint. The imagery used invokes symbols or allegories, sometimes with an extreme distance from the concepts or events it seeks to evoke. They represented a monument to a hero of the Belgian revolution of 1830, the figure of King Albert with an overprint for the benefit of the red cross, prestigious buildings of three martyred cities, the flag of a prestigious regiment, the figure of the patriotic cardinal, or, to celebrate the centenary today, the emblematic Menin gate in Ypres, or quite simply a poppy. From this five-year war and the disasters it caused, only distant, stripped, ethereal echoes reach us through the stamps. Their potential for evocation is thus most probably in the realms of inner thought, reflection, or meditation rather than emotion. In any case, this is a hypothesis that might be examined more closely.

4 Vivid traces from younger generations

The last two studies developed in the book have chosen to examine vivid traces of the century-old conflict. One of them asks what remains of this conflict in the minds of young people today. The other one examines how young people respond to museum tours and documentaries commemorating the Great War. These two studies therefore inform us about representations, affects and attitudes that will probably be perpetuated in the rest of the 21st century by the young people interviewed and by their descendants.

The first of these studies of living traces reveals to us the extent to which, among French and German students, the representations of the First World War (responsibilities, violence, past and present suffering) are pacified. Moreover, the answers on both sides are surprisingly similar. Where have the ancestral hatreds gone among the descendants of these two countries who have torn each other to the extreme on three occasions in less than a century? And above all, what a stunning contrast there is between these peaceful responses and the painful and resentful responses of young Serbs and young Croats. These two groups were equal in exalting victimization and denouncing aggression. In a few soberly worded questions, the study reveals two remarkably contrasting worlds. In the first, the conflict is a thing of the past. The new generations possess the memory of the conflict without this memory weighing either on their present or on their future. In the second world revealed by the study, on the contrary, the conflict of the past remains "under the skin" in young respondents. And their answers reveal how precarious the future of intergroup relations is likely to be for them and their descendants. The authors of the study then evoke the exemplary history of the memory work carried out by successive generations of leaders from France and Germany. Who could doubt that it is in this work that the rationale for the study's findings lies? May this history be known, understood and meditated upon in all countries and in all human communities.

The last study reported in these pages examines how young people reacted to their visit to an exhibition with the evocative title "14–18, it's our history". The organizers of such exhibitions are generally concerned to denounce the misdeeds of war and promote pacifism. The authors of the study were surprised to find that young Flemish people differed from young French-speaking people in the level of their identification with the characters represented as well as in the level of emotions felt. It therefore seems that the two groups saw the exhibition from different perspectives.

This questions the title of the exhibition: "Our" history? Or different stories? Another major surprise to the results was the observation that after the visit, the attitudes of the young visitors were less pacifist than before the visit. In short, this visit did worse than expected. There is in any case a basic principle of emotion regulation that can be used in this context. It states that as long as an event is seen from the same viewpoint, it generates the same emotion. By telling "our history", the authors of the exhibition evoked this war from the point of view of how it was experienced in the country at the time – the perspective of the poor little Belgium that was attacked. From this perspective, the visitor's emotional response can only be vindictive. It would then be advisable to return to the lessons of the previous chapter. If they want to achieve objectives in the sense of pacifism, the authors of exhibitions must offer their visitors multiple perspectives dominated by the concern for decentralization. Undoubtedly, the primary concern must be to enrich the visitors' eyes so that they can work their way out of the rut of naïve knowledge. Was it this effect that was produced by Lanoye's war poetry verses? In any case, unlike visiting the exhibition, the emotions aroused by these poems stimulated pacifist attitudes.

5   Final word

The research program reported in this book is remarkable for the diversity of the traces it has questioned in its examination of the collective memory of this now century-old war. The authors have in turn studied diaries kept by soldiers while they were at the front, diaries kept by prominent historians under deportation, the emotional impact that war poetry still has today, the traces that remain on the streets and walls of cities particularly affected by war, the traces left in the iconography of postage stamps, the impact on the contemporary public of exhibitions and documentaries devoted to the war, and finally, the memory that emerges when the younger generations are directly surveyed in countries that were once involved in the conflict. What a program! Its development over several years has enabled its authors to provide us with a particularly vast panorama of what remains today in our memory of that era from which we cannot detach our gaze. This panorama allows us to glimpse how what seems unthinkable today was experienced by those who were exposed to it. It also permits us to analyze the distant echoes of the tremendous emotions, of glory or pain that were felt there. Finally, it enables us to examine how we resonate today when we re-expose ourselves to these echoes.

Authors

Pierre Bouchat is Doctor in psychology from *Université libre de Bruxelles* (ULB) and currently university lecturer and researcher at UCLouvain. He is interested in the social representations of history and focuses especially on the links between collective memories of the Great War and current pacifist attitudes among young Europeans.

Elke Brems is Professor of Literature and Translation at KU Leuven – Brussels. She is interested in cultural transfer, literary translation and 20th century Dutch literature. Her area of expertise is a. o. Reception Studies, focusing on how literary texts are received by readers and cultures. She is the head of the Research Unit of Translation Studies at the University of Leuven.

Chantal Kesteloot is Doctor in contemporary history. She obtained her PhD in 2001 at ULB with a thesis on the Walloon movement and Brussels from 1912 to 1965. In 1992 she joined the permanent team of the Center for Historical Research and Documentation on War and contemporary Society (CegeSoma). She is currently in charge of the Public History sector. Her main areas of interest are the legacies of the wars and Belgian history as well as issues of nationalism and national identities.

Olivier Klein is Professor of Social Psychology at ULB. He is interested in social influences bearing upon memory, in the use of historical analogies in social judgment and in social representations of historical events. He has especially studied colonial memory in Belgium and the representations of World War I in Europe. He has been an active member of the European research network COST titled *Social Representations of History in the European Union*, in which he led a working group on cognitive approaches to appraisals of History. He also recently co-edited a special issue of *Memory Studies* titled *Recent Advances in Historical Cognition*.

Olivier Luminet is Professor of Psychology at UCLouvain and ULB and Research Director at the Belgian National Fund for Scientific Research (F.R.S-FNRS). One aspect of his research examines moderating impact of emotional expression/inhibition on emotional processing and health. Another aspect is related to the effects of emotions on individual and collective memories, including flashbulb memories. Recently, he focused his work on events related to Belgian history such as the splitting of the University of Louvain, intergenerational memories of WWII and honour and shame among Belgian soldiers during WWI. In 2012 he edited a special issue of *Memory Studies* titled *The Interplay between Collective Memory and the Erosion of Nation States. The Paradigmatic Case of Belgium*.

Reine Meylaerts is Professor of Comparative Literature and Translation Studies at KU Leuven where she teaches courses on European Literature, Comparative Literature and Plurilingualism in literature. Her current research interests concern translation policy, intercultural mediation and transfer in multilingual cultures, past and present. She is the author of numerous articles and chapters on these topics. She is also review editor of *Target. International Journal of Translation Studies*. She was coordinator of 2011–2014: FP7-PEOPLE-2010-ITN: *TIME: Translation Research Training: An integrated and intersectoral model for Europe*. She is former Secretary General (2004–2007) of the *European Society for Translation Studies* (EST) and Chair of the Doctoral Studies Committee of EST.

Bernard Rimé is Emeritus Professor in Psychology at UCLouvain. His main research field is on emotions, where he has published widely. One of his main publications is *Le partage social des émotions* (Presses universitaires de France, 2009).

Valérie Rosoux is Senior Research Fellow at the Belgian National Fund for Scientific Research (F.R.S.-FNRS). She teaches *International Negotiation*, and *Conflict Transformation* at UCLouvain. In 2010–2011, she was a Senior Fellow at the United States Institute of Peace (Washington DC). As a post-doctoral researcher, she worked at The Johns Hopkins University School of Advanced International Studies (SAIS) in 2002, the Center for International Studies and Research (CERI), Institut d'Études Politiques of Paris (2001) and the University Laval, Canada (2000). Valérie Rosoux has a master degree in Philosophy and a Ph.D. in International Relations. Her research interests focus on the uses of memory in international relations, especially in the Franco-German, Franco-Algerian, Rwandan and South African cases.

Rose Spijkerman is PhD candidate in History at Ghent University. In her research she focuses on the study of emotions in history, particularly the ones linked to honor and shame in the Belgian army during the First World War.

Myrthel Van Etterbeeck is PhD candidate in Literature at KU Leuven – Brussels. Her research deals with the memory of the Great War in the Belgian Dutch and French literature during the interwar period.

Karla Vanraepenbusch studied history at *Vrije Universiteit Brussel* and Museum Studies at the *Université de Neuchâtel* in Switzerland. She is currently preparing a PhD thesis at CegeSoma and UCLouvain. Her research concerns the material memory traces of the First World War in Antwerp and Liège.

Laurence van Ypersele is Professor at UCLouvain. She teaches Contemporary History and works on World War I and its memory. Member of the board of the Historial de la Grande Guerre of Péronne (France), she wrote several books: *Le roi Albert, His-*

toire d'un mythe (Quorum, 1995; Labor, 2006), *Question d'histoire contemporaine: Conflits, mémoires et identités* (PUF, 2006), *Je serai fusillé demain. Les dernières lettres des patriotes belges et français fusillés par l'occupant, 1914–1918* (Racine, 2011), and *Brussels, War and Memory, 1914–2014* (La Renaissance du livre, 2014).

Antoon Vrints is Assistant Professor at the Department of History (Research Unit Social History after 1750) of Ghent University. He is specialized in the history of conflict regulation and the social history of the First World War. He published on these topics following monographs: *Bezette stad. Vlaams-nationalistische collaboratie in Antwerpen tijdens de Eerste Wereldoorlog* (Brussels, 2002), *Het theater van de straat. Publiek geweld in Antwerpen tijdens de eerste helft van de twintigste eeuw* (Amsterdam, 2011). Moreover, he recently coedited the first counterfactual history of Belgium. Antoon Vrints is member of the editorial board of *Stadsgeschiedenis* and *Wetenschappelijke Tijdingen*.

Geneviève Warland is Reader in History at UCLouvain and Research Assistant in the project *Recognition and resentment: experiences and memories of the Great War in Belgium*. Her PhD (2011) dealt with the public role of history and the conceptions of nation and Europe as interpreted by the contemporary philosophers J.-M. Ferry and J. Rüsen, on the one side, and by the historians P. J. Blok, Karl Lamprecht, Ernest Lavisse and Henri Pirenne on the other. She has worked as guest lecturer at the University of Frankfurt/Main and at the University of Paderborn. Her research interests focus on the history of historiography in Europe in the 19th and 20th centuries, especially on the role of historians as scientific mediators and on the expression of emotions in their writings.